Autorenkollektiv

Analytical Problems

Autorenkollektiv

Analytical Problems

With 58 Figures and 16 Tables

Akademie-Verlag Berlin
1986

Die Originalausgabe erscheint im Springer-Verlag Berlin · Heidelberg · New York · Tokyo
in der Schriftenreihe „Topics in Current Chemistry",
Volume 134

Vertrieb ausschließlich für die DDR und die sozialistischen Länder
Akademie-Verlag Berlin

ISBN 3-05-500203-2 Springer-Verlag Berlin · Heidelberg · New York · Tokyo
ISBN 3-05-500203-2 Springer-Verlag New York · Heidelberg · Berlin · Tokyo

ISBN 3-05-500203-2

Erschienen im Akademie-Verlag Berlin, DDR-1086 Berlin, Leipziger Straße 3—4
Lizenznummer: 202 · 100/535/86
Printed in the German Democratic Republic
Gesamtherstellung: VEB Druckerei „Thomas Müntzer", 5820 Bad Langensalza
LSV 1235
Bestellnummer: 763 639 9 (3072/134)
12400

Editorial Board

Table of Contents

Surface Enhanced Raman Scattering of Biomolecules

Eckhard Koglin and Jean-Marie Séquaris

Institute of Applied Physical Chemistry, Nuclear Research Center (KFA) Jülich, P.O. Box 1913, D-5170 Jülich/FRG

Table of Contents

A review of Surface Enhanced Raman Scattering (SERS) and Surface Enhanced Resonance Raman Scattering (SERRS) from biomolecules adsorbed on a metal surface is given. Advantages and applications of these new vibration spectroscopic methods particularly in characterize in-situ the chemical identity, structure, orientation, chemical and electrochemical reactions of biological specimens adsorbed at charged surfaces are discussed. The technical aspects of the instrumentation and procedure as also the fundamentals of the SERS theory are exposed. Different applications show that SERS- and SERRS spectroscopy are powerful in-situ methods to study the interfacial behaviour of biomolecules. Moreover, the high enhancement factor of the Raman scattering intensity creates a new technique for obtaining high resolution vibrational spectra of biomolecules from rather diluted aqueous solutions down to 10^{-8} M.

1 Introduction

The structure and dynamics of chemisorbed biomolecules are of great importance in order to elucidate the behaviour of these molecules at electrically charged surfaces. Recently, it has been suggested that Raman spectroscopy at solid/liquid interfaces becomes a general tool for the study of the physicochemical phenomena that take place in such environments [1-8]. In his early overview on Surface Enhanced Raman Scattering (SERS) Van Duyne [1] estimated that the expected scattering intensity from the adsorbed molecules is 10^5–10^6 times stronger than for nonadsorbed species at the same bulk concentration. Such enormous enhancement totally overcomes the traditional low sensitivity problem associated with Normal Solution Raman Scattering (NSRS). This enables researchers to characterize *in-situ* the chemical identity, structure, orientation and chemical reactions of species adsorbed at surfaces applying SERS.

Today a rather detailed knowledge of the conformational changes of nucleic acids and proteins in the solution state is available with NSRS and this knowledge is continuously growing [9-12]. On the other hand much less information exists about the interfacial behaviour of these biopolymers, due to the lack of suitable methods. However, the following important processes are typically interfacial:

(I) control of the genetic information,
(II) mechanisms of blood clotaing,
(III) redox enzymatic reactions at mitochondrial membranes.

In 1979, the SERS-spectroscopy was first applied to the study of adsorbed biopolymers in the case of nucleic acids [13]. This was the starting signal for the rapid expansion of SERS into the field of biochemistry from the hitherto existing corner restricted to the investigation of some organic substances, predominantly pyridine derivatives, and some simple inorganic adsorbates.

Using biomolecules with chromophoric groups the Raman bands are both resonance (RRS) — and surface enhanced (RRS + SERS = SERRS). Instead of the usual term SERS, the Raman effect is, in this case, called surface enhanced resonance Raman scattering (SERRS). SERRS spectroscopy was first applied to biochemistry of heme chromophores by Cotton et al. [14]. Since then, SERS and SERRS have been extended to systematic investigations of biomolecules in the adsorbed

What is the advantage of SERS-spectroscopy in biological science? The high enhancement factor of the Raman scattering intensity by the adsorbed biomolecules creates a new technique for obtaining high resolution vibrational spectra of biomolecules from very diluted aqueous solutions down to 10^{-8} M. This means that only very small amounts of material are needed, e.g. of compounds which are not available in large amounts, because they are difficult to prepare and hence very expensive and valuable. Recording the NSRS spectra of many biomolecules is impossible because of their very low solubility in water. However, vibration spectra of biomolecules with a solubility lower than 5×10^{-4} g in 100 g H_2O have been obtained by means of SERS-spectroscopy [25,31,41]. The decisive point of this new spectroscopic method was the distance of the Raman enhancement from the surface. The sterical investigations of the biopolymers DNA and poly-A adsorbed at positively charged silver surfaces (electrodes, colloids) have indicated that the sensitivity of the enhancement is limited by the short-range enhancement to distances near the surfaces [26,40]. Thus, SERS-spectroscopy is a very sensitive method used to detect moieties of an adsorbed biopolymer situated close to a charged surface. The purpose of this contribution is to review the recent advances in the application of SERS- and SERRS spectroscopy in biological science.

2 Experimental Features

After the first detection of the enhanced Raman signals from pyridine adsorbed on a silver metal electrode [42] it is now well established that this phenomenon is caused by an enhancement of the Raman cross section of adsorbates at an electrode-electrolyte interface [43–68], on metal colloids [69–93] and at a metal-vacuum surface [94–98].

All investigators have outlined that "surface roughness" is a prerequisite for such an enhancement in the Raman scattering intensity. This roughness can be created by various types of processes: electrochemical [2], chemical reduction [69], mechanical polishing [99], vapour deposition [100], lithography [94,101], evaporation [102] and photochemical [103]. Metals, which have been successfully employed as substrates for SERS belong qualitatively into several groups.

i) Noble metals, e.g., Ag, Cu and Au, at which d-bands lie well below the Fermi level.

ii) Transition metals, e.g., Ni, Pd, Pt, of which d-bands overlap the Fermi level and thereby contribute to a strong covalent bonding of adsorbates.

iii) Metals, such as Al, Na and K, which do not have d-bands and are free-electron-like. Up to now SERS experiments with biomolecules are carried out only in an electrochemical cell with Ag electrodes or in a Ag colloid solution.

For the study of adsorbed biological, significant species a typical experimental arrangement is shown in Fig. 1. Generally for "Electrode SERS spectroscopy" a conventional three-electrode configuration is used, with the potentiostat maintaining the potential of the working electrode relative to the reference electrode and a function generator as programmer for the oxidation (dissolution) — reduction (deposition)

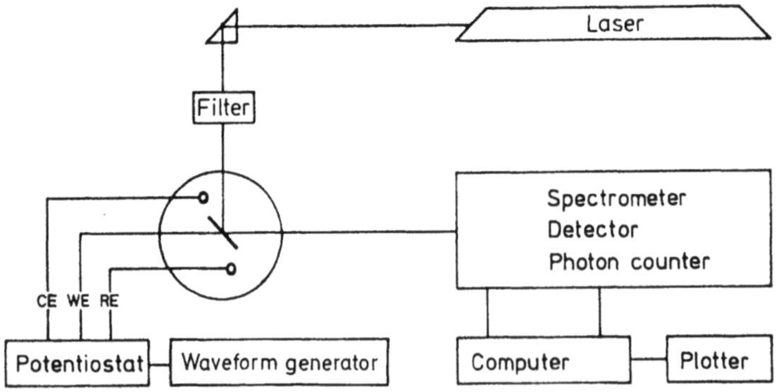

Fig. 1. Typical Raman spectroelectrochemistry equipment system. WE, working electrode; CE, counter electrode; RE, reference electrode

Table 1. Biomolecules investigated by SERS and SERRS

Purine	
Sugars:	Ribose, Deoxyribose
Nucleic Bases:	Adenine (A), Guanine (G), Cytosine (C), Thymine (C)
Nucleosides:	Adenosine, Guanosine, Cytidine, Uridine, Thymidine
Nucleotides:	(d)AMP, ADP, ATP, (d)GMP, (d)CMP, UMP, TMP
Dinucleoside Monophosphates:	ApA, ApC, ApG, ApU
Polynucleotides:	Poly A, Poly C, Poly U, Poly A · Poly U, Poly I · Poly C
Deoxyribopolynucleotides and Nucleic Acids:	Poly d(AT), Poly d(GC), Poly dG · Poly dC, Native and denatured DNA
Amino Acids:	Phenylalanine, Trypthophan, Tyrosine, Histidine, Glutamine, Glycine, Alanine
Aminobenzoic Acid:	p-Aminobenzoic Acid (PABA)
Citric Acid:	Sodium Citrate
Porphyrin Chromophores:	porphyrins, bile pigments, metalloporphyrins, hemoproteins
Flavin Chromophores:	Flavoproteins, glucose oxidase
Retinal Chromophore:	Bacteriorhodopsin

cycles (ORC). "Colloid SERS spectroscopy" is carried out with a conventional Raman cell for liquids or with capillary tubes. Most surface Raman spectra were measured using a computer controlled double monochromator with a cold photomultiplier, operated in the photon counting mode. The efficient optical system of the spectrometer is combined with a powerful laser light source.

A list of biomolecule adsorbates studied presently is given in Table 1. The number of materials investigated, however, grows rapidly. The activity in this field of SERS-spectroscopy is used for two types of Raman scatterers: laser excitation far removed from the electronic absorption maxima and excitation of species at wavelengths near to or at absorption maxima. SERS studies of species adsorbed on metal surfaces with absorption bands near the UV region (DNA and the derivatives, proteins without chromophoric groups) have shown that Raman signals can be enhanced by as much as 10^4–10^7 fold [19,25]. When combined with resonance Raman scattering from an appropriate chromophoric adsorbate, total Raman enhancement factors might reach values in the 10^{10} to 10^{12} range [21,91].

2.1 Electrode SERS

The electrochemical cells used for SERS studies on polycrystalline silver electrodes are shown in Fig. 2. In the spectroelectrochemical cell the Ag working electrode is placed in such a position that the laser light can be focused onto its surface and the backscattered light can then be efficiently collected. The optoelectrochemical cell is usually a quartz glass cylinder with a diameter of about 1.5 cm and a volume of 2 ml [39]. The polycrystalline Ag working electrode is positioned in the center of the cell for optimal substance diffusion and electrochemical conditions (cf. Fig. 2a). The cell can be used in experiments where the angle of incidence is varied by rotating

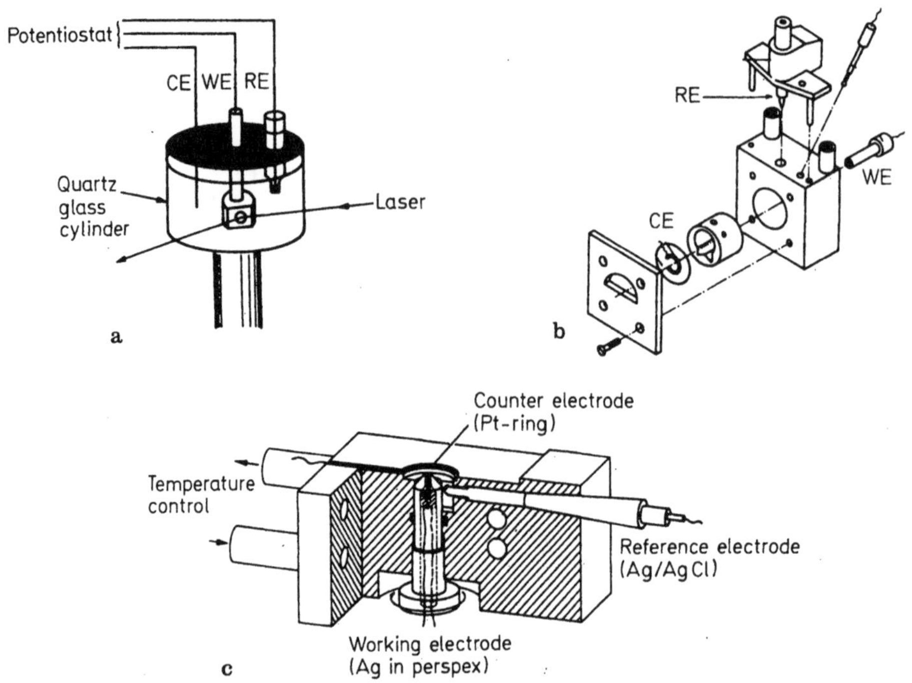

Fig. 2a–c. Raman spectroscopic cell designs for electrode surface studies: **a** Ervin et al., Ref. [16]; **b** and **c** Otto et al., Ref. [36]

the cell round the axis of the working electrode. In this cell design, the Raman scattering is measured at 90° to the incident laser radiation. The reference electrode in the cell is a Ag/AgCl electrode or a saturated calomel electrode (SCE). The third electrode of this three-electrode cell is simply a platinum wire as the counter electrode.

Surface enhanced Raman signals from the electrode can be observed using different pretreatment procedures:

a) The surface is pretreated by running the electrochemical oxidation-reduction cycle (ORC) in the bulk solution containing the biomolecules.

b) The electrode roughening procedure is carried out in the electrolyte solution in the absence of the biomolecule and the biomolecule solution is then added to the cell.

c) The silver electrode is removed from the cell after the electrochemical cycle, dried and the spectra are measured in air. One of the most important problems in the use of the SERS effect for the study of adsorbed conformations of nucleic acids, proteins and peptides is conservation of their conformational state during the ORC. Thus, to avoid conformational changes of the large biomolecules during the electrochemical cycle procedure (b) should be prefered.

A demonstration of the advantage of high sensitivity in SERS spectroscopy is given in Fig. 3. This figure displays the SERS spectrum of the DNA base cytosine [39]. The laser power used to excite the sample was only 10 mW at 514.5 nm from an argon ion laser. An important observation is that the band positions obtained in SERS spectra are essentially the same as in NSRS spectra. The largest frequency shift

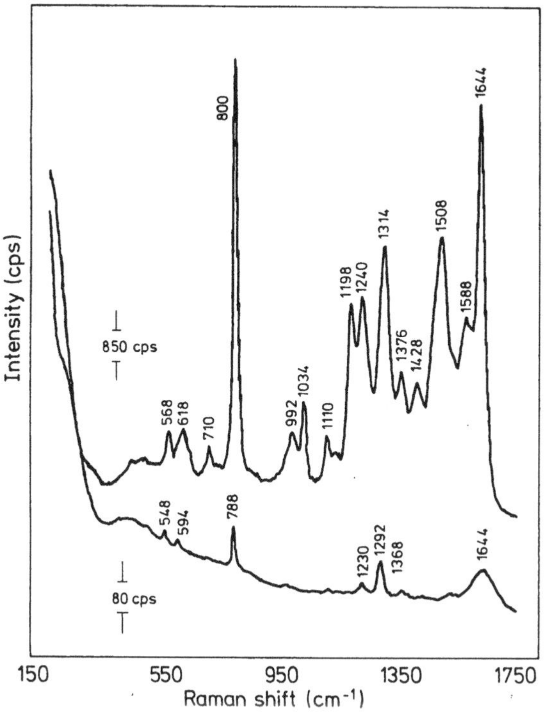

Fig. 3. SERS spectrum of cytosine (above). Conditions: laser excitation line 514.5 nm; laser power at the Ag electrode 10 mW; E_s −0.6 V, 0.1 M KCl and 10^{-3} M Na_2HPO_4; pH 8; cytosine concentration 1×10^{-3} M. (Lewinsky, Ref. [39]).
NRS spectrum of cytosine (below). Conditions: laser excitation line 514.5 nm; laser power 120 mW; 10^{-2} M cytosine in H_2O; accumulation time 2 s/cm^{-1}; 6 scans

is about 30 cm^{-1}. Therefore, the previously assigned vibrational bands of the NSRS spectra can be compared with the SERS spectra. The enhancement factor of the inplane ring; breathing mode of cytosine at 800 cm^{-1} is about 10^6. With a polished and chemically cleaned silver electrode a strong Raman signal from the vibrational lines of a biomolecule appears only after an electrochemical oxidation reduction cycle, a socalled "activation cycle". Such a cycle consists of:

1) The oxidation of the Ag electrode $Ag^0 \rightarrow Ag^+ + e^-$ where the amount of Ag oxidation is monitored by the total charge passed through the electrode.

2) During the reduction half cycle, a roughened silver surface is reformed by $Ag^+ + e^- \rightarrow Ag^0$. Scanning electron microscopy (SEM) of electrode surfaces after this oxidation-reduction procedure have revealed that the initially smooth surfaces have acquired bumps on the scale of 25 to 500 nm [8]. These bumps can be approximated as speres, hemispheres and prolate spheroids [8].

This "SERS active" surface consists of randomly distributed surface bumps with a surface topography in the 25 nm region (conventional SEM resolution range), the submicroscopic size range (2–20 nm) and even in the atomic scale roughness from a single atom to 2 nm. These structures produce large electromagnetic fields on the surface when the incident photon energy is in resonance with the localized surface plasmons (submicroscopic spheres and spheroids) and the single atoms or clusters enhance the Raman polarizability (cf. Chapt. 3).

Recently, two small-volume electrochemical cells for the measurements of surface enhanced Raman scattering of very small amounts of biological material were developed [33]. The mini-SERS cell (cf. Fig. 2b) with a volume of about 0.8 ml is used for a normal Raman spectrometer and the angle between the incoming laser beam and the electrode surface can be chosen. The minicell consists of a brass frame and a Teflon inner part. The silver working electrode with a diameter of 3 mm is fitted into a Teflon rod which can be inserted from the back of the cell.

The cell design shown in Fig. 2c has been used for micro-SERS spectroscopy of chromosomes and related material [36]. This microcell is for use in a Raman micro-spectrometer using epi-illumination. By choice of the objective used in the microscope, the focus of the laser beam is about 6 µm in diameter for a typical chromosome micro-SERS-spectrum. The working electrode, with a diameter of 0.5 mm, is fitted into a perspex rod and can be screwed into a frame for positioning the electrode surface to the objective of the microscope. This small microcell needs only 0.08 ml of sample.

2.2 Colloid SERS

Metal colloids in an aqueous solution are ideal markers for cell surfaces and intracellular components for microscopic observation (light and fluorescence microscopy, transmission and scanning electron microscopy) and for studying molecular organization and cell function [104]. It also has numerous medical uses as a drug and as a test for various diseases [105]. For more specific information about the interfacial behaviour of biomolecules adsorbed on metal colloids several studies of complex molecules by means of colloid SERS- [25,27,41], and SERRS spectroscopy [22,106] have been published. This is an application of metal colloids which may become of great practical value, particularly in the vibration spectroscopy of biomolecules in the adsorbed state. The advantage of this colloid SERS spectroscopy is the simple experimental pretreatment procedure and the Raman measurements in conventional liquid cells or in capillaries. An additional advantage as compared with the electrode SERS spectroscopy is that the molecular structure is not influenced through the oxidation-reduction cycle during pretreatment.

The silver colloids are prepared according to Creighton et al. [69]. They are formed by rapidly mixing a solution of $AgNO_3$ with icecold $NaBH_4$. This aggregated sols exhibit visible absorption spectra in which the 390 nm peak is attributable to small particle resonant Mie scattering [70]. This yellow unaggregated colloid is stable for several weeks. Transmission electron microscopy shows that these colloids consist of 7 to 15 nm average diameter faceted crystals [82]. The addition of a solution containing a biomolecule leads to a decrease in the main absorption band of the hydrosol at 380–390 nm and to the appearance of long-wavelength bands (cf. Fig. 4). These long-wavelength bands originate from aggregates of silver micelles formed during the adsorption process. The electron microscopic analysis of the hydrosol-phenylalanine complex (Phe) has shown that the silver micelles form aggregates of about 150–200 nm in diameter [27].

Aggregation of the colloid is a required first step to obtain SERS spectra of adsorbed molecules [76,79]. This aggregation can be initiated by adding negatively charged ions (Cl^-, ClO_4^-, NO_3^-). A SERS spectrum occurs when the negatively charged species are displaced from the silver surface by more strongly bound adsorbates with the rate determined by the nature and concentration of the displacing species [92]. Weitz et al.

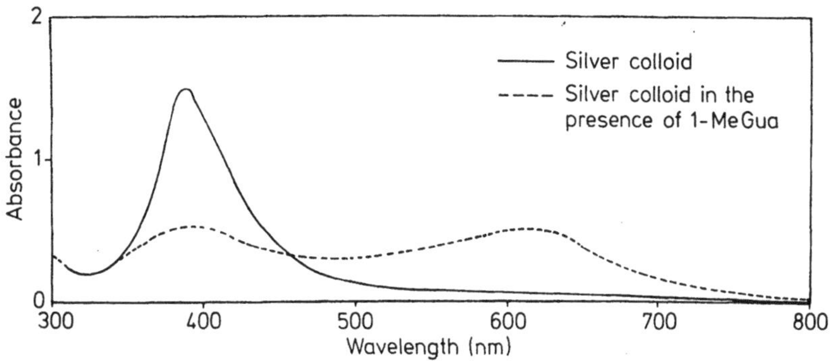

Fig. 4. Absorption spectra of silver sol (solid line) and silver sol in presence of 1-MeGua (broken line). 7×10^{-6} M of 1-MeGua

have reported useful informations about the structure of colloidal aggregates, kinetics of aggregation and theoretical developments [93].

The disadvantage of the colloid system is its tendency to flocculate and precipitate at the bottom of the spectroscopic cell. It was recently demonstrated that this annoyance can be avoided by application of the silver colloidal hydrosols on filter paper [107], chromographic paper [108] and silica gel plates [109]. With this new technique, subnanogram amounts of various dyes [107] and nonresonant biomolecules [109] were detected. It was found that the aggregated Ag sols (i.e. colloidal silver metal particles with adsorbed biomolecules) exhibited strong SER scattering of incident light in the blue-green region. The excitation profile investigations of an amino acid-Ag-sol complex have shown that the excitation maximum of the complex coincides well with the maximum of the long-wavelength absorption band [27]. Moreover, the shift of the absorption band maximum at increased concentrations of the amino acid (Phe) was accompanied by the same shift in the excitation maximum [27].

The SERS spectra of 9-methylguanine (-9MeGua) in Fig. 5 demonstrate the high sensitivity of the colloid SERS technique. The normal Raman spectrum (Fig. 5a) could only be obtained at a rather high concentration of 10^{-2} M and a laser power of 300 mW. The characteristic ring-breathing mode is located at 634 cm^{-1} and two skeletal vibrations were observed at 1374 cm^{-1} and 1410 cm^{-1}. The broad band at 1634 cm^{-1} is attributed to the water H—O—H bending mode and this band almost blurrs the typical guanine vibrations in this spectral region.

The SERS spectra of 9-MeGua in the presence of Ag sol particles are shown in Fig. 5c. The SERS is so sensitive that the concentration could be reduced to 7×10^{-7} M, although the laser power is only 120 mW. The most characteristic features of this spectrum are located at 660 cm^{-1} and 1338 cm^{-1} and are due to the guanine ring-breathing mode and a skeleton vibration. In addition, one notes that the water bending vibration is not enhanced and the guanine vibrations now stand out clearly in this spectral range.

Figure 5d demonstrates the subnanogram detection of 9-MeGua (nonresonant in the visible region) on silica gel plates used for thin layer chromatography. 1 µl (125×10^{-12} g) of the 9-MeGua colloid complex was applied to the silica gel plate and the plate spot (2 mm in diameter) was then investigated with a typical 90° Raman scattering arrangement. Using this technique, subnanogram amounts of various methylated guanine derivates were detected and identified directly with the colloid SERS spectroscopy [109]. To the knowledge of the authors, this was the first application of SERS in biochemistry for the *in situ* detection and identification at subnanogram levels.

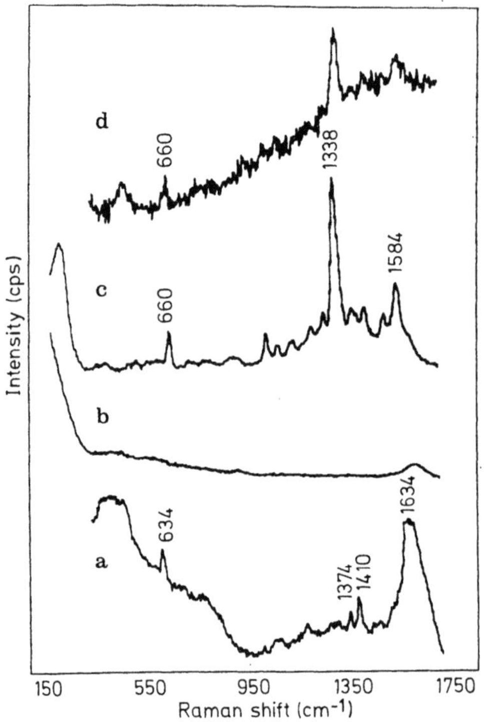

Fig. 5a–d. NRS and SERS spectra of 9-methylguanine (9-MeGua); 514.5 nm excitation, monochromator slit width 5 cm^{-1}.
a) NRS spectrum of 9-MeGua, 10^{-2} M in 0.5 M HCl. Laser power 300 mW; accumulation time 3 s/cm^{-1}; 5 scans;
b) SERS spectrum of silver colloid solution (blank spectrum). Laser power 120 mW; accumulation time 2 s/cm^{-1}; 1 scan;
c) SERS spectrum of silver colloidal aggregate solution with 9-MeGua, 7×10^{-7} M at pH 5. Laser power 120 MW; accumulation time 2 s/cm^{-1}; 1 scan;
d) SERS spectrum of solution **c)** applied on HPTLC silica gel plate (120 pg of 9-MeGua). Laser power 120 mW; accumulation time 2 s/cm^{-1}; 3 scans

3 Characteristics of SERS

3.1 Raman Scattering of Adsorbates

The purpose of this section is to provide some background to the theories by introducing theoretical expressions for Raman scattering intensities and outlining some of the more important features of the various theories: "classical" electromagnetic enhancement (EM enhancement) and "nonclassical" contributions (chemical effects).

The intensity of a Raman line corresponding to a transition between an initial state, i, and a final state, f, is given by [110]:

$$I_{fi} = I_{fi}(\omega_s) = \frac{2^3\pi}{3^2c^4}\,\omega_s^4 I_L \sum_{\varrho,\sigma} |\alpha_{fi}^{\varrho\sigma}|^2 \tag{1}$$

where $\omega_s = 2\pi c\bar{v}_s$ (in cm^{-1}) is the frequency of the scattered light, $\omega_s = \omega_L - \omega_R$; ω_L: incident laser frequency; ω_R: Raman active normal mode excited by the inelastic scattering process, I_L is the intensity of the incident laser light, ϱ and σ are the polarizations of the Raman and incident light respectively, and $\alpha^{\varrho\sigma}$ is the ϱ, σ th component of the polarizability tensor. Intensities of scattering processes are alternatively expressed in terms of differential cross-sections $d\sigma/d\Omega$:

$$\Omega \frac{d\sigma(\omega_s)}{d\Omega} = \frac{2^3\pi}{3^2c^4} \omega_s^4 \sum_{\varrho,\sigma} |\alpha_{fi}^{\varrho\sigma}|^2 \tag{2}$$

so that I_{fi} becomes

$$I_{fi} = \Omega \frac{d\sigma}{d\Omega} I_L \tag{3}$$

The Raman scattering tensor α_{fi} is

$$\alpha_{fi}^{\varrho\sigma} = \sum_e{}' \frac{\langle\psi_f|\underline{e}_\varrho\mu|\psi_e\rangle\langle\psi_e|\underline{e}_\sigma\mu|\psi_i\rangle}{(E_e - E_i) - \hbar\omega_L + i\Gamma_e} + \frac{\langle\psi_f|\underline{e}_\sigma\mu|\psi_e\rangle\langle\psi_e|\underline{e}_\varrho\mu|\psi_i\rangle}{(E_e - E_f) + \hbar\omega_L + i\Gamma_e} \tag{4}$$

where μ is the dipole moment operator, and e_ϱ and e_σ are the scattered and laser polarization vectors. ψe represents an intermediate state in the Raman scattering process. E_i is the initial energy and E_f the final energy.

The normal Raman scattering (NRS) regime is defined by the condition $\hbar\omega_L \ll (E_e - E_i)$. Resonance Raman scattering (RRS) is defined by the condition $\hbar\omega_L \approx (E_e - E_i)$. In RRS the value of $d\sigma/d\Omega$ corresponding to the by resonance enhanced value of $\alpha_{fi}^{\varrho\sigma}$ can be 10^2 to 10^6 times greater than in the corresponding NRS case.

In 1977 two groups, Jeanmaire and Van Duyne [43] and Albrecht and Creighton [45] showed that the Raman cross section for pyridine adsorbed onto electrochemically roughened silver electrodes was enhanced 10^6 times:

$$\{I_{fi}(\omega_s)\}_{ads} \approx 10^6\{I_{fi}(\omega_s)\}_{free} \tag{5}$$

There is some experimental evidence to indicate that much of the enhancement is associated with surface roughness (local microstructures) in the range of 1 to 100 nm. At resonance with these microparticle modes the local electric field at the incident frequency ($\hbar\omega_L$) becomes large near and on the particle surface. Furthermore, the re-radiation efficiency of Raman active molecules situated near the surface also becomes enhanced when the inelastically scattered frequency ($\hbar\omega_s$) is also in resonance with these microparticle modes. The Raman scattering intensity of the adsorbed molecule is then given by [8]

$$\{I_{fi}(\omega_s)\}_{ads} = I_L(\omega_L) \cdot L^2(\omega_L) \cdot L^2(\omega_s) \cdot \Omega \cdot \left(\frac{d\sigma_{eff}}{d\Omega}\right)_{ads} \cdot N_{sur} \tag{6}$$

Here, $L^2(\omega_L) \cdot L^2(\omega_s)$ describes the electromagnetic surface-averaged intensity enhancement factors at the incident and Stokes Raman frequencies, respectively (i.e. the "classical" enhancement by surface plasmon type resonance). $(d\sigma_{eff}/d\Omega)_{ads}$ takes into account a "chemical" effect due to electronic interaction between the chemisorbed molecule and the surface. N_{sur} is the number of adsorbed molecules.

The dominant mechanism seems to be the EM effect with enhancements approximately estimated to be in the range of 10^4 to 10^6. The chemical mechanisms appear to contribute a combined factor in the range from 10 to 10^2.

3.2 The EM Model for SERS

The basic concept of the purely electro-magnetic model considers a Raman active molecule (scatterer) near a metallic particle [111-126] and is shown schematically in Fig. 6. The main features of these theories are seen by considering a single dielectric ellipsoid with a laser excitation field $E_L(\omega_L)$ directed along the principal axis of the ellipsoid. Then the field E_{ins} inside the particle is uniform and given by [140]:

$$E_{ins}(\omega_L) = \frac{\varepsilon_s}{\varepsilon_s + (\varepsilon_m - \varepsilon_s)\,A_c} E_L(\omega_L) \qquad (7)$$

Here ε_m and ε_s denote the dielectric functions of the metallic sphere and its surrounding, respectively. A_c is a depolarization factor depending solely on particle shape.

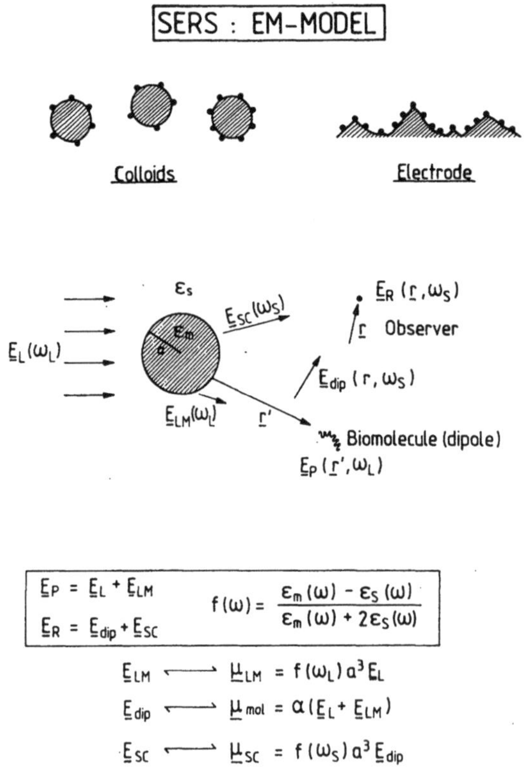

Fig. 6. Schematic picture indicating the origins for the EM-enhancement

$\varepsilon_m(\omega) = \varepsilon_1(\omega) + i\varepsilon_2(\omega)$ is the expression for the complex dielectric constant. The maximum of the internal field E_{ins} occurs at a frequency ω_{sp}, where

$$\varepsilon_1(\omega_{sp}) \approx (1 - 1/A_c)\,\varepsilon_s \tag{8}$$

The condition corresponds to the excitation of localized surface plasmons. Silver can satisfy this condition for visible light.

The expression (7) for E_{ins} is identical to that of the electric field, due to an ideal dipole at the center of the sphere ($A_c = 1/3$)

$$\mu(\omega_L) = \alpha E = \frac{\varepsilon_m(\omega_L) - \varepsilon_s(\omega_L)}{\varepsilon_m(\omega_L) + 2\varepsilon_s(\omega_L)}\, a^3 E_L \tag{9}$$

The general elastically scattered field of the sphere is calculated by the Lorenz-Mie theory [128] and is denoted $E_{LM}(r', \omega)$.

Considered is a Raman scattering molecule located at coordinate r' outside of a spherical particle of radius a. If the electromagnetic wave of frequency ω_L is incident on that small sphere, the total field outside the sphere is equivalent to $E_L(r', \omega_L)$ plus the field $E_{LM}(r', \omega_L)$. This field polarizes the molecule and induces a dipole moment.

$$\mu_{mol} = \alpha_{mol}\{E_L(r', \omega_L) + E_{LM}(r', \omega_L)\} = \alpha_{mol} E_p(r', \omega_L) \tag{10}$$

The electric field of this dipole μ_{mol} is $E_{dip}(r', \omega_s)$ for the observer at r. Beside this direct radiation, the vibrating molecule also polarizes the metal sphere and uses it as an antenna to amplify its Raman radiation.

E_{dip} induces a dipole μ_{sc} in the metal particle with the radius a

$$\mu_{sc}(\omega_s) = \frac{\varepsilon_m(\omega_s) - \varepsilon_s(\omega_s)}{\varepsilon_m(\omega_s) + 2\varepsilon_s(\omega_s)}\, a^3 E_{dip}\,. \tag{11}$$

In the dipole approximation, the field outside the spere (E_{sc}) is the same as that generated by this dipole. The electric field at the observer r is

$$E_R = E_{dip} + E_{sc}\,. \tag{12}$$

The calculated enhancement of this purely physical EM effect as function of the distance of the molecule from the spere, reflects the long range nature of this model [112]. The enhancement depends strongly upon the particle shape and the dielectric constants ε_m and ε_s [113,127]. For small spheres, in resonance with the localized surface plasmons, the local field strength averaged over the surface is about 1000 times the incident field strength. Detailed calculations for isolated prolate ellipsoids have been reported [122,123]. It seems clear that even more calculations exploring the limits of these electro-magnetic effects are needed in order to compare the experimental results with this EM model.

3.3 The Chemical Effects in SERS

The central problem in understanding the chemical contribution to the overall enhancement reduces to the calculation of the polarizability of the adsorbate metal surface complex. The mixing of molecular states with metal states may bring about a large effective polarizability. The polarizability α depends on the normal mode amplitude of the molecular vibration Q. In the image field theory of SERS [129] the effective polarizability $\alpha_{eff}(Q)$ depends on the distance between the point molecule and the metal surface and on ε_s and ε_m. In order to obtain Raman enhancement the distance between molecule and metal is in the range of 1.5 to 4 Å.

Recently, Ueba [130–132] presented a calculation of the Raman scattering polarizability of an adsorbed molecule on a metal surface, where charge transfer excitation participates as an intermediate state of the Raman process. A typical estimation of pyridine chemisorbed on Ag through the N lone pair electron shows an enhancement of about 10^2. This seems to indicate that the charge transfer mechanism (CT) operates in conjunction with the EM effect.

Another contribution from charge transfer transitions to the enhanced Raman scattering was treated by Persson [133]. In this theory the factor in the Raman enhancement is estimated to 30.

A different approach was described by Otto et al. [6,134] and Burstein et al. [135]. Their "Adatom Model" postulates an extra Raman enhancement mechanism for adsorbates at active sites of "atomic scale roughness". The adatom acts as an element of small or atomic scale roughness causing localized breakdown in the selection rules for electron-hole pair excitation. The model is based on a Raman scattering mechanism by charge transfer [135] (cf. Fig. 7). An electron on the metal side is excited from

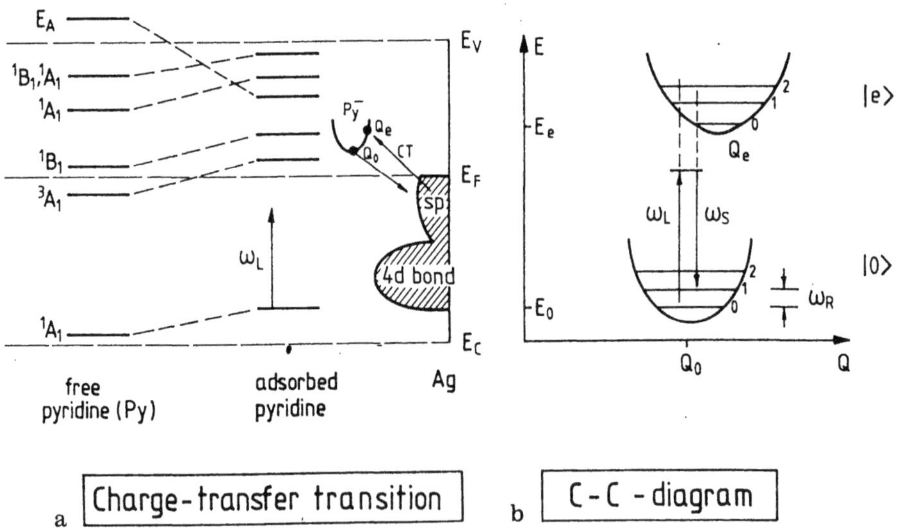

Fig. 7a and b. Charge transfer Raman mechanism.
a) Schematic energy level diagram for pyridine adsorbed on Ag.
b) Energy-configuration coordinate diagram showing the vibronic transitions in Raman scattering

the incident photon. This excited electron tunnels into the electron affinity levels of the adsorbed molecule. Since the electron is trapped in an antibonding orbital (e.g. π^* of adenine: A) the resulting negative ion A^- has a different equilibrium geometry compared with the neutral adsorbate A. Therefore, the charge transfer process induces a nuclear relaxation in the adsorbate which, after the return of the electron to the metal, results in a vibrational excited neutral molecule. Such a resonance scattering type of mechanism would then result in a short-range enhancement of Raman scattering. This process involves a virtual optical transition from a vibrational level in the ground electronic state $|0\rangle$ to an intermediate state, that corresponds to a vibrational level in the excited electronic state $|e\rangle$, followed by a virtual optical transition from the intermediate state to a different vibrational level in the ground state $|0\rangle$ (cf. Fig. 7).

The transition polarizibility α_{RS} (Raman scattering matrix element) can be expressed in terms of:

i) $\langle e|p \times A_i|0\rangle$ and $\langle 0|p \times A_s|e\rangle$ the momentum matrix elements for the transition between $|0\rangle$ and $|e\rangle$;

ii) $\langle V_e|V_0\rangle$, and $\langle V_0'|V_e\rangle$ Franck-Condon type overlap integrals over the wavefunctions of the vibrational levels involved in the optical transition, which depends on $Q_e - Q_0$ and on the strength of the electron vibration mode interactions involved;

iii) E_0 and E_e the energies of the vibronic levels in the ground and excited state, respectively, and Γ the Lorentzian broadening of the electronic excitation [136,137].

Different experiments indicate the importance of surface complex formation in determining the nature of the chemical component of SERS [7,59,64,138]. These investigations have shown that the atomic singularities are important elements in the SERS. Recent experiments [139] showed that the electrochemically roughened silver electrode presents a surface containing Ag^+ ions which are stabilized by coadsorbed Cl^- ions. An adatom on a positively charged surface would be similar to the Ag^+ ion. The formed surface complex between adsorbate and the metal substrate, demonstrates a charge transfer excitation resonance between the active site and the probe molecule leading to unusually large SERS at the interface.

4 Applications of SERS Spectroscopy

4.1 The Short-Range Sensitivity of SERS

The natural geometry of biomolecules can be exploited to clarify the SERS sensitivity dependence on distance from the surface. This aspect of SERS spectroscopy is important for the interpretation of the SERS spectrum of a biopolymer. The electromagnetic model predicts very rapid decay of SERS with increasing distance [112,113]. Thus, in small molecules with a dimension of approximately 0.6 nm (benzene) all vibrations of the molecule can be enhanced. In large biomolecules with diameters of about 6 nm (hemoglobin protein) only groups which are attached directly to the surface will yield SERS. This important aspect is illustrated by SERS studies of three examples: mono-, di-, and polynucleotides.

a) Mononucleotides

Figure 8 compares the SERS spectra of cytidine-3′-monophosphate (3′-CMP) as function of the applied electrode potential. The following vibration modes are expected for the 3′-CMP/Ag-surface system:

i) enhanced internal modes of the components of the 3′-CMP molecule (phosphate, ribose, and cytosine base),

ii) interfacial vibrations of the adsorbed molecule interacting with the silver surface,

iii) vibrations of the counterions Cl^- interacting with the silver surface, i.e. Ag—Cl vibrations.

The possible interfacial orientations of 3′-CMP on the electrode can be explained by the interaction of the electric field of the electrode with the charge and dipole

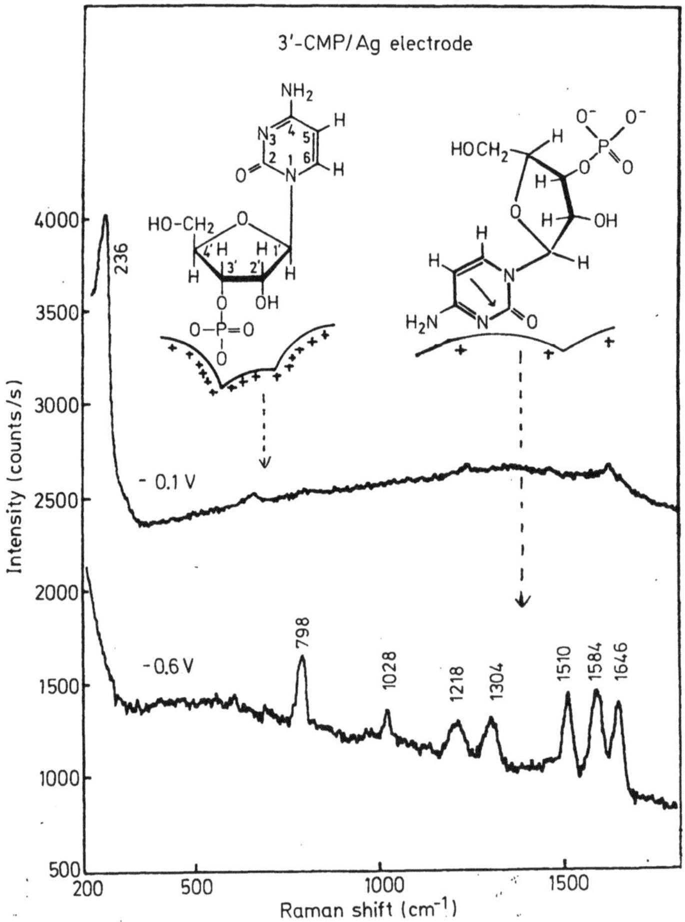

Fig. 8a and b. SERS spectra of cytidine 3′-monophosphate (3′-CMP). 3′-CMP concentration 2×10^{-3} M, 0.15 M KCl, 2×10^{-3} M. Tris buffer (pH 7.2), laser excitation line 514.5 nm, laser power at the electrode 10 mW, prior activitation of the silver electrode: 1 × 5 mCb between —0.1 V and +0.2 V (Ref. [40]).

a) Adsorption potential E_s —0.1 V vs. Ag/AgCl reference electrode.

b) Adsorption potential E_s —0.6 V vs. Ag/AgCl reference electrode moment of the adsorbed molecule. On the positively charged electrode (—0.1 V) the charge of the $—OPO_3^{2-}$ groups determines the orientation. This suggests that the 3′-CMP molecule is adsorbed end-on mostly with the $—OPO_3^{2-}$ moiety directed toward the electrode surface. The phosphate group is coordinated directly to the silver surface. The cytosine base is oriented towards the solution.

The SERS spectrum of 3′-CMP at an adsorption potential of —0.1 V vs. Ag/AgCl shows only a strong enhanced band at 236 cm^{-1} (cf. Fig. 8a). This band can be assigned to the interfacial vibration of the phosphate moiety with the positively charged silver surface: $—OPO_3^{2-}$/Ag-surface. This assignment is possible by the experimental SERS results of the investigations of the mononucleotide components [14,39] (see also Chapt. 4.2). Indeed, under the same experimental conditions the cytosine base and cytidine (cytosine bound to ribose) give no strong SERS signals in the spectral range of 200–300 cm^{-1}. Yet the 3′-CMP mononucleotide containing the base-, the sugar-, and the phosphate unit shows a very strong band at 236 cm^{-1}. The Ag—Cl vibration is hidden in this strong $—OPO_3^{2-}$/Ag vibration.

These experimental results show that the relative enhancement might be a strong function of the distance of the various parts of a biomolecule from the electrode surface. Adsorbed ribose is expected to lie within 0.6 nm from the surface whereas the cytosine base is probably more than 1 nm removed from the surface when the phosphate group is attached directly to the surface. Fig. 8b shows that while the intensity of the band at 236 cm^{-1} strongly decreases upon a shift of the potential from —0.1 V to —0.6 V, new bands at 798, 1028, 1218, 1304, 1510, 1584 and 1646 cm^{-1} appear in the SERS spectrum of 3′-CMP. The band at 798 cm^{-1} is the characteristic ring-breathing mode of the cytosine moiety (cf. Fig. 3). The other observed bands in the 1000–1650 cm^{-1} region are attributed to the skeleton vibrations of the cytosine base and are assigned in Ref. [141–143]. This spectrum suggests that the 3′-CMP molecule is now adsorbed end-on with the cytosine unit directed to the surface at the adsorption potential E_s —0.6 V. The hydrophilic phosphate group is now preferentially oriented towards the solution at this more neutral surface.

b) Dinucleoside monophosphates

Figure 9 shows the SERS spectra of the dinucleoside monophosphates adenylyl-(3′–5′)-uridine (ApU) and adenylyl-(3′–5′)-cytidine (ApC) at different adsorption potentials in the characteristic spectral range of the ring-breathing modes. The adsorbed base modes alone on the electrode surface are at 736 cm^{-1} in adenine, 798 cm^{-1} in cytosine and 795 cm^{-1} in uracil. The corresponding frequencies in the dinucleoside monophosphates ApC and ApU are at 734 cm^{-1} for adenine, 792 cm^{-1} for cytosine and 796 cm^{-1} for uracil.

The NSRS spectrum of ApU in aqueous solution was presented by Prescott et al. [192]. In this NSRS spectrum the intensities at 785 cm^{-1} (U ring-breathing mode) and at 732 cm^{-1} (adenine ring-breathing mode) are essentially the same. On the contrary, the SERS spectra show significant intensity differences at various potentials. At E_s —0.1 V vs. Ag/AgCl, very strong scattering was produced by the adenine moiety, indicating a high surface population of the adenine unit of the dinucleoside monophosphates. This shows that the dinucleosides are adsorbed end-on mostly with the adenine residue and the phosphate group directed towards the surface. The

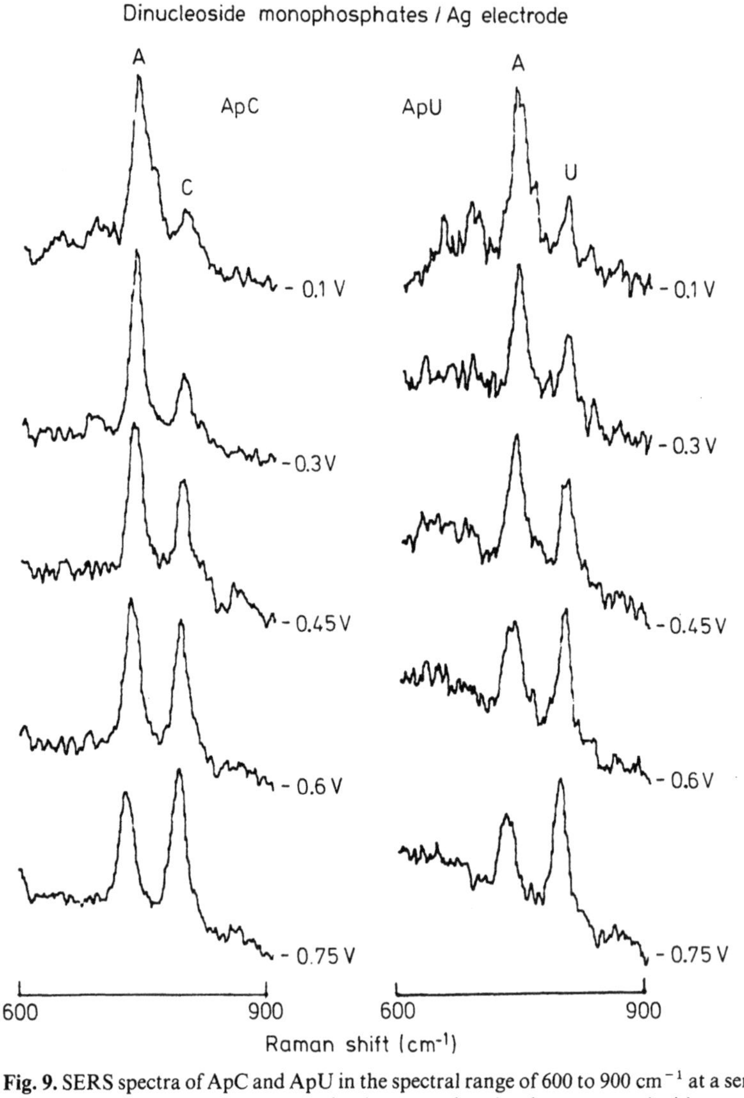

Fig. 9. SERS spectra of ApC and ApU in the spectral range of 600 to 900 cm^{-1} at a series of adsorption potentials. For every spectrum an activation procedure has been repeated with a new solution. Other experimental conditions as in Fig. 8 (Ref. [40])

other base (C in ApC, U in ApU) is repelled from the surface therefore attaining a more solution-sided position.

While the intensity of the adenine band at 734 cm^{-1} decreases upon a cathodic shift of the potential from —0.1 to —0.75 V, the cytosine band at 792 cm^{-1} in ApC and the uracil band at 796 cm^{-1} in ApU increase in intensity. When the applied voltage is set to E_s —0.6 V the ring-breathing mode signals of adenine/cytosine and adenine/uracil are approximately equal in intensity, indicating that at this potential the base residues populate the surface equally.

At E_s of —0.75 V, near the zero charge potential, the population of the surface is dominated by the uracil base in the ApU dinucleoside. Thus, these potential dependent investigations of the dinucleoside monophosphates have shown that the base moieties of these dimers interact directly with the surface and their adsorptions depend on the electrode charge.

The maximum distance between the adsorbed base and the solution-oriented base is about 1.2 nm [193,194]. Thus, these experimental results confirm that only short-range Raman enhancement plays an important role for these dimeric biomolecules [40].

These results also confirm previous voltammetric findings on the adsorption behaviour of mononucleotides and dinucleotide monophosphates at the mercury electrode surface [196–199]. Taking into account the respective potentials of zero charge (p.z.c.) —0.6 V and about —0.8 V for the mercury and silver electrodes, the conclusions on the orientation of the nucleic acid components in the adsorbed state can now be visualized in situ by the SERS spectroscopy. At a low charged surface, around the p.z.c., the presence of adsorbed compact layers for the rather concentrated solutions 2×10^{-3} M of mononucleotides and dinucleoside monophosphates deduced from the a.c. (alternating current) and sweep voltammetric measurements agrees with the highest intensities detected for the SERS bands characteristic of the nucleic bases moieties. Furthermore the weak Raman enhancement for the ribose phosphate chain vibrations supports the previously proposed structure of a condensed film where the stacking forces between nucleic base moieties, in parallel to each other, favour a perpendicular orientation of the hydrophobic ring moieties to the metallic surface. In a similar way SERS results obtained at high positively charged surface, corresponding to more anodic adsorption potentials permit to get specific informations on the diluted adsorption layer evaluated from voltammetric measurements. The competitive interaction of the phosphate group moiety associated with a more parallel flat adsorption of the nucleic base part to the positively charged surface through a π electron binding can thus explain a lower surface concentration of the mononucleotides and dinucleoside monophosphates at a positively charged surface.

c) Polynucleotides

In view of these results obtained with a rough silver electrode, the Raman scattering from biomolecules absorbed on dispersed silver particles of positively charged silver colloids has been reported [25,30,41]. From the results of the strong SERS signals of the adenine molecule with the colloidal silver surface [30], attention was turned to a polynucleotide based solely on the adenine-monophosphate, i.e. polyriboadenylic acid poly-A. This biopolymer forms a double stranded helix at acid pH [144]. The strands are arranged with the sugar-phosphate backbone on the outside and the adenine base facing the center. The SERS spectrum of this polynucleotide and its building stones (adenine, adenosine-5′-monophosphate and ribose-5′-phosphate) adsorbed at silver colloids are shown in Fig. 10.

For the interpretation of the poly-A SERS bands it was necessary to assign precise frequencies of the SERS band of the monomeric units. Adenine and adenine 5′-monophosphate exhibited characteristic ring-breathing modes at 726 cm^{-1} and 721 cm^{-1}. Prominent SERS bands for the ribose-5′-phosphate were obtained at 600 cm^{-1}, 914 cm^{-1} and 1282 cm^{-1}.

A comparison of these results with the SERS spectrum of poly-A has shown that

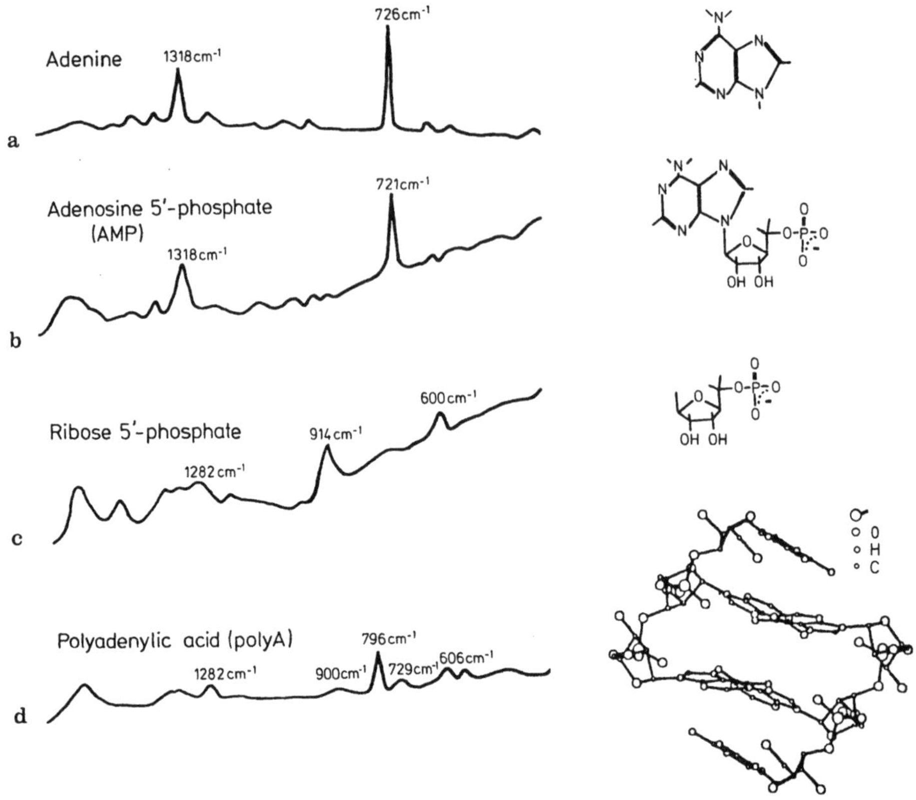

Fig. 10. SERS spectra of poly-A and its building stones: adenine, adenosine 5'-monophosphate and ribose 5-phosphate. Freshly prepared silver colloids, pH 4.5; 4×10^{-4} M adenine, 5'-AMP or ribose 5-phosphate added; poly-A concentration 1.6 mg/ml; Laser excitation line 514 nm, laser power 200 mW. (The drawing of poly-A in d shows the adenine base and the sugar-phosphate backbone outside the molecule)

the double stranded poly-A helix structure at pH 4.5 and low ionic strength exhibited SERS signals only from the helical strands. The appearance of a band at 796 cm^{-1} in the SERS spectrum of poly-A corresponding to the stretching of the ribose-phosphate backbone confirms that the ribose-phosphate group is preferentially adsorbed. The adenine molecule located at a distance of about 0.5 nm from the phosphate group displays only weak SERS signals.

These investigations of the mono-, di- and polynucleotides emphasize that the high sensitivity of the SERS method is limited to the macromolecular components coming into direct contact with the surface.

4.2 Native DNA

Inside living systems there exist a number of electrical charges carrying interfaces which are associated with all the biological events in life. The range of biological interfaces extends from the fields of molecular biology through to prothetic surgery.

The biopolymer interactions, the enzymatic activities and the surgical implant compatibilites are but a few examples of biochemically relevant interfacial reactions. All these systems are governed by the water activity and the electrical properties in the interfacial regions. The complexity of the biological parameters has inspired the development of simple and convenient models such as the metal electrode/aqueous electrolyte interface for the study of important physicochemical parameters of the interfacial interactions of biomolecules. This model interface was applied to elucidate the main contours of the interfacial behaviour of nucleic acids, particularly native double stranded deoxyribonucleic acid (DNA), the carrier of the genetic code [145–153]. Such studies are important for the understanding of DNA behaviour in the living cell. Indeed the interfacial recognition of DNA by other biopolymers, as proteins, during the expression and control of the genetic information is one of the more striking problems of the molecular biology of the gene.

By application of the voltammetric method at a mercury electrode/electrolyte solution interface, the action of adsorption forces and the interfacial electric field on the helical structure of DNA has been revealed and the potentialities and essential findings have been summarized in a recent review by Nürnberg [154].

In order to confirm and study in situ the respective conformational changes of DNA in the adsorbed state, the SERS spectroscopy was applied later [19]. Native DNA exhibits some 30–40 normal solution Raman scattering bands in the spectral range of 200–1800 cm^{-1} [155,156]. The more intense bands are caused by vibrations of the base residues adenine (A), guanine (G), cytosine (C) and thymine (T).

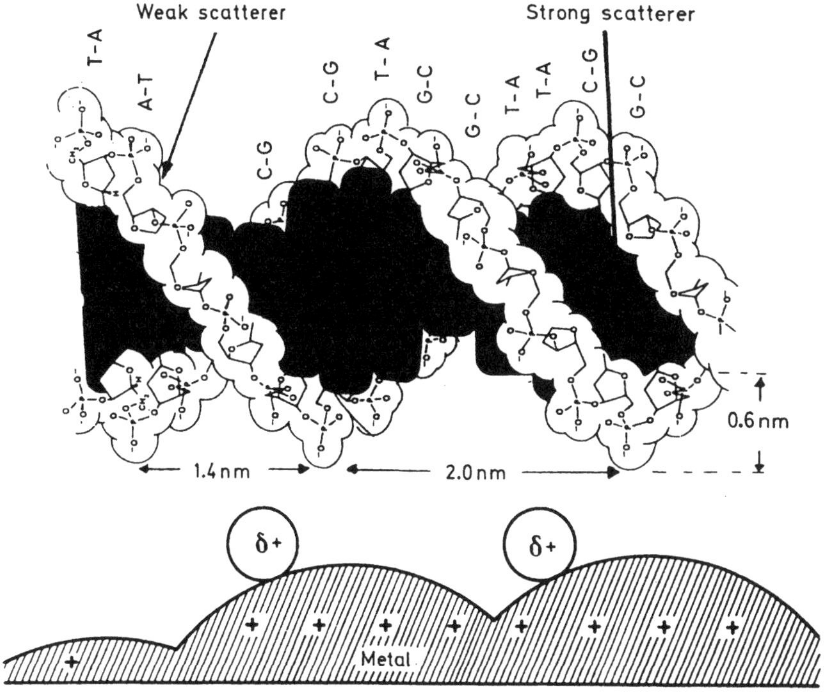

Fig. 11. Spatial arrangement of DNA adsorbed at the positively charged silver surface

For the interpretation of the Raman scattering of DNA close to a charged surface the natural geometry of this biopolymer at the positively charged surface is shown in Fig. 11. This biopolymer consists of a double stranded helix [193,194] with a weak Raman scatterer (sugar-phosphate-group) on the outside of the molecule and a strong Raman scatterer (nucleic bases A, G, C, and T) located in the center of the helix. The distance from the center of DNA to the phosphate group is about 1 nm.

The SERS spectrum of native calf thymus-DNA is shown in Fig. 12. The normal Raman scattering spectra of DNA in solution require a hundred times more concentrated solution than the SERS spectrum presented in Fig. 12. For the interpretation of the SERS spectrum of DNA it is necessary first to assign precise frequencies of the SERS bands of the nucleic bases A, G, C, and T.

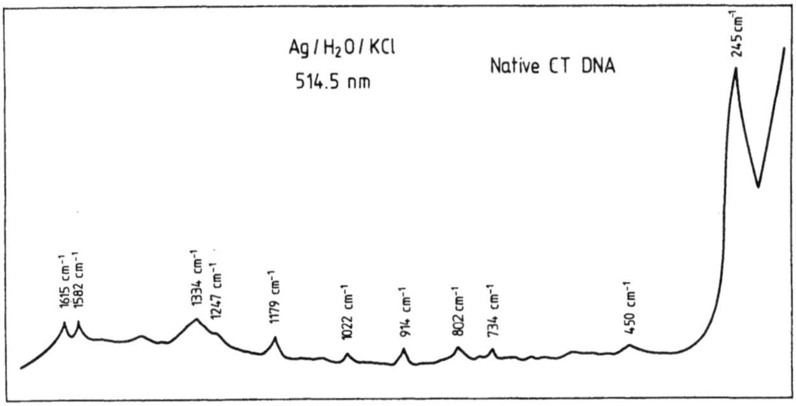

Fig. 12. SERS-spectrum of native CT-DNA. DNA concentration 200 $\mu g \times mL^{-1}$, 0.15 M KCl, 10^{-3} M cacodylate pH 6.8. Laser excitation line 514 nm, laser power at electrode 100 mW. Prior activation of silver electrode by two triangular voltage sweeps between —0.1 and +0.2 V at a sweep rate of 50 mV s^{-1}

4.2.1 DNA Bases

Figure 13 shows the SERS spectrum of a solution containing adenine, guanine, cytosine and thymine in the presence of Ag colloids. This SERS spectrum shows that these building stones of DNA when adsorbed to the silver surface exhibit strong SERS bands. Prominent and characteristic bands are the SERS ring-breathing modes in the spectral range of 600 to 800 cm^{-1}. The most intense SERS band in this region is located at 732 cm^{-1} and is attributed to the adenine ring-breathing mode. In NSRS spectra of DNA the line near 680 cm^{-1} identifies guanine residues in the nucleic acid chain. The corresponding band of guanine in the SERS spectrum of the base mixture solution is at 657 cm^{-1} (cf. Fig. 13). Normal Raman spectra of all pyrimidines have an intense line near 780 cm^{-1}. The corresponding bands of thymine and cytosine in the SERS spectra are at 797 cm^{-1} and are not resolved. In Fig. 13 the SERS spectrum shows a specific strong enhancement of the vibration band corresponding to the adenine base. This result points to a specific adsorption of the adenine

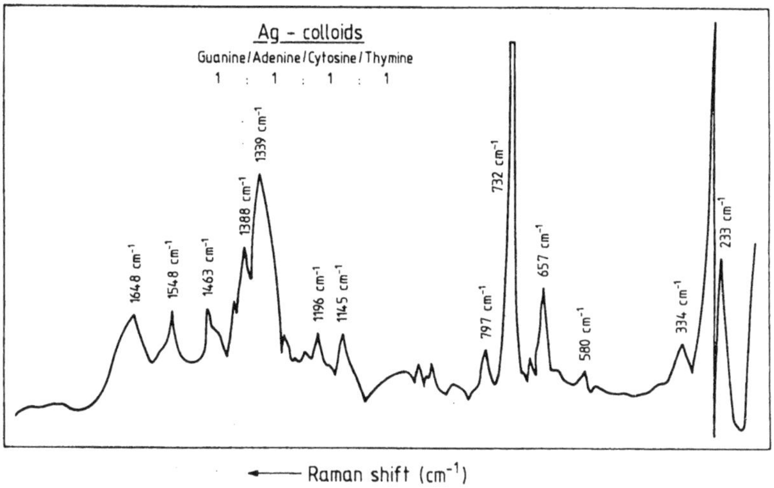

Fig. 13. SERS-spectrum of a solution containing adenine, guanine, cytosine and thymine. Freshly prepared silver colloids, pH 4.5, 4×10^{-6} M adenine, guanine, cytosine and thymine added; laser excitation line 514 nm, laser power 100 mW

Table 2. SERS-ring-breathing modes (cm^{-1}) characteristic for DNA (a, b, c, d and e see Ref. [143, 200, 201, 23, 24])

Bases	Cal.^{a}	Solid^b	Solution^c acid, alkal.	Electrode^d	Colloids^e
Guanine	651	651	642, 650	648	653
Adenine	718	725	722, 725	736	728
Thymine	795	791	788, 788	782	789
Cytosine	793	794	795, 795	798	797

base on the charged silver surface. In Table 2 the calculated and the measured NSRS frequencies (cm^{-1}) for the characteristic ring-breathing modes in the solid state and in solution are compared [30]. SERS frequencies (cm^{-1}) for nucleic bases adsorbed at the electrode and at colloidal particles are also shown.

4.2.2 Mononucleotides

The next DNA building units are the nucleotides, dAMP, dGMP, dCMP, and dTMP (base + deoxyribose + phosphate group).

Figure 14a shows an example of the SERS spectrum of 5′-AMP and its building stones adenine (Fig. 14c) and adenosine (Fig. 14b) adsorbed at a positively charged silver electrode in the spectral range of 100 to 1700 cm^{-1}. The most characteristic internal band systems of the 5′-AMP spectrum are located at 730 and 1340 wavenumbers. They exhibit a significantly enhanced intensity. Moreover, one intense band is observed at 240 cm^{-1}. This band has been assigned to the interfacial vibration of the phosphate group with the positive silver surface $—PO_3^{2-}/Ag$ (cf. Fig. 14d). The

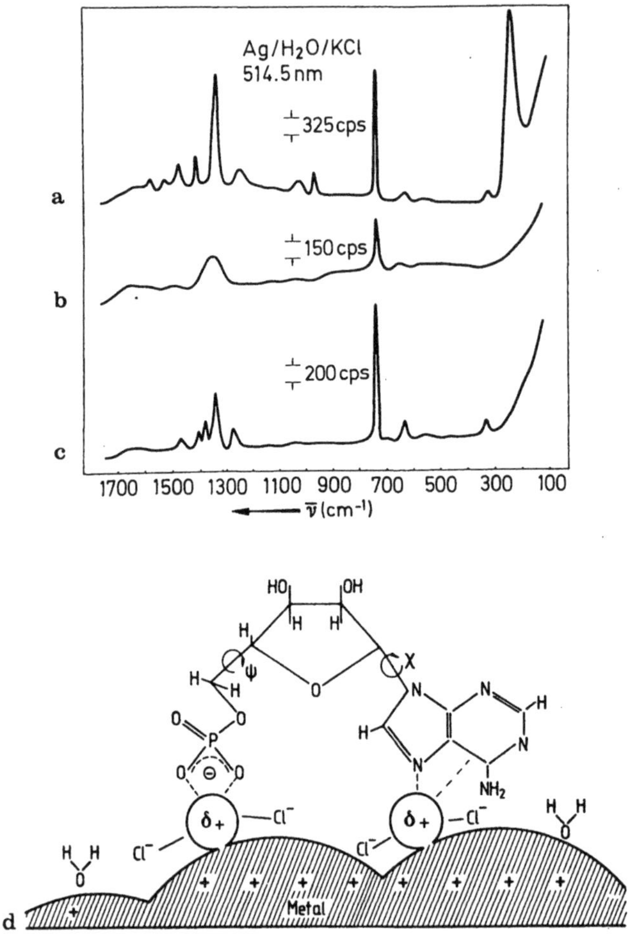

Fig. 14a–d. Surface Raman spectra of
a) adenosine-5′-monophosphate (5′-AMP),
b) adenosine and
c) adenine under identical experimental conditions: 20 mW, E_s of −0.1 V (1 cycle), 0.1 M KCl and 10^{-3} M Na_2HPO_4, pH 8.2; 1.9×10^{-3} M 5′-AMP **a)**; 2.1×10^{-3} M adenosine **b)**; 2.2×10^{-3} M adenine **c)**.
d) Schema of a possible configuration of the adsorbed 5′-AMP at a positively charged silver surface

reason for this assignment is illustrated in Fig. 14a, where first the 5′-AMP mononucleotide with the base, the sugar, and the phosphate unit shows a very strong band at 240 cm^{-1}. Under the same experimental conditions the adenine base and adenosine (adenine bound to ribose) give no strong SERS signals in the spectral range of 200 to 300 cm^{-1} (cf. Fig. 14b, c). From these experimental results of the DNA monomeric units it is now possible to assign the SERS bands in the DNA spectrum. In this spectrum bands appear predominantly at 245 cm^{-1} and 802 cm^{-1} which can be respectively assigned to a silver-phosphate group vibration ($-PO_2^-/Ag$) and to the backbone vibration of the polymeric deoxyribose-phosphate chain. The bands at 914 cm^{-1},

$1022\ cm^{-1}$, $1179\ cm^{-1}$ and $1247\ cm^{-1}$ are typical SERS vibrations of the ribose-phosphate skeleton. The presence of these Raman bands in the SERS spectrum of DNA indicates a preferential interaction of the nucleic residues located on the outer side of the helical structure.

4.2.3 Double-Stranded Polynucleotides

The results reported in the previous section refer only to the adsorption behaviour of a native CT-DNA with a high molecular weight of about 10×10^6 and an intact double stranded structure at rather anodic adsorption potentials and consequently a positively charged silver surface. Indeed it must also be mentioned that depending on the quality of the DNA preparation (molecular weight distribution, presence of strand breaks) and generally at more cathodic adsorption potentials, SERS signals can be detected [39] due to direct contact of nucleic bases with the silver surface. In Fig. 15, SERS spectra of synthetic DNA partial model analogues, poly(dG-dC) × poly(dG-dC) and poly(dA-dT) · poly(dA-dT), containing respectively guanine-cytosine and adenine-thymine base pairs are compared with the SERS spectrum of bacterial ML-DNA (28% A-T, 72% G-C) from Micrococcus Lysodeikticus after adsorption at —0.6 V vs. Ag/AgCl. The presence of characteristic breathing mode vibrations for the nucleic bases residues in the $600\ cm^{-1}$–$800\ cm^{-1}$ spectral region (cf. Tab. 2) clearly indicates an adsorption of the nucleic bases at the electrode sur-

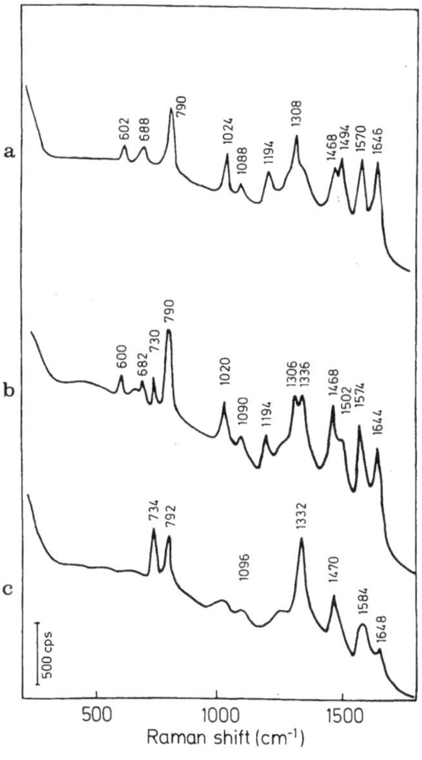

Fig. 15a and b. SERS spectra of poly(dG-dC) · poly(dG-dC) **a)**, of native ML-DNA **b)** and of poly(dA-dT) · poly(dA-dT) **c)**. DNA concentration $140\ \mu g\ ml^{-1}$, $50\ \mu g\ ml^{-1}$, $80\ \mu g\ ml^{-1}$ respectively; 0.15 M KCl, 10^{-3} M Tris pH 8; adsorption potential —0.6 V vs. Ag/AgCl; activation procedure repeated three times from E_s —0.2 V, charge current 6 mCb; 514.5 nm excitation, laser power 15 mW (Lewinsky, Ref. [39])

face. Under these adsorption potential conditions, local destabilization of the adsorbed DNA structure, induced by interfacial forces originate from charged silver surface [145-151,154,159]. A prerequisite for the direct contact of a DNA base residue with the surface is the interfacial destabilization, leading to the breaking of the Watson-

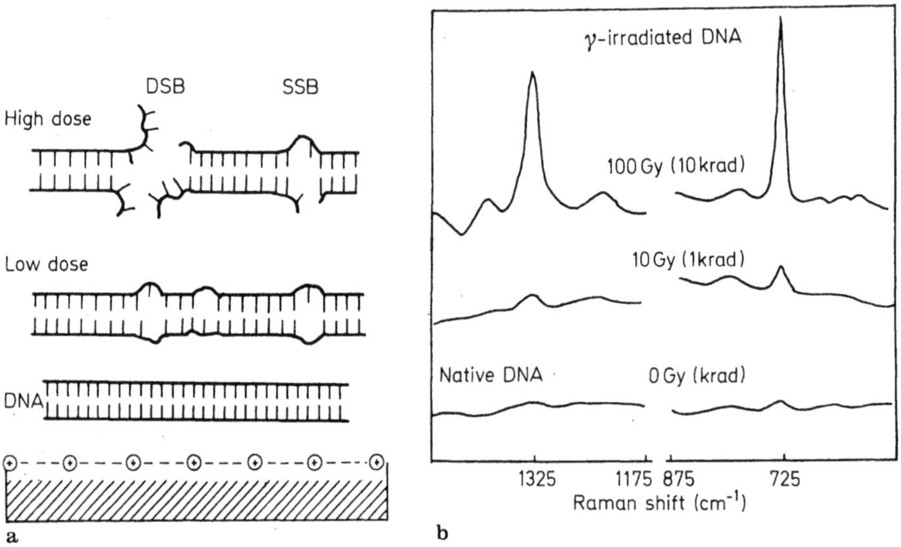

Fig. 16a and b. Damages in DNA by γ-radiation.
a) Scheme of damages in native DNA by ionizing radiations;
SSB: single strand breaks,
DSB: double strand breaks.
b) SERS spectra of native and γ-irradiated DNA **b)**. 0.1 M KCl + 2×10^{-3} M Na_2HPO_4; 300 μg DNA/ml; pH 8.0; irradiated with γ-rays from a ^{60}Co-source. Laser excitation line 514 mm laser power at electrode 50 mW. Prior activation of silver electrode by two voltage sweeps between −0.2 und +0.2 V at a sweep rate of 50 mV s^{-1} (Lewinsky, Ref. [39])

Table 3. Tentative assignment of SERS bands of DNA from Micrococcus Lysodeikticus (ML-DNA); other conditions see Fig. 15

ML-DNA (cm^{-1})	d(A-T)	d(G-C)	r(A-C)	Tentative of Assignement
600	—	+	—	Cytosine
682	—	+	—	Guanine
730	+	—	+	Adenine
790	+	+	+	Cytosine, Thymine
1020	+	+	+	Cytosine
1090	+	+	+	Phosphate
1194	—	+	+	Cytosine
1306	—	+	+	Cytosine
1336	+	—	+	Adenine
1468	+	+	+	Nucleic bases
1502	—	+	+	Cytosine
1574	+	+	+	Nucleic bases
1644	+	+	+	Cytosine, Thymine

Crick hydrogen bonds between two adjacent bases in an interstrand base pair. This causes partial opening of the double helical structure and enables the orientation of the unpaired bases towards the surface (cf. Fig. 16a). In Table 3 the assignment of the SERS bands from ML-DNA have been listed after comparison with poly(dA-dT) · poly(dA-dT), poly(dG-dC) · poly(dG-dC), and poly(rA-rC).

4.3 Modified DNA

4.3.1 γ-Radiation

It is interesting to compare the SERS results of the intact double helical structure of native DNA and the SERS spectra of γ-irradiated DNA. It is well known that ionizing radiation, e.g. γ-radiation, causes damage in DNA by the action of radicals formed in radiation chemical reactions with the solvent water. The hitherto known kinds of damage are single strand breaks and at higher doses an increasing number of double strand breaks followed by release of oligonucleotide units [152,153] (cf. Fig. 16a).

The SERS spectra of the intact and γ-irradiated DNA in the spectral range of the characteristic ring-breathing modes and the skeletal vibrations are shown in Fig. 16b. The most striking features are the pronounced lines at 734 cm^{-1} and 1334 cm^{-1} in the γ-irradiated DNA. These characteristic bands can be assigned to the vibrations of adsorbed adenine bases. It follows that the nucleic base adenine becomes accessible to the electrode surface. As only short-range interactions play an important role in the enhancement factor, this finding confirms that in the γ-irradiated DNA some adenine residues from destabilized base pairs become free for direct adsorption at the surface. Even at a γ-radiation dose as low as 10 Gy or 1 krad a destabilization of the double helical conformation of the irradiated DNA (300 μg DNA/ml) can be detected which confirms spectroscopically previous voltammetric findings [152,153].

4.3.2 Chemical Methylation

In this context it is mentioned that a similar SERS approach has also revealed the mechanism of alkylating substances causing mutagenic chemical damages in native DNA [41]. Methylation occurs preferentially, though not exclusively, at the N(7) position of guanine labilizing the affected G-C nucleic base pairs [158–160]. Several studies have shown that methylated DNA is unstable [161,162]. The breakdown is due to the formation of apurinic sites followed by strand scission at these weakened points [158–162].

Figure 17 shows the SERS spectra of native and methylated DNA. In the SERS spectrum of the native DNA (cf. Fig. 17a) the Raman bands at 736 cm^{-1} and 1332 cm^{-1} corresponding to adenine residues are more intense than the bands in the SERS spectrum shown in Fig. 12. As has already been mentioned, the Raman intensity of the adenine vibration can vary somewhat depending on the electrochemical pretreatment of the silver electrode and the available quality of the DNA samples. Before discussing the specific changes in DNA SERS spectra, due to the methylation, it is necessary to know the SERS data of the methylated guanine bases. The observed frequencies and relative intensities of the SERS bands of guanine and its derivates are given in Table 4. The methylation of guanine leads to a specific change in the SERS spectrum. The strong enhanced ring modes at 1386 cm^{-1} and 1467 cm^{-1}, characteristic for guanine, disappear in the 7-methylguanine (7-MeGua), the guanine ring-breathing mode at 653 cm^{-1} decreases and new enhanced bands appear at 703 cm^{-1} and 1354 cm^{-1}. The band at 703 cm^{-1} which is not seen in the spectrum of guanine can be assigned to the N(7)C(5) stretching vibration or the N(7)C(5)C(6) band vibration. Apparently by introducing a methylgroup at the N(7)-nitrogen this band becomes Raman active.

At the adsorption potential of —0.2 V vs. Ag/AgCl which corresponds to a highly positively charged surface, the SERS spectrum of adsorbed DNA is characterized by a strong band at 236 cm^{-1} (cf. Fig. 17a). This specific low frequency vibration,

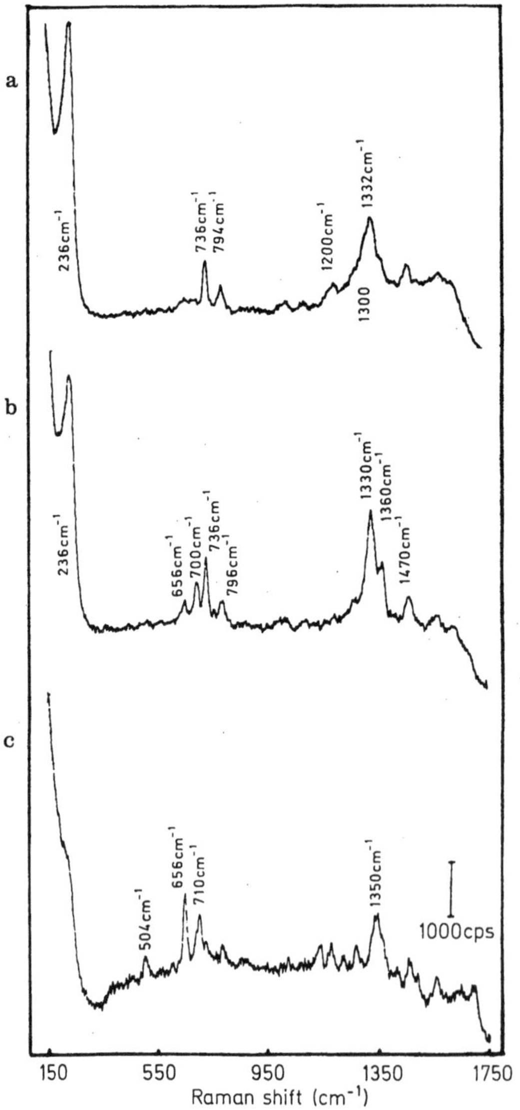

Fig. 17a–c. SERS spectra of native CT-DNA **a)**, methylated CT-DNA (8%-MeGua) before **b)** and after heating at 70 °C **c)** adsorbed on Ag electrode. Concentration of DNA 200 μg mL^{-1}, 0.15 M NaCl, 2×10^{-3} M Tris, pH 8, adsorption potential E_s —0.2 V vs. Ag/AgCl reference electrode (Ref. [41])

Table 4. SERS frequencies (cm^{-1}) of guanine derivatives adsorbed at silver colloids

Gua(I) C 3.6×10^{-6} M	1MeGua(II) C 3.3×10^{-6} M	9MeGua(III) C 1.4×10^{-6} M	7MeGua(IV) C 4.2×10^{-6} M	3MeGua(V) C 8.4×10^{-6} M	0^6MeGua(VI) C 4.5×10^{-6} M	6ClGua(VII) C 5×10^{-6} M
234 v	232 v	223 v	232 v	222 v	224 v	236 v
336 w	326 w				339 w	
380 w	366 w	361 w	396 w	368 m	395 w	368 w
455 w	476 w	495 w	455 w	462 m	429 w	452 w
506 w	526 w	522 w	505 m	501 w		
552 w			559 w	559 m	570 w	536 w
		607 m				*582* s
					620 v	
653 v	*655* v	*656* s	*651* v	*638* v		
	714 w		*703* v	735 m		
745 w	762 w	730 w		765 m	752 w	752 w
856 w	814 w		871 w			844 w
964 m	938 m	911 m		921 w	946 w	938 w
	978 w			995 w		963 w
1054 w	1028 w	1047 m		1055 m		
		1092 w				
1145 s	1147 m		1139 s	1154 m	1134 w	
		1200 w	1183 s			
1224 m	*1231* s	1235 w	1218 m	1221 s		
1260 w	1291 m	1285 m	1272 s	*1243* v	1240 w	
1317 s				1285 s		
						1300 s
1356 s	*1356* s	*1335* v	*1354* v	1349 s	*1334* v	
1386 v	1375 m	1396 m		*1387* v	1386 m	1384 m
	1405 m		1421 s	*1421* v		
1467 v	1460 m	1446 m	1462 m			
1512 m		1498 m	1495 s	1510 m	1506 w	1496 w
1538 s	1549 m					
1574 m		*1580* s	1565 s			
1594 m	1589 w			1592 s		1608 w
1655 m					1628 w	
1708 s	*1700* s		*1703* v			

w, m, s, v indicate weak, medium, strong and very strong intensities respectively.

already mentioned in 4.2, has been attributed to the electrostatic interaction of negatively charged phosphate groups with the surface. It is seen that after reaction of alkylating agents with DNA the 236 cm^{-1} band decreases (cf. Fig. 17b). This intensity change can be interpreted as a decrease of the adsorption of modified DNA through the phosphate groups.

The effects of chemical methylation lead to further specific variations in the spectral range of 600 to 800 cm^{-1} and 1300 to 1500 cm^{-1}.

The SERS spectrum of methylated DNA shows new Raman bands at 656 cm^{-1}, 700 cm^{-1} and 1360 cm^{-1} which correspond to characteristic vibrations of 7-MeGua residues in adsorbed methylated DNA (cf. Table 4). Furthermore, the decrease of the band at 1200 cm^{-1} and the 1300 cm^{-1} shoulder of the band centered at 1332 cm^{-1} in the SERS spectrum of native DNA upon methylation can be related to a conformational change of DNA at the location of modified nucleic base pairs 7-MeGua-cytosine. Thus, at a rather positively charged surface, the SERS spectra reveal substantial changes in the adsorption behaviour of methylated DNA.

The cleavage of 7-MeGua, accompanied by strand breaks, can be obtained by heating the DNA solution. Fig. 17c shows the SERS spectrum of methylated DNA after heating at 70 °C. Comparing this SERS spectrum with the 7-MeGua vibrations (cf. Table 4) it appears that most Raman bands of the heated methylated DNA can be assigned to vibrations of the released 7-MeGua.

Considering a competitive adsorption at the surface, it must be assumed that the strong hydrophobic character of the 7-MeGua prevails over more hydrophilic properties of the oligonucleotide units from the degraded DNA.

4.3.3 Temperature Effects on Native DNA

Thermal denaturation of calf-thymus DNA has also been studied by SERS-spectroscopy [19,39]. The examinations of the SER scattering of thermally denatured DNA indicates that the nucleic bases bands are sensitive to the termal transition from the helical double stranded structure to the disordered single stranded structure. In this thermally destabilized DNA the strands are open and the corresponding bases can easily re-orientate therfore becoming available for direct interaction with the surface. Generally at every adsorption potential there is a sensitive increase of the intensity of the Raman bands of the nucleic bases in the SERS spectra. In summary, one may say that SERS is useful to determine the structural changes of DNA under the action of physical or chemical disturbances.

4.3.4 Pt-coordination Compounds

Rosenberg's discovery [163] of the surprising antitumoral properties of certain platinum compounds has led to a number of investigations of the interaction of a series of these compounds with DNA [164–168]. The results suggest that specific strand cross-links of the DNA through covalent bands of Pt compounds to the nucleic bases could be responsible for the antitumoral activity.

SERS-spectroscopy has been used to clarify the specific binding modes of the powerful anti-tumor agent cis-$Pt(NH_3)_2Cl_2$ and an inactive Pt-complex [Pt-(dien)Cl]Cl [32]. The presence or absence of specific SERS bands of platinum compounds yields information concerning the stereochemistry of Pt binding to DNA. This is a further

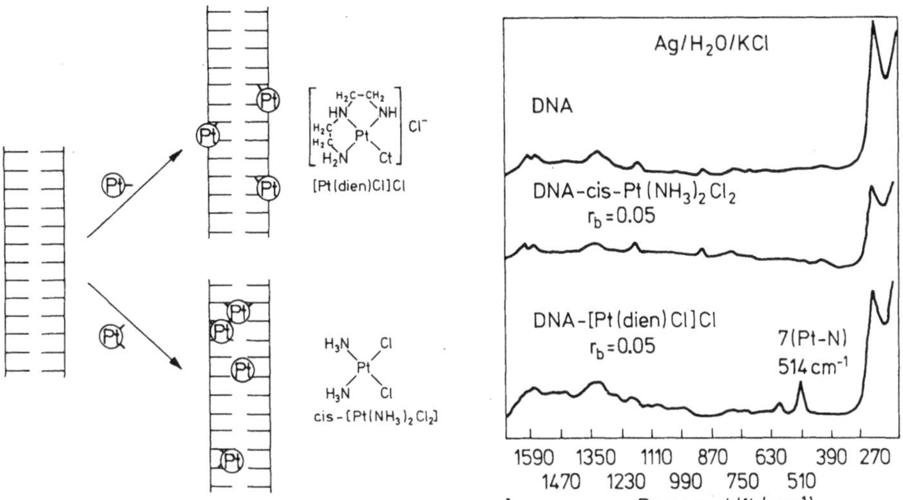

a b

Fig. 18a and b. Interaction of DNA with Pt-complexes
a) Schematic diagram of inner and outer complexes of Pt-coordination compounds with CT DNA.
b) SERS spectra of native CT DNA by [Pt-(dien)Cl]Cl and cic-$Pt(NH_3)_2Cl_2$. DNA concentration 200 μg × mL^{-1}, 0.15 M KCl, 10^{-3} M cacodylate pH 6.8, inserted r_b values represent the number of platinum atoms bound per nucleotide. Laser excitation line 514 nm, laser power 200 mW, 3 successive rapid (50 mV × sec^{-1}) cyclic voltammetric scans from starting potentials E_s −0.2 V to +0.2 V versus a Ag/AgCl reference electrode

utilization of the to short-range forces restricted SERS (cf. Fig. 18a). Fig. 18b compares the SERS spectra of native DNA (top) and DNA complexed with cis-$Pt(NH_3)_2Cl_2$ (middle), [Pt-(dien)Cl]Cl (bottom). The appearance in the SERS spectra of a strong band at about 245 cm^{-1} attributed to the surface adsorbed $-PO_2^-$-group vibration is a clear indication of the adsorption. In the Pt-DNA complexation the characteristic Pt-N stretching band at 514 cm^{-1} is missing in the SERS spectrum of the cis-$Pt(NH_3)_2Cl_2$ interacting with DNA. The absence of SERS signals, if interactions occur outside the short range where the SERS is restricted, suggests that this antitumoral Pt-complex is coordinated in the interior of the double helical structure, probably between adjacent guanines [168]. On the other hand, the characteristic symmetric Pt-N stretching vibration at 514 cm^{-1} observed in the case of the inactive [Pt-(dien)Cl] interaction with DNA indicates a preferential binding outside the double helical structure.

The studies of the inner and outer complexes of Pt-compounds with DNA clearly demonstrate the ability of SERS to differentiate binding modes substances to DNA.

4.4 Micro-SERS of Chromosomes

In addition to DNA and RNA large amounts of associated proteins known as histones, as well as other proteins, are present in the chromosomes. The relatively low cross-section for Raman scattering of chromosomes is the reason for the lack of normal Raman investigations. Recently, the first Raman spectra of intact chromosomes

(Chinese hamster lung cells) have been obtained by means of Micro-Raman spectroscopy [169]. The Micro-Raman spectra of these chromosomes exhibited significant Raman bands which could be assigned to the DNA or to the protein contents of the chromosomes.

All Raman bands measured in DNA fibres or crystals appear in this chromosome Micro-Raman spectrum. In addition, typical vibrations of the protein component were observed (phenylalanine, tyrosine, S—S group and the amide I mode). Recently, Micro-SERS has been applied for the first time to investigate the chromosomes adsorbed at the silver electrode [36]. This Micro-SERS spectrum of Chinese hamster metaphase chromosomes shows a number of intense bands. The enhancement factor obtained was estimated to be about 100 for the 790 cm^{-1} DNA backbone vibration. The most intense bands in this SERS spectrum are located at 730 cm^{-1} and 1330 cm^{-1} and can be attributed to the adsorbed adenine base vibration of the DNA. The characteristic protein vibrations in the normal Raman spectrum are missing in the SERS spectrum.

The peptide backbone vibration (amide I) and the ring-breathing mode of phenylalanine at 1004 cm^{-1} are not enhanced in this chromosome. An interpretation of this missing enhancement is that only the DNA has a strong interaction with the surface. The protein contents do not interact directly with the surface. These Micro-SERS investigations have shown that SERS can clarify structural changes of chromosomes in the adsorbed state.

4.5 Other Substances of Biochemical Significance

a) Anabolic Drugs

Natural and synthetic hormones are used worldwide to improve meat production [170]. There are, however, possible hazards for the consumer. Therefore, in most European countries the use of hormonal anabolics is restricted or even prohibited by law. Among the banned synthetic anabolics diethylstilbestrol (DES) takes the most important place at the moment. Analytical control is carried out in various ways. Frischkorn and Smyth [171,172] have described an HPLC method with electrochemical detection for the determination of growth promoting hormones in meat.

Obtaining normal solution Raman spectra of some anabolic agents is impossible, because of its very low solubility in water. However, vibrational spectra of these compounds have been obtained by means of SERS in the presence of colloidal silver particles [31]. The anabolic DES shows at 8×10^{-5} M bulk concentration a very strong Raman scattering with enhanced bands at 1174, 1468 and 1606 cm^{-1}.

Fig. 19 shows the SERS spectrum of DES-3,4-oxide, a potential metabolite of DES. A comparison with the SERS spectrum of DES shows that one has characteristic changes in the SERS spectrum after DES-oxidation. The characteristic DES band at 1606 cm^{-1} is shifted to 1572 cm^{-1} in the DES-3,4-oxide spectrum. The strong SERS band at 1468 cm^{-1} in DES is decreased in the DES-3,4-oxide SERS spectrum and a new characteristic SERS band appears at 534 cm^{-1}.

b) p-Aminobenzoic acid

p-Aminobenzoic acid (PABA) is important in the bacterial biosynthesis of folic acid [195]. The SERS spectrum of PABA adsorbed on aqueous colloidal silver particles

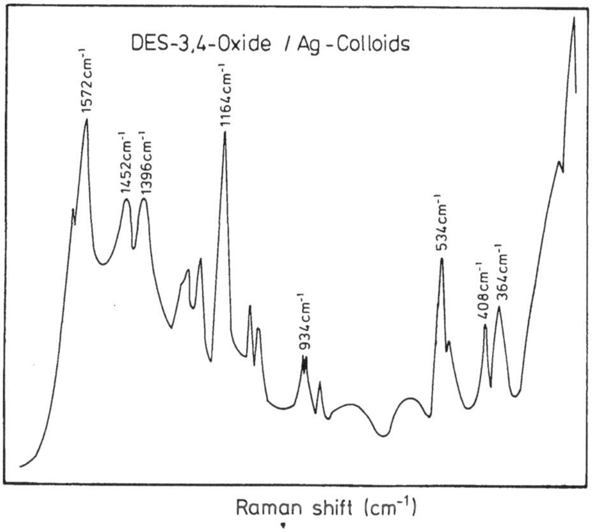

Fig. 19. SERS spectrum of DES-3,4-oxide adsorbed on Ag colloids. Ag colloids with 5×10^{-5} M DES-3,4-oxide, laser excitation line 514 nm, laser power 200 mW

was reported by Suh et al. [28]. A SERS spectrum obtained with a silver colloid sample containing a very low PABA concentration is shown in Fig. 20. The observed concentration and temperature behaviour of the SERS spectrum suggests the existence of PABA in two forms on the surface. The PABA molecule is adsorbed flatly in its anionic form, bound through the benzene ring. In the spectral range of 100 cm^{-1} to 300 cm^{-1} a typical interfacial band between the $—COO^-$ group and the Ag surface is missing. This is an additional indication that the flat adsorption is prefered. The enhancement factor was estimated to be 4×10^6.

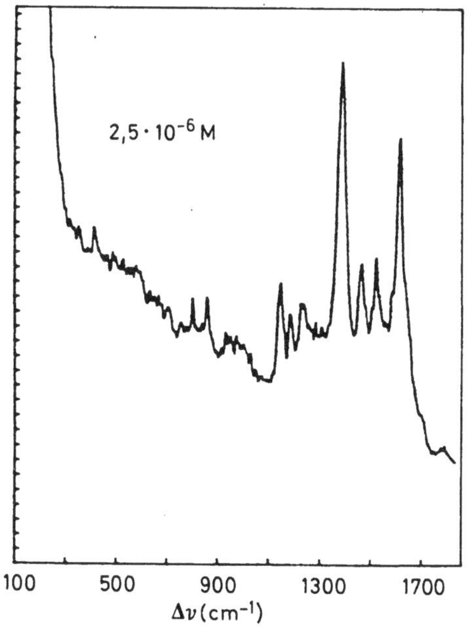

Fig. 20. SERS spectrum of a low concentration (2.5×10^{-6} M) of p-Aminobenzoic acid adsorbed on silver sol particles. (Suh et al., Ref. [28])

c) Citric acid

The citric acid plays an important role in the citric acid cycle (TCA or Krebs cycle) to separate carbons from reducing equivalents, which are concentrated as reduced coenzymes [195].

Citrate adsorbed on colloidal silver is a model system for the explanation of SERS on metal colloids with the electromagnetic model [70,79,86,88]. The citrate ion is chemisorbed and coordinated to surface silver atoms in the deprotonated form. Adsorbed citrate exhibits intense SERS bands at 1400 (vs), 1026 (s), 953 (m), and 840 cm^{-1}. Maximum measured enhancement of about 2×10^5 agree with electrodynamic calculations. The strongly enhanced band at 1400 cm^{-1} is assigned to $\nu_s(COO^-)$. The $\nu_{as}(COO^-)$ vibration at 1580 cm^{-1} in NSRS is absent in the SERS spectrum. The position of the carboxylate symmetric stretching band is characteristic of both bonding strength and geometry of coordination in the individual metal complex. The COO^- groups may coordinate with the metal atoms on the surface in one of the following ways:

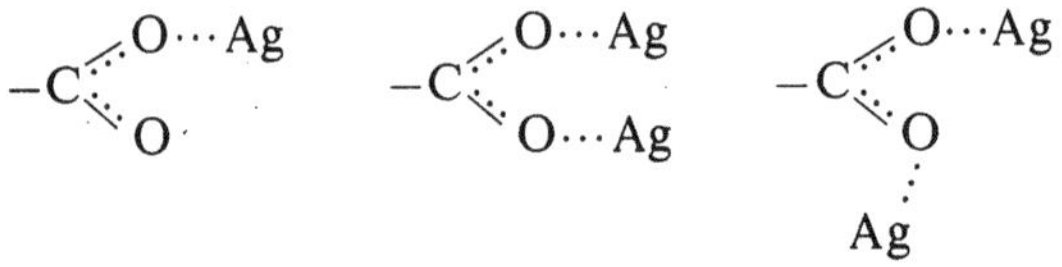

(a) (b) (c)

I

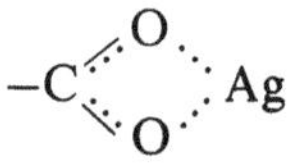

II

In the case of structure I the carboxylate group (symmetry C_{2v}) is known to become more asymmetric as the metal-oxygen bond becomes stronger, leading to a lower frequency shift of $\nu_s(COO^-)$, which correlates with the distorted configuration (C_s symmetry: I a) in the adsorbed state. The 15 cm^{-1} downward shift to 1400 cm^{-1} of the $\nu_s(COO^-)$ mode exhibits monodenate coordination (I a–c). The bidentate chelate mode of binding configuration (II) gives higher $\nu_s(COO^-)$ band frequencies than in configuration (I) and is therefore not considered to be an alternative assignment for any of the citrate carboxylate-silver surface coordination configurations in the sodiumcitrate-Ag sol [86].

d) Hydrogen-Deuterium exchange in 5′-AMP and guanine

The mechanism of hydrogen exchange has shown that DNA is subject to local structural fluctuations, which result in frequent opening and closing of the structure [173,174]. A study of the isotopic exchange thus reveals interesting aspects of the kinetics of structural fluctuations of the DNA. In particular the study of deuterium exchange by means of NSRS-spectroscopy has shown that the Raman spectrum provides a method for the determination of the exchange rate constant in purine nucleotides [175,176]. The study of hydrogen-deuterium exchange by means of SERS-spectroscopy was first applied to biomolecules in Ref. [18]. The SERS effect for 5′-AMP on Ag-

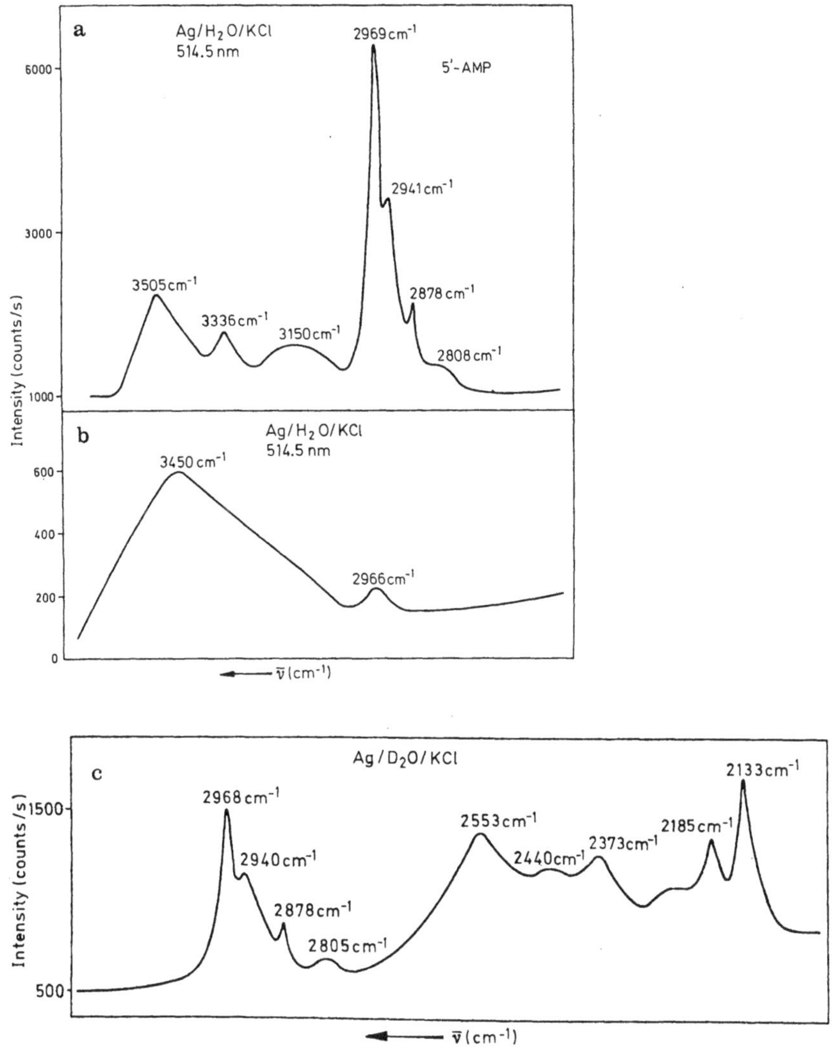

Fig. 21a–c. SERS spectra in the C-H and C-D vibrational range.
a) SERS spectrum of 5′-AMP in H_2O after one cycle of electrochemical activation from E_s —0.1 V to 0.2 V and back;
b) The background surface spectrum taken before the activation cycle, 2×10^{-3} M 5′ AMP in 0.1 M KCl + 10^{-3} M Na_2HPO_4, pH 5.2;
c) SERS spectrum of 5′-AMP in D_2O medium after one cycle of electrochemical activation from E_s —0.1 V to 0.2 V and back. 2×10^{-3} M 5′-AMP in 0.1 M KCl + 10^{-3} M Na_2HPO_4, pD 5.1

electrodes in the C—H vibrational range is illustrated in Fig. 21 by comparing the NSRS spectrum in H_2O solution (cf. Fig. 21 b) and SERS spectrum in the adsorbed state after electrochemical roughening (cf. Fig. 21 a).

Before electrochemical activation of the silver electrode, one observes the broad and intense stretching mode of water (3450 cm^{-1}). This O—H scattering masks the vibrations of the 5′-AMP molecule in the NSRS spectrum (cf. Fig. 21 b). After activation, the intensity of the 5'-AMP vibrations are many times greater than that of the water vibrations. The enhancement of water vibrations is generally very small and thus the SERS spectrum give very intense and well-resolved Raman lines of the adsorbed molecules in the spectral range of 2800–3400 cm^{-1} (cf. Fig. 21a). When D_2O is the solvent for 5'-AMP the isotopic hydrogen exchange between protons of the 5'-AMP and the deuterons of the solvent takes place. The SERS bands of 5'-AMP in D_2O solution are more or less sensitive to the kinetics of hydrogen-deuterium exchange. The spectral effect produced by this deuteration is shown in Fig. 21c. All O—H stretching vibrations of water molecules at the Ag surface are shifted from 3505 cm^{-1} to 2553 cm^{-1}. The SERS vibrations of D_2O at 2553 cm^{-1} are weak and the scattering does not obscure the scattering signals of 5'-AMP. This permits the observation of hydrogen-deuterium exchange in this spectral range (2000–2800 cm^{-1}).

The observation of the H—D exchange in the spectral range near the laser excitation frequency by means of SERS spectroscopy is illustrated in Fig. 22. This SERS spectrum of guanine dissolved in D_2O shows a remarkable increase of intensity of new bands and a decrease of intensity of other bands. A detailed analysis of this isotopic exchange from C—H to C—D is given elsewhere [25]. In the deuterated guanine SERS spectra are two characteristic vibrations at 1330 cm^{-1} (δND_2) and 1267 cm^{-1} (δND).

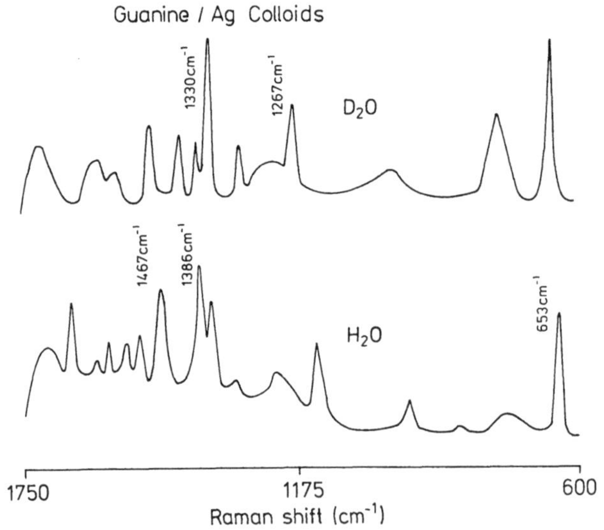

Fig. 22. SERS spectra of guanine adsorbed on Ag colloids in D_2O at pD 4.1 (top) and in H_2O at pH 4.5 (bottom). Ag colloids with 1×10^{-6} M guanine, laser excitation 514.5 nm, laser power 150 mW

4.6 Amino Acids

A typical protein chain is formed by the peptide repeating unit $(—CO—NH—C_\alpha HR—)_n$ where R is an aliphatic or aromatic substituent of the amino acid and often referred to as the "amino acid side chain". Most of the observed Raman bands of proteins come from these amino acid side chains, particularly the aromatic side chains [11,12,155,156]. For the interpretation of SER scattering of proteins it is first necessary to discuss the surface enhanced Raman spectra of aromatic amino acids. SERS spectra of aromatic amino acids adsorbed at silver electrodes were first presented by Nabiev et al. [20]. SERS spectra of phenylalanine (Phe), tryptophane (Trp), tyrosine (Tyr) and histidine (His) in a bulk concentration range of 0.5–1.0 mg/ml were obtained. This concentration is two orders of magnitude less than those required for obtaining the non-resonance Raman spectra of amino acids.

Fig. 23 compares these SERS spectra of Phe, Trp, Tyr and His in an aqueous solution of 0.025 M KCl and pH 7 at an electrode potential E_s —0.6 V. All amino acids investigated show strong enhanced Raman spectra in the spectral range from 500 to 1700 cm^{-1}.

Recently the SERS spectra of on silver hydrosols adsorbed aromatic amino acids have also been studied [27]. The Raman spectra are enhanced from 100 to 200 times in the presence of silver colloids with primary sol particles 14 nm in size. The hydrosol-Phe interaction shows the strongest SERS spectrum. The frequency shifts between the NSRS- and SERS spectra are small (1–15 cm^{-1}). The following SERS bands are characteristic for the aromatic amino acids: Phe, 1005, 1034 and 1049 cm^{-1}; Trp, 762, 1340 and 1377 cm^{-1}; Tyr, 831, 988, 1169 and 1299 cm^{-1}; His, 670 and 1310 cm^{-1}.

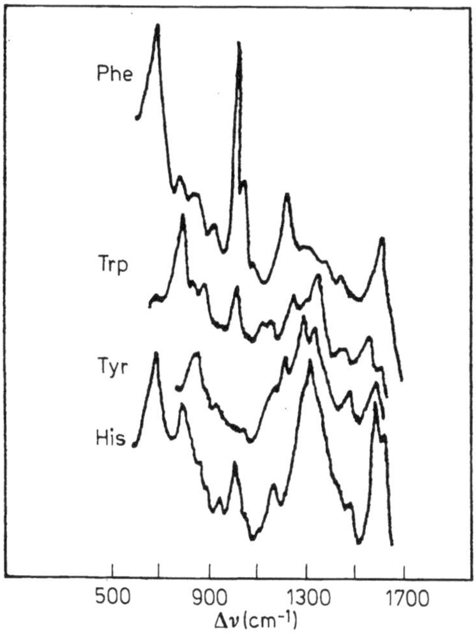

Fig. 23. SERS spectra of aromatic amino acids adsorbed on Ag electrodes. Phe: phenylalanine, Trp: tryptophan, Tyr: Tyrosine, His: histidine (Nabiev et al., Ref. [20])

4.7 Proteins

There have been a number of recent investigations in the field of normal Raman spectroscopy with laser excitation of proteins in aqueous solutions [11,12,155,156]. Raman spectroscopy uncovers information of the peptide backbone, geometry of disulfide bonds, and influences of the solution environment of side chains such as tyrosine (Tyr), tryptophane (Trp) and methionine. Moreover, Raman spectroscopy can detect the presence of the disulfide bond (—S—S—), the methionine residue, and the sulfhydryl group (—SH), tasks which are tedious by conventional chemical methods.

A correlation between normal Raman spectra and conformational properties of proteins (peptide backbone arrangement such as "α-helix", "β-sheet structure", "β-turn configuration", "γ-turn configuration" and "random coil") is often applicable to Raman group frequencies of amides to ascertain the protein chain conformation. With this Raman technique one detects frequency shifts corresponding to the vibrational modes arising from various types of chemical bonds. The amide I (1650 to 1675 cm^{-1}) reflects mainly C=O stretching motions and is hardly affected by hydrogen bonding; whereas amide III (1230–1310 cm^{-1}) originates from C—N stretching and N—H bending motions of the peptide backbone. Other modes in the Raman spectrum arise from motions in the bonds of the amino acid side chains.

How can SERS spectroscopy elucidate the protein structure? What is the basis for it? As was mentioned before, SERS signals of macromolecules are only detected from components being in direct contact with the surface. Thus, SERS signals from proteins give specific information about the direct interaction of the surface active protein sites with a charged surface.

In order to see how these results of the short-range enhancement (cf. Chapt. 4.1) can be used to study the interfacial behaviour of the enzyme lysozyme, the SERS spectrum of this protein in the adsorbed state at a charged silver surface is shown in Fig. 24. The spectrum observed at —0.6 V vs. SCE exhibited very high signal-to-noise ratios for a solution concentration as low as 0.2 mg/ml. This concentration is about two hundred times smaller than in the NSRS spectroscopy [177, 178].

A number of characteristic SERS bands originate from the amino acid side chains: Trp, Tyr and Phe. The peptide backbone vibrations are not enhanced in this protein (low scattering intensity in the spectral range of 1650–1675 cm^{-1}: amide I). The presence of the strong SERS bands of Trp, Tyr and Phe and the absence of the amide vibrations indicate a preferential interaction of these amino acid side chains with the surface. The strong (S—S) vibration at 509 cm^{-1} in the NSRS spectrum is also missing in the SERS spectrum. This indicates that the disulfide bonds do not interact directly with the surface.

Another demonstration of the utility of SERS for studying somewhat larger proteins is shown in Fig. 25 where the SERS spectrum of bovine serum albumine (BSA) could be observed on silver electrodes at a concentration of 20 μg ml^{-1} [179]. The NSRS spectrum of BSA was first presented by Bellocq. et al. [180] at a 1000 fold higher concentration of 20 mg ml^{-1} and a laser power of 100 mW.

Bovine serum albumine is a large protein with a molecular weight of 64000, cross-linked by 16 disulfide bonds [181]. It has 26 phenylalanine, 17 histidine, 19 tyrosine and 2 tryptophane residues. The aromatic rings of these residues give rise to several characteristic ring frequencies in the NSRS spectrum [180]. The ring-breathing vibration of the monosubstituted phenyl ring is seen at 1004 cm^{-1}. Other phenyl lines occur at 623 and 1032 cm^{-1}. Lines due to tyrosine appear at 820 and 852 cm^{-1}. The lines of tryptophane are obscured in the BSA spectrum, because of the low proportion of tryptophan in the molecule. The 16 S—S bonds in the molecule give very weak

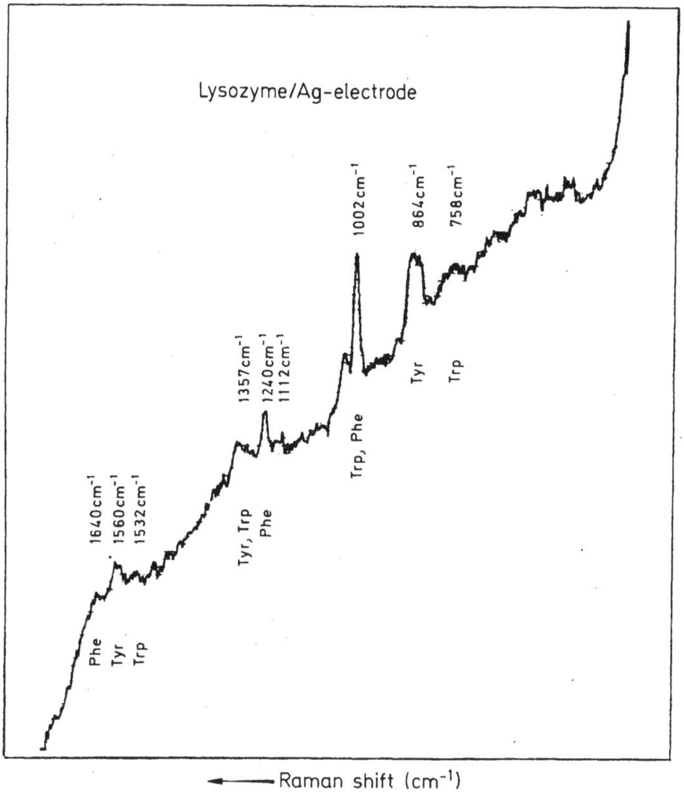

Fig. 24. SERS spectrum at the Ag electrode 0.1 M KCl, 280 μg ml^{-1} lysozyme recorded using 514.5 nm excitation and 6 mW power (Kisters, Ref. [179])

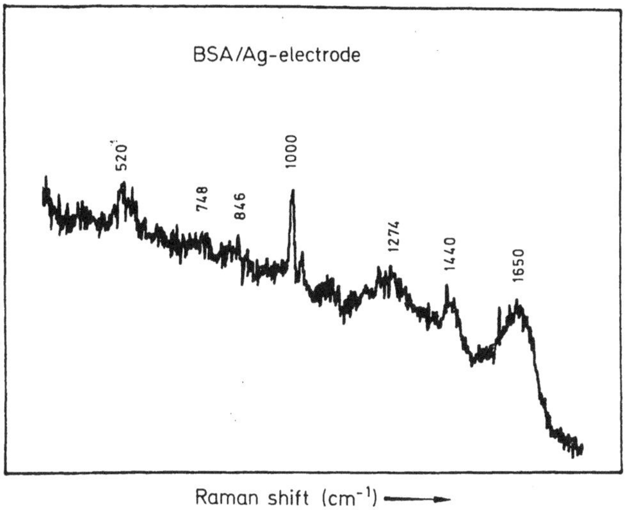

Fig. 25. SERS spectrum of bovine serum albumin (BSA) adsorbed on the Ag electrode. Conditions: 20 μg ml^{-1} BSA, 0.15 M KCl, 2 mM Tris, exc., 514.5 nm, laser power 10 mW, E_s —0.9 V (Kisters, Ref. [179])

NSRS bands in the characteristic frequency range of 500 to 600 cm^{-1}. The amide I vibration is obscured by the water band at 1650 cm^{-1} and the amide III vibration shows only a shoulder at 1280 cm^{-1} and a broad 1250 cm^{-1} band.

In the SERS spectrum of BSA the strongest bands are located at 526, 846, 1000, 1274, 1440 and 1650 cm^{-1}. The presence of the SERS bands of Phe (1000 cm^{-1}) and Tyr (846 cm^{-1}) indicates an interaction of these amino acid side chains with the surface.

The frequency of the amide I vibration of the peptide group falls in the range 1600–1700 cm^{-1} and this spectral range is not obscured by the water band, because of the low enhancement of the HOH bending mode in the SERS spectroscopy. Thus, the SERS band of BSA at 1650 cm^{-1} can be tentatively assigned to the amide I vibration of the adsorbed peptide bond. In the region of the amide III vibration, a broad SERS band appears at 1274 cm^{-1}. The strong band at 1440 cm^{-1} is readily assigned to the deformation of the CH_2 and CH_3 groups.

5 Surface Enhanced Resonance Raman Scattering (SERRS)

In the above described SERS studies of biological compounds, the laser excitation wavelength used is far from the electronic absorption band of the substance or moiety adsorbed at the metal surface. For example, in the case of DNA, the maximum of its absorption band at 258 nm lies in the U.V. spectral region far from the predominately used 514.5 nm laser excitation line. Under these conditions (see Chapt. 3), a very small percentage of the scattered photons exchange energy with the vibrational states of sample molecules to give Raman photons. This phenomenon, due to the low sensitivity of the NRS spectroscopy, can be overcome with coloured biological samples. Indeed, under the conditions of a coincidence or near-coincidence of the electronic absorption bands of the substances with the laser excitation wavelength, the increased probability of photon-molecule energy exchange with vibrational states leads to intensity or resonance enhancement compared to the NRS spectroscopy [182]. This resonance Raman enhancement of a factor 10^6 permits the Resonance Raman Scattering (RRS) spectroscopy to measure vibrational spectra of biological chromophores at very low concentrations at the suitable excitation wavelength. However, the intrinsic fluorescence accompanying the photon absorption, expressed in a low signal-to-noise ratio of the Raman signal, considerably limits the application of this technique. Notwithstanding this practical point of view, the RRS spectroscopy was specifically developed to study the behaviour of the chromophores of biomolecules. Monitoring of different electronic states from metalloporphyrins during the biological activity of hemoproteins have for example helped to clarify their catalytic activities during the respiratory mechanism [157]. Accurate structural pictures and functional insights for the biological chromophores make RRS spectroscopy one method of choice in molecular biophysics. Since the discovery that adsorption on roughened silver electrodes or silver colloids can increase Raman scattering, RRS spectroscopy has acquired new applications. The combination of both scattering enhancements which would reach an upper factor of about 10^{12}, has been considered by various research groups [91,183–185]. In the biological area, the first applications of the Surface Enhanced Resonance Raman Scattering (SERRS) spectroscopy, are provided by

Table 5. Resonance Raman spectroscopy of biological chromophores (SERRS studies are underlined)

Chromophores with tetrapyroll skeletons		Other chromophores	
Respiratory activity	Other activity	Respiratory activity	Other activity
hemoproteins (*cytochromes*, *myoglobin*, . . .)	*bile pigments* *chlorophylls* vitamine B12	hemocyanin hemerythrin iron-sulphur proteins "blue" copper proteins *flavoproteins*	carotenoids *vidual pigments* iron-sulfur proteins transferritin *flavoproteins*

Cotton et al. [14]. Already in their preliminary work, the authors explored the potentialities and goals of the SERRS technique for possible applications to bioanalytical problems. The first possibility is enhanced sensitivity for the RR scattering of scarce materials. A second possibility can be added specifically to redox-active chromophores in proteins. Indeed, this new spectroelectrochemical method permits the simultaneous study of an electrochemical reaction in a biological system in conjunction with a specific measurement of subtile variations in the vibrational spectrum of the chromophores. Another striking feature of the SERRS spectroscopy is that fluorescence of the adsorbate can be completely quenched by the metal surface which generates a high-quality Raman spectrum [22]. Another common application of SERRS spectroscopy is the study of the adsorption behaviour and conformation of biomolecules at the metal/electrolyte interface.

Before reviewing the different biological applications of the SERRS spectroscopy, it is necessary to recall in Table 5 the by RR spectroscopy most investigated biological chromophores. A classification is proposed which would facilitate the organization of actual SERRS studies. The chromophores have first been divided into two main groups depending on whether they contain tetrapyrole skeletons or not. Among them, the porphyrin skeleton is encountered mostly in hemoproteins and chlorophyll pigments chelated with iron or magnesium respectively [195]. In order to discriminate their functional activities in free forms or linked to proteins, a second subdivision is made between chromophores which participate directly or indirectly in the respiratory mechanism. The actual studies with SERRS generally concern chromophores of which the structures are well characterized and RR spectra have been analyzed as a function of their complexation states, eventual central metal oxydation and spin states, adducts, biologically active sites and laser excitation wavelenghts [157,182]. In the first part of this chapter, the SERRS results with porphyrinic chromophores and their analogues will be reviewed gradually from their free forms to their complexation states embedded in protein structures. In the second part, results obtained with flavin and retinal chromophore will also be briefly described.

5.1 Porphyrin Chromophores

5.1.1 Water-Soluble Porphyrins

Porphyrins absorb strongly in the visible spectral regions and are therefore ideal candidates for study using resonance Raman methods.

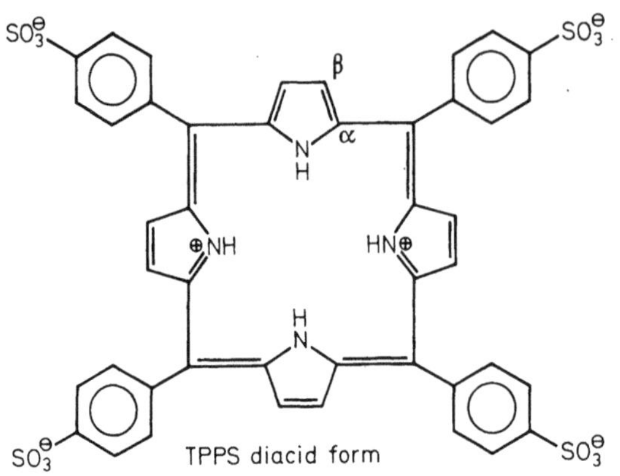

Fig. 26. Structure of meso-tetrakis(4-sulfonatophenyl)porphin (TSPP) in its diacid form (Itabashi et al., Ref. [187])

Water soluble porphyrins, meso-tetrakis(4-carbonylphenyl) porphyrin [TCPP] and tetrasodium-mesotetrakis(4-sulfonato-phenyl) porphyrin [TSPP], Fig. 26, have been investigated by the SERRS technique. From SERRS spectra, at concentrations of 10^{-6} M, it can be shown that depending on pH and substituents, sulfonate or carboxylate groups in TSPP and TCPP, respectively, the adsorption of the tetraphenyl porphyrin strongly differs. In the case of TSPP, the SERRS signal of the neutral form [186] reaches a maximum at 0 V vs. SCE while the maximum intensity of the acid form [187] is observed near —0.2 V. The strong potential dependence of the SERRS spectrum of the acid form of TSPP is explained by the authors by different electrochemical processes at the silver electrode which can be interpreted in terms of dissociation of aggregated TSPP to monomers around —0.3 V and of partial Ag incorporation in TSPP near —0.4 V, Fig. 27. This last process was first proven with the neutral forms [16] of TSPP and TCPP during the anodization step of the electrode. Indeed, the presence of metal-sensitive bands in SERRS spectra, also found in RR spectra of silver tetraphenylporphyrine in solution, support a metallation during the activation procedure of the electrode. These metal sensitive Raman bands decrease as the potential of the electrode becomes more negative. It suggests some demetallation of the incorporated Ag atom under reducing conditions. However, the disappearance of the Raman bands is also due to the adsorption or reorientation of the adsorbates. Thus, variations in adsorption behaviour at the silver surface as a function of potential for neutral TSPP and TCPP, have been related to the complexing and specific adsorption capacities of the substituant groups sulfonate (TSPP) or carboxylate (TCPP) with Ag^+ ions and the Ag metal electrode. The rapid desorption of TSPP at negative potentials —0.5 V vs. SCE is explained by a coulombic repulsion between the sulfonate groups and a negatively charged electrode. On the other hand, in the case of TCPP, the neutralization of the carboxylate groups by a rather strong complexation with Ag^+ during the activation procedure would limit the electrostatic factors in the adsorption behaviour.

5.1.2 Bile Pigments

The bile pigments are derived from degradation of porphyrins in liver cells of animals. They are also of physiological importance in plants since they are related to the chromophoric groups of phytochromes, phycocyanin and phycoerythrin [195]. They essentially consist of four pyrrol molecules but they do not form a closed ring like the porphirin ring. The difficulty to get RR spectra of these fluorescent products incited Lippitsch [22] to apply the SERRS-colloid spectroscopy to discriminate fluores-

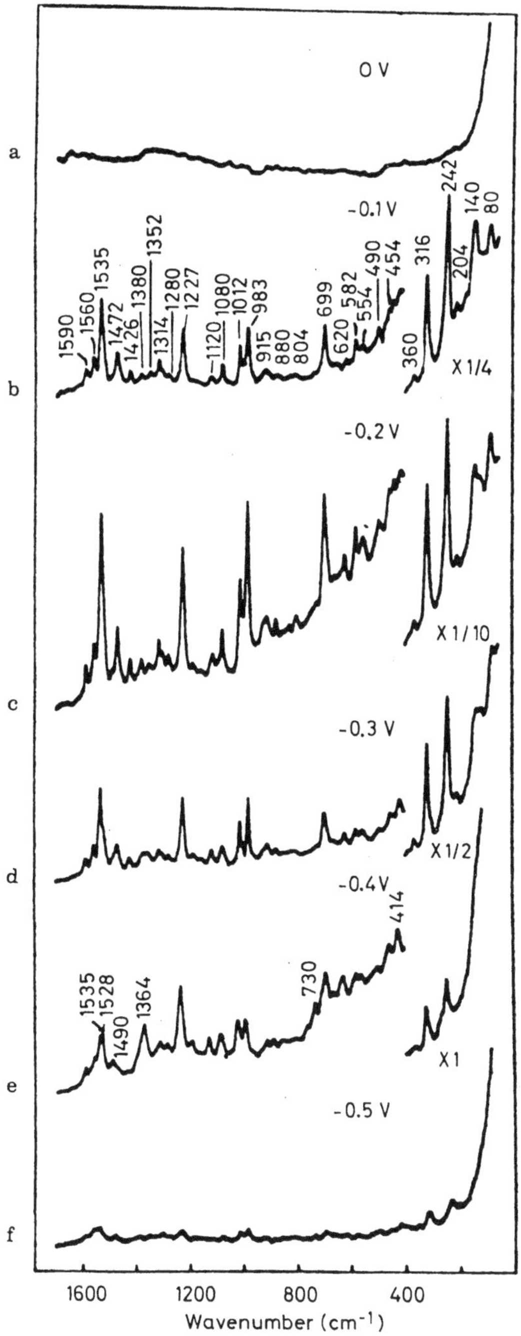

Fig. 27. SERS spectra of TSPP adsorbed on the Ag electrode at different electrode potentials in 0.05 M H_2SO_4. Excitation wavelength: 488.0 nm (20 mW). (A) 0 V; (B) —0.1 V; (C) —0.2 V; (D) —0.3 V; (E) —0.4 V; (F) —0.5 V (versus Ag/AgCl electrode). (Itabashi et al., Ref. [187])

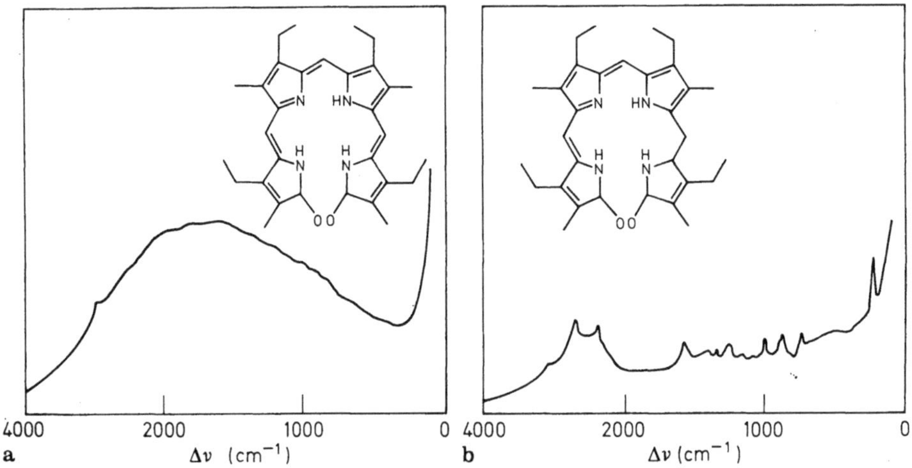

Fig. 28a and b. Raman- and SERS spectra of aetiobiliverdine.
a) Conventional Raman spectrum of a solution of aetiobiliverdine (10^{-4} M) in ethanol (+ solvent band).
b) Raman spectrum of aetiobiliverdine (2×10^{-7} M) adsorbed to a silver sol. Solvent background subtracted. (Lippitch, Ref. [22])

cence with respect to Raman scattering by surface enhancement of the latter. The author has thus obtained well resolved vibrational spectra at a concentration of 2×10^{-7} M for aetiobiliverdine-IV-γ, (see Fig. 28) and dimethylpyrromethone, a partial structure of the former product. Considering more recent works [24,106], these results are the first demonstration of a quenching effect of fluorescence from adsorbates at a silver colloid surface.

5.1.3 Metalloporphyrins

Metalloporphyrins consist of porphyrin ring structures complexed to a central atom. Among them, hemin structures with central iron atoms at different oxidation states and chlorophyll pigments containing magnesium are most abundant [195]. The interest in their spectroelectrochemical studies is multiple. Thus, their adsorption and electrochemical behaviour at the electrode surface can be used not only to model their functions in a biological matrix but also to improve the practical application of porphyrin coated electrodes as catalysts or sensitizers in photoelectrochemical cells [186].

5.1.3.1 Hemin

SERRS spectra of adsorbed Fe(III) protoporphyrin IX chloride (FePPCl) in aqueous base media (pH 10.5) [188,190] and its dimethylester form in acetonitrile [188] were recently published. Using a rather low excitation wavelength at 406.7 nm, near the strong electronic absorption B (or Soret) of metalloporphyrin, Sanchez and Spiro [188] were able to monitor the oxidation state of the Fe ions as a function of the silver electrode potential, see Fig. 29. From metal sensitive Raman bands, attributed to Fe(III) and Fe(II) complexes, the authors found good agreement between the voltammetric and the RR results. The mid-point of the transition for aqueous hemin, —0.65 V vs. SCE, measured by the ratio of the SERRS band intensities at 1370 cm^{-1} Fe(III) and 1360 cm^{-1} Fe(II) agrees with the average of the anodic and cathodic potentials (−0.72 V and −0.58 V), see Fig. 30, 31. Furthermore, the irreversible character of the cyclic voltammetric redox process at a silver electrode, characterized by a potential peak separation larger than 0.06 V can also be illustrated by the non-Nernstian behaviour of the ratio of the RR band intensities. This behaviour may reflect differential rates of adsorption and desorption of the oxidized and reduced species.

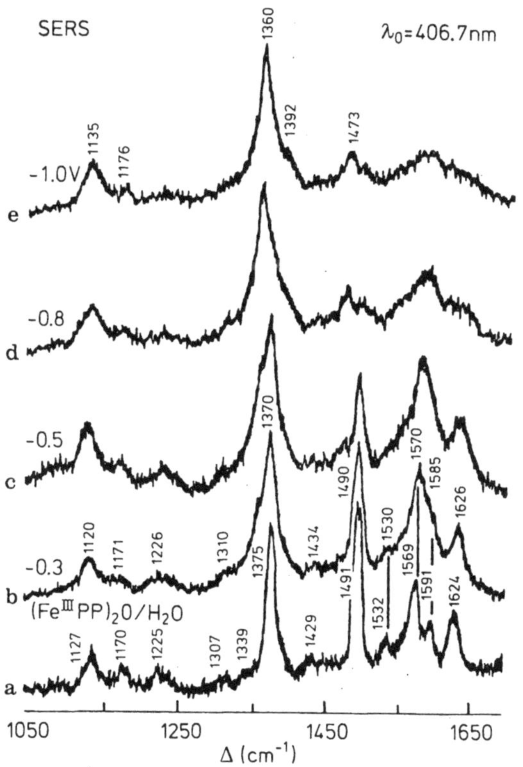

Fig. 29. 406.7 nm-excited Raman spectra of hemin chloride (15 m*M*) in aqueous base (bottom spectrum, a), and of a roughened silver electrode surface in contact with hemin chloride (0.15 m*M*) in aqueous base and held at the indicated potentials versus SCE (b–e). Experimental conditions laser power, 30 mW, spectral slitwidth 5 cm^{-1}, accumulation time 1 s, scan rate 1 cm^{-1}/s (Sanchez and Spiro, Ref. [188])

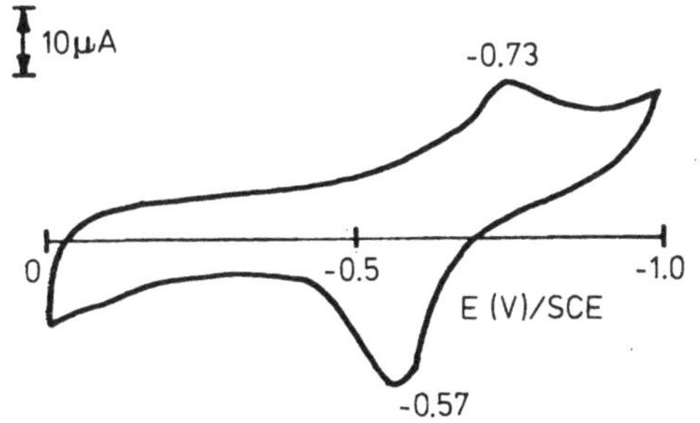

Fig. 30. Cyclic voltammogram for a roughened silver electrode in aqueous (pH 10.5) hemin chloride (0.5 m*M*) containing 0.1 *M* KCl as supporting electrolyte. Scan rate 100 mV/s (Sanchez and Spiro, Ref. [188])

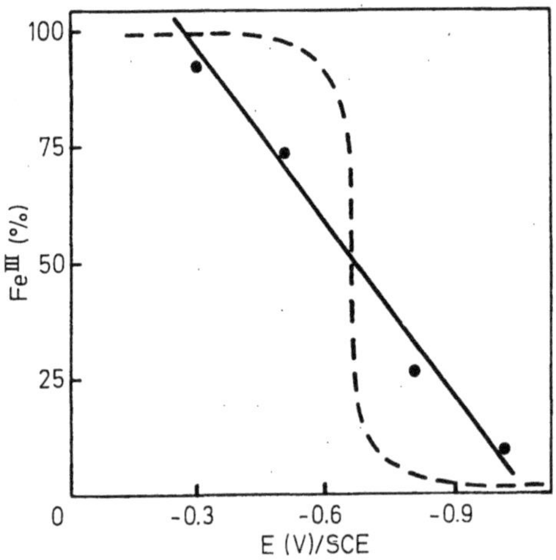

Fig. 31. Fraction of the hemin adsorbed from aqueous base remaining as Fe(III) hemin versus the electrode potential, as estimated from the intensities of the V_4 SERR bands at 1370 cm^{-1} Fe(III) and 1360 cm^{-1} Fe(II). The dotted curve is the expected equilibrium (Nernstian) behavior for a redox couple with a formal potential of —0.65 V versus SCE (Sanchez and Spiro, Ref. [188)])

The RR enhancement mechanism is comparable in the solution and at the electrode surface. Therefore, the authors conclude that the silver surface does not markedly disturb the electronic state distribution in the adsorbed heme but only acts as an amplifier of the RR factors. Such observations and confirmations of an interfacial quenching of fluorescence have also been made by McMahon and Melendres [190)] in the SERRS study of the properties of FePPCl as oxygen reduction catalyst. However, it was shown, that in the presence of oxygen no SERRS band assigned to a reduced heme Fe(II) can be detected at —0.6 V vs. SCE though rapid cyclic voltammograms give evidence of the reduction process. The authors [190)] thus proposed the following mechanism at —0.60 V to account for the electrochemical and Raman observations in the presence of oxygen:

$$\underset{\text{high-spin Fe}}{\text{Fe(III)PPOH}} + e^- \rightarrow \text{Fe(II)PPOH}$$

$$\text{Fe(II)PPOH} + O_2 \rightarrow \underset{\text{low-spin Fe}}{O_2\text{Fe(III)PPOH}^-}$$

This mechanism requires the rapid oxidative regeneration of Fe(III) by oxygen so that the Fe(II) intermediate is never observed in the SERRS spectrum. Shifts to higher frequency observed for the structure-sensitive bands of FePPCl adsorbed at —0.6 V have been attributed to a change from high-spin-5-coordinated Fe(III) to low-spin-6-coordinated Fe(III). The sixth ligand which is consistent with this mechanism is the reduced oxygen O_2^-. This mechanism would thus participate in the observed modest catalysis of the O_2 reduction reaction in the presence of porphyrin.

5.1.3.2 Chlorophyll Pigments

Chlorophylls are key pigments participating in the absorption of light in photosynthesis. They consist of a magnesium porphyrin derivative in which one pyrrol ring is partially reduced. An isocyclic ring is also present [195)]. Although no SERRS spectrum of the chlorophyll pigment alone has been published until now, it has already been shown by Cotton and Van Duyne [24] that a selective choice of excitation wavelengths can discriminate the RR spectra of the chlorophyll pigments from Rhodopseudomonas spheroides reaction centers. Indeed this reaction center complex contains, besides protein, different pigments (bacteriochlorophylls, bacteriophephytins, quinone) which are all susceptible to RR effects. Thus, the strong adsorption of bacteriochlorophyll (BChl) at —0.7 V vs. SCE, the 457.9 nm excitation laser line

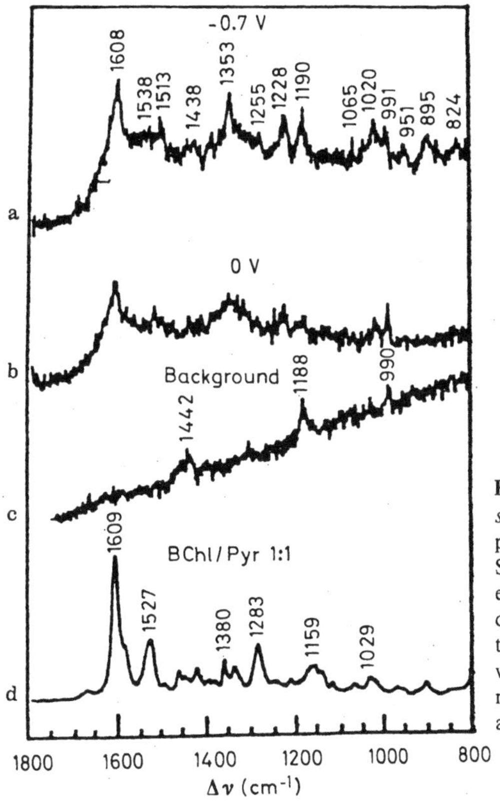

Fig. 32a–d. Resonance Raman spectra of *Rps. sphaeroides* reaction centers as a function of potential of the silver electrode: **a)** —0.7 V vs SCE; **b)** 0.0 V vs SCE; **c)** Blank (buffer, electrolyte, and LDAO); **d)** BChl (10^{-2} M) dissolved in CH_2Cl_2 with sufficient pyridine to form BChl pyridine; laser excitation wavelength 457.9 nm; laser power 20 mW; monochromator bandpass 5 cm^{-1} (Cotton and Van Duyne, Ref. [24])

and the quenching of the fluorescence by the electrode surface are independent factors which favour not only an enhancement of the RR effects, but also the specificity of the observed vibrations, see Fig. 32. Bacteriophephytin (BPh) pigment which corresponds only to the chlorophyll porphyrinic structure without the magnesium atom can be in the same way specifically characterized from the reaction center complex by using a different excitation wavelength of 530.9 nm after adsorption at a more positive potential 0 V, see Fig. 33. These results obtained by a combination of specific excitation wavelengths with the potential dependence of the SERRS signals, have demonstrated the feasibility of utilizing SERRS spectroscopy to study individual chromophores in complex biological structures.

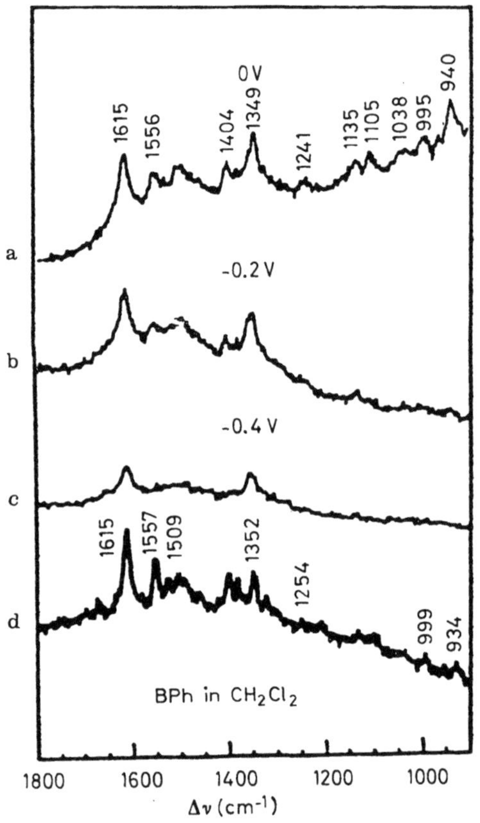

Fig. 33a–d. Resonance Raman spectra of *Rps. sphaeroides* reaction centers as a function of potential of the silver electrode: **a)** 0.0 V vs SCE; **b)** —0.2 V vs SCE; **c)** —0.4 V vs SCE; **d)** BPh (10^{-2} M) in $CH\,Cl_2$; laser excitation wavelength 530.9 nm; other scan parameters were identical to those in Fig. 31 (Cotton and Van Duyne, Ref. [24])

5.1.4 Hemoproteins

Hemoproteins bound to the protein surface consist of iron-containing porphyrinic chromophores. By varying the oxidation state of the iron atom, these proteins participate in various biological reactions involving oxygen [157].

5.1.4.1 Myoglobin

Myoglobin (Mb) is a hemoprotein capable of reversible fixation of O_2 in muscles of vertebrates and invertebrates. Cotton et al. [14] have thus compared the oxidation and spin-state markers of RR bands in solution and at a Ag electrode. From SERRS spectra of adsorbed Mb at two adsorption potentials, E_s —0.6 V and —0.2 V vs. SCE, they conclude that the reduction of Fe(III) to Fe(II) occurs at —0.6 V followed by its reoxidation at —0.2 V. In the same paper they also report the first SERRS spectra of cytochrome c.

5.1.4.2 Cytochrome

Various members of the cytochrome family participate in the electron transfer to the oxygen in the respiratory chain by means of the alternative oxidation and reduction of the central ions from the hemin structure [195].

a) Cytochrome c

As in the case of Mb, Cotton et al. [14] have reported SERRS spectra of highly dilute solutions (10^{-6} M) of cytochrome c (Cytc) at two different potentials (E_s —0.2 V and —0.6 V vs. SCE) using the 514.5 nm excitation wavelength. Findings similar to SERRS investigations of Mb can be outlined. The position of the spin-oxidation state marker bands of Cytc on the silver electrode surface indicates that the heme Fe is in its low spin reduced state at —0.6 V. The Fe(III) bulk Cytc solution RR spectrum is only observed by stepping the electrode potential to a more positive value of —0.2 V vs. SCE, see Table 6.

Table 6. Comparison of oxidation and spin-rate marker bands of Cyt c in solution and at a Ag electrode[a]. (Ref. [14])

Ferri Cyt c[b] (low spin)	Cyt c at Ag electrode, —0.2 V	Ferro Cyt c[c] (low spin)	Cyt c at Ag electrode —0.6 V
1636	1638	1622	1625
1582	1588	1584	1589
1502	1502	1493	1498
1376	1377	1362	1365

[a] Frequencies are in cm^{-1}; [b, c] from Ref. [14] and Refs. cited therein.

As discussed before in the case of nucleic acids the authors have also considered the incidence of the interfacial conformation of the hemoproteins on the appearance of the SERRS signals from the chromophores. Although under their Raman conditions no protein vibration can be observed, the possibility of heme loss or protein denaturation are envisaged to explain a direct interaction of the heme chromophores with the electrode surface in the case of the adsorbed Mb. extensive denaturation of Cytc at the electrode appears unlikely to the authors on the basis of the close correspondence of the surface and solution spectra. Furthermore, the sluggish electron transfer kinetics measured by cyclic voltammetry in the case of Cytc is also an argument in favour of some structural hindrance for the accessibility to the heme chromophore in the adsorbed state of Cytc. This electrochemical aspect of the behaviour of Cytc has very recently incited Cotton et al. [29] and Tanigushi et al. [34,189] to modify the silver and gold electrode surface in order to accelerate the electron transfer. The authors show that in the presence of 4,4-bipyridine [29], bis (4-pyridyl)disulfide and purine [34] an enhancement of the quasi-reversible redox process is possible. The SERRS spectroscopy has also permitted the characterization of the surface of the modified silver electrode. It has been thus shown, that in presence of both pyridine derivates the direct adsorption of the heme chromophore is not detected [29,34] while in presence of purine a coadsorption of Cytc and purine occurs [34].

In the case of the Ag-bipyridyl modified electrode [29] the cyclicvoltammetric and SERRS data indicate that the bipyridyl forms an Ag(I) complex on Ag electrodes with the appropriate redox potential to mediate electron transfer between the electrode and cytochrome c.

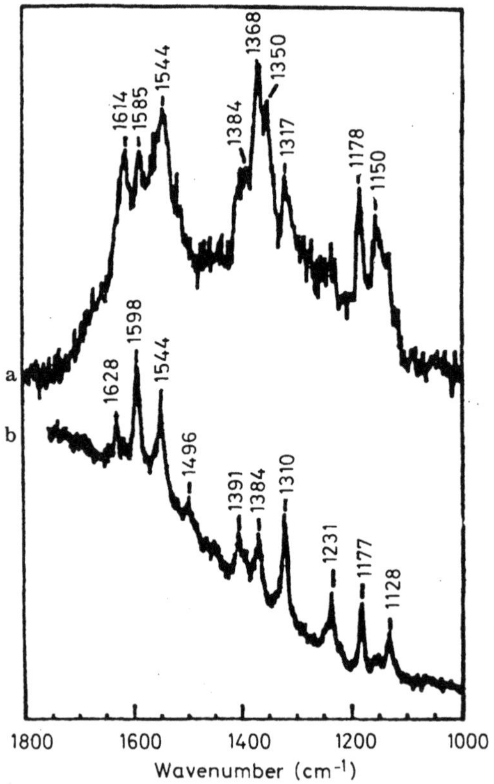

Fig. 34 a and b. RR spectra of *Pseudomonas aeruginosa* cytochrome cd_1 complex, 514.5 nm excitation. **a)** SERRS spectrum, 3×10^{-6} M in 0.1 M Na_2SO_4, adsorbed on Ag at −0.6 V vs SCE. Laser power 20 mW; monochromator slit width 2 cm^{-1}. **b)** Solution RR spectrum of reduced complex; 5.5×10^{-4} M; laser 20 mW; monochromator slit width 2 cm^{-1} (Cotton et al., Ref. [21])

b) Cytochrome cd_1

In the case of cytochrome cd_1 (Cyt cd_1) found in many facultative, anaerobic denitrifying bacteria, the SERRS spectroscopy [21] has been used to obtain preliminary heme structure/environment comparisons between cyt cd_1 from two bacteria sources, Pseudomonas and Paracoccus. The difficulty encountered in preparing sufficient quantities of cyt cd_1, can be thus solved by the low product consuming SERRS method. By exciting selectively with the 514.5 nm and 460 nm lines of an Ar^+ laser, it is possible to produce successively an enhancement of RR scattering of reduced heme c, see Fig. 34, and heme d_1, see Fig. 35, in the protein complexes (3×10^{-6} M) adsorbed on Ag at −0.6 V vs. SCE. A comparison between the SERRS spectra of cd_1 proteins from the bacteria suggests differences in the heme chromophore and peripheral substituents.

5.2 Flavin Chromophores

Flavin molecule by its redox properties plays an important role in energy providing reactions. Flavin occurs as riboflavin or as a nucleotide in flavin mononucleotide (FMN) and combined to adenine nucleotide in flavin adenine dinucleotide (FAD) [195]. Very recently it was shown by Spiro et al. [106] that free fluorescence SERRS spectra from flavoproteins adsorbed at silver colloids (average size of 7.5 nm) can be obtained

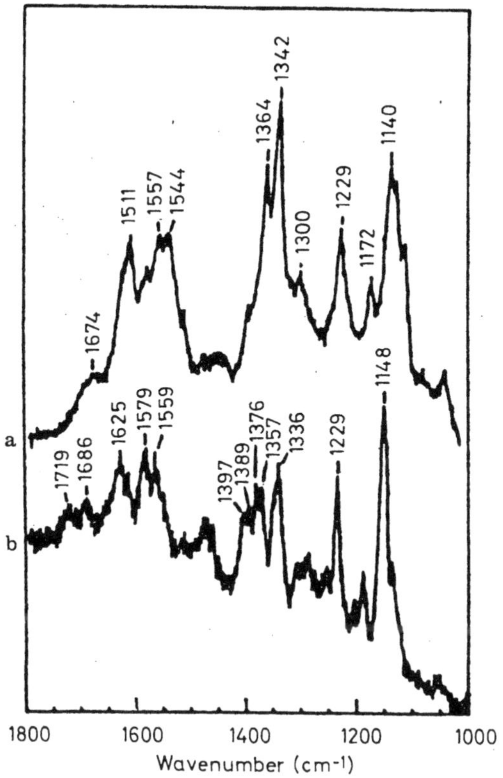

Fig. 35a and b. RR spectra of *Pseudomonas aeruginosa* cytochrome cd_1 complex, 457.9 nm excitation. **a)** SERRS spectrum, 3×10^{-6} M in 0.1 M Na_2SO_4, adsorbed on Ag at −0.6 V vs SCE. Instrumental parameters the same as Fig. 31a. **b)** Same as in Fig. 31b (Cotton and Van Duyne, Ref. [24])

at concentrations of 10^{-6} M. In the case of the glucose oxidase, whose intrinsic fluorescence masks the normal RR spectra, it is possible to achieve a high quality flavin SERRS spectrum, see Fig. 36. A number of approximately 20 binding sites per particle was evaluated by varying the enzyme concentration in solution. Indeed, considering the fluorescence quenching effect by the silver surface, the saturation of the silver surface by the enzyme molecules can be easily monitored by a rapid increase of the background fluorescence, due to the unadsorbed enzymes. Furthermore, the authors have demonstrated by testing the enzyme activity, that the adsorption and laser excitation hardly alter the essential chemical activites of the chromophore.

5.3 Retinal Chromophore

Very recently first SERRS results about bacteriorhodopsin have been communicated by Nabiev et al. [191]. Bacteriorhodopsin is a membrane protein found in bacteria which functions as a light driven proton pump. Using the short-range mechanism of SERS (Chapt. 4.1) the active site (retinal chromophore) position of the protein in the membrane has been estimated with high accuracy [191]. It is interesting to note, that adsorption of bacteriorhodopsin on silver colloids seems to fix light-induced cyclic transformations in the protein active sites.

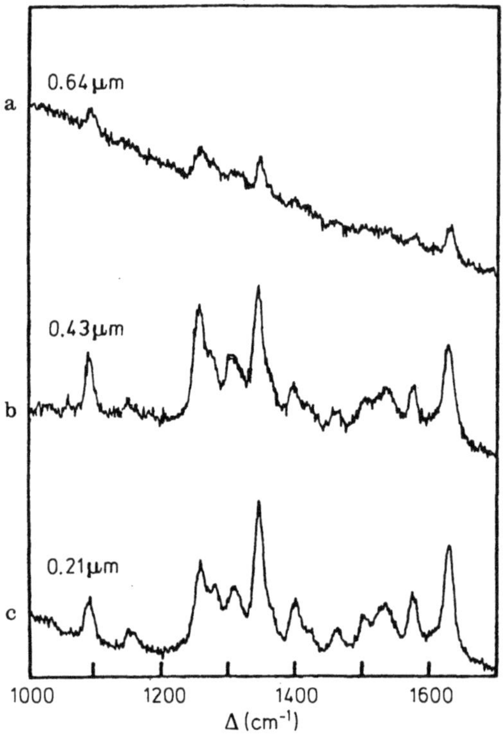

Fig. 36. SERRS spectra of glucose oxidase in Ag sols (0.33 mM Ag) containing the indicated protein concentrations (half the flavin concentrations). Conditions: laser power 20 mW, spectral slit width 5 cm^{-1}, accumulation time 3 s/cm^{-1}. The data were collected digitally and are unsmoothed. The silver colloids were prepared by the procedure of Creighton et al. [69], and the proteins were added subsequently (Copeland et al., Ref. [106])

6 The Future

The examples of SERS and SERRS measurements in the biochemical field reviewed in this article were selected to illustrate the sensitivity, molecular specificity of adsorption process, accuracy, ease of sample preparation, and significant manifold applications of Raman analysis by SERS and SERRS for biomolecules in the adsorbed state.

One main advantage for biochemistry is, that Raman spectra are obtainable from highly dilute solutions of biomolecules, indicating that SERS and SERRS have great potential for detecting Raman scattering from extremely small concentrations of biological materials. Furthermore, the sensitivity of the SERS and SERRS spectra of biomolecules to its environment enables a detailed investigation of the state of the biomolecule at the surface.

Another advantage of the SERS spectroscopy is to obtain vibrational spectroscopic informations in electrolyte solution under conditions close to the real biological situation. The continuous development of laser sources with new excitation wavelength lines renders it possible to expand the study of adsorbed biomolecules on different metal surfaces which can also be chemically or electrically modified to adjust specific adsorption properties. Such a crucial event in medical applications as the behaviour of implants in contact with blood can be thus envisaged by the study of the adsorption of blood proteins and its physiological consequences. The possibility to monitor the interfacial electric field of the electrode surface can also be used to understand and hence mimic the catalytic properties of energetic relevant enzymes. The accessibility to SERS enhancement factors also offers a new approach either to probe a sterical configuration of Raman active products in complexation with nucleic acids and proteins, or to detect their transport through organized biochemical structures. Membrane systems adsorbed on the electrode and included metallic colloids in phospholipid vesicles would thus offer a new method for the direct study of membrane transport. In more complex biological systems the up to now microscopic marking with metallic colloids would offer biochemical information on the immediately surrounding biological medium.

7 Acknowledgements

The authors are indebted to H. W. Nürnberg for his continous encouragement and critical reading of the article. They thank P. Valenta for interesting and helpful discussions. Gratefully acknowledged is also the collaboration of former and present co-workers, K. M. Ervin, J. C. Fritz, B. Kisters, H. H. Lewinsky, and P. Valenta Jr., as well as many helpful discussions with other researchers in the to electrochemistry related SERS field, T. M. Cotton, J. A. Creighton, W. Krasser, S. Krimm, M. E. Lippitsch, F. F. M. de Mul, A. Otto, B. Pettinger, J. Pockrand and D. Weitz. We are grateful to J. J. McMahon, J. R. Nabiev, T. G. Spiro and I. Taniguchi for sharing preprinted information. All these colleagues have provided us with their unpublished and published results.

8 References

1. Van Duyne, R. P.: J. Phys. (Paris) 38, *C-5*, 239 (1977)
2. Van Duyne, R. P.: in: Chemical and Biochemical Applications of Laser (C. B. Moore, Ed.), Vol. *4*, Academic Press, New York 1979, p. 101
3. Cooney, R. P., Mahoney, M. R.: in: Advances in Infrared and Raman Spectroscopy (Clark, R. J. H., Hester, R. E., Eds.), Vol. *9*, Heyden, London 1982, p. 188
4. Chang, R. K., Furtak, T. E.: Ed. Surface Enhanced Raman Scattering, Plenum Press, New York 1982
5. Birke, R. L., Lombardi, J. R., Sanchez, L. A.: Adv. Chem. Ser. *201*, 69 (1982)
6. Otto, A.: Surface Enhanced Raman Scattering, Classical and Chemical Origins, in: Light Scattering in Solids, Vol. 4, (Cardona, M., Güntherodt, G., Eds.), Springer 1983
7. Furtak, T. E.: Advances in Laser Spectroscopy , 175 (1983)
8. Chang, R. K., Laube, B. L.: CRC Crit. Rev. Solid State Mater. Sci. *12*, 1 (1984)
9. Peticolas, W. L.: Biochem. *57*, 417 (1975)
10. Johnson, B., Peticolas, W. L.: Ann. Rev. Phys. Chem. *27*, 465 (1976)
11. Thomas, G. J.: in: Infrared and Raman Spectroscopy, (Brame, E. G., Grasselli, J. G., Eds.), Vol. *1*, Marcel Dekker, New York and Basel 1977, p. 717
12. Tu, A. T.: Raman Spectroscopy in Biology, Wiley-Interscience 1982
13. Koglin, E., Séquaris, J. M., Valenta, P.: Proc. 14th European Congr. on Molecular Spectroscopy, 3.–7. 9., Frankfurt/M. 1979, p. 122
14. Cotton, T. M., Schultz, S. G., Van Duyne, R. P.: J. Am. Chem. Soc. *102*, 7960 (1980)
15. Koglin, E., Séquaris, J. M., Valenta, P.: J. Mol. Struct. *60*, 421 (1980)
16. Ervin, K. E., Koglin, E., Séquaris, J. M., Valenta, P., Nürnberg, H. W.: J. Electroanal. Chem. *114*, 179 (1980)
17. Venkatesan, S., Erdheim, G., Lombardi, J. R., Birke, R. L.: Surf. Sci. *101*, 387 (1980)

18. Koglin, E., Séquaris, J. M., Valenta, P.: Z. Naturforsch. *36c*, 809 (1981)
19. Séquaris, J. M., Koglin, E., Valenta, P., Nürnberg, H. W.: Ber. Bunsenges. Phys. Chem. *85*, 512 (1981)
20. Nabiev, J. R., Efremov, E. S., Trakhanov, S. D., Marinyuk, V. V., Lazorenko-Manevich, R. M.: Bioorgan. Khim. *7*, 941 (1981)
21. Cotton, T. M., Timkovich, R., Cork, M. S.: FEBS Lett. *133*, 39 (1981)
22. Lippitsch, M. E.: Chem. Phys. Lett. *79*, 224 (1981)
23. Koglin, E., Séquaris, J. M., Valenta, P.: J. Mol. Struct. *79*, 185 (1982)
24. Cotton, T. M., Van Duyne, R. P.: FEBS Lett. *147*, 81 (1982)
25. Koglin, E., Séquaris, J. M., Valenta, P.: in: Surface Studies with Lasers, Springer Series in Chemical Physics 33, (Aussenegg, F. R., Leitner, A., Lippitsch, M. E., Eds.), Springer Verlag 1983, p. 64
26. Koglin, E., Séquaris, J. M.: J. Phys. (Paris) *C10*, 487 (1983)
27. Nabiev, J. R., Savehenko, V. A., Efremov, E. S.: J. Raman Spectrosc. *14*, 375 (1983)
28. Suh, J. S., Dilella, D. P., Moskovits, M.: J. Phys. Chem. *87*, 1540 (1983)
29. Cotton, T. M., Kaddi, D., Iorga, D.: J. Am. Chem. Soc. *105*, 7462 (1983)
30. Koglin, E., Séquaris, J. M., Fritz, J. C., Valenta, P.: J. Mol. Struct. *114*, 219 (1984)
31. Koglin, E., Séquaris, J. M., Valenta, P., Nürnberg, H. W.: Fresenius Z. Anal. Chem. *317*, 698 (1984)
32. Séquaris, J. M., Koglin, E., Malfoy, B.: FEBS Letters *173*, 95 (1984)
33. Otto, C., Van Welie, A., de Jong, E., de Mul, F. F. M., Mud, J., Greve, J.: J. Phys. E: Sci. Instrum. *17*, 624 (1984)
34. Taniguchi, J., Iseki, M., Yamaguchi, H., Yasukochi, K.: J. Electroanal. Chem. *175*, 341 (1984)
35. Copeland, R. A., Fodor, S. P. A., Spiro, T. G.: J. Am. Chem. Soc. *106*, 3872 (1984)
36. de Mul, F. F. M., Otto, C., Mud, J., Greve, J.: Proc. IX. Int. Conf. Raman Spectroscopy, Tokyo 1984, p. 294
37. Koglin, E., Séquaris, J. M., Lewinsky, H., Valenta, P., Nürnberg, H. W.: ibid., p. 592
38. Sanchez, L. A., Spiro, Th. G.: J. Phys. Chem., *89*, 763 (1985)
39. Lewinsky, H. H.: Doctor Thesis, Univ. Frankfurt/M. and KFA Jülich 1985
40. Koglin, E., Lewinsky, H. H., Séquaris, J. M.: Surf. Sci., *158*, 370 (1985)
41. Séquaris, J. M., Fritz, J., Lewinsky, H. H., Koglin, E.: J. Coll. Interf. Sci., *105*, 417 (1985)
42. Fleischmann, M., Hendra, P. J., McQuillan, A. J., Paul, R. L., Reid, E. S.: J. Raman Spectrosc. *4*, 269 (1976)
43. Jeanmaire, D. L., Van Duyne, R. P.: Electroanal. Chem. *84*, 1 (1977)
44. Cooney, R. P., Fleischmann, M., Hendra, P. J.: J.C.S. Schem. Comm. *7*, 235 (1977)
45. Albrecht, M. G., Creighton, J. A.: J. Am. Chem. Soc. *99*, 5215 (1977)
46. Pettinger, B., Wenning, U., Kolb, D. M.: Ber. Bunsenges. Phys. Chem. *82*, 1326 (1978)
47. Allen, C. S., Van Duyne, R.: Chem. Phys. Lett. *63*, 455 (1979)
48. Creighton, J. A.: in: Vibrational Spectroscopy of Adsorbates, Springer Series in Chemical Physics 15, (Willis, R. F., Ed.), Springer, Berlin—Heidelberg—New York 1980, p. 145
49. Allen, C. S., Schatz, G., Van Duyne, R.: Chem. Phys. Lett. *75*, 201 (1980)
50. Billmann, J., Kovacs, G., Otto, A.: Surf. Sci. *92*, 153 (1980)
51. Kötz, R., Yeager, E.: J. Electroanal. Chem. *113*, 113 (1980)
52. Schulz, G. G., Janik-Czachor, M., Van Duyne, R. P.: Surf. Sci. *104*, 419 (1981)
53. Fleischmann, M., Robinson, J., Waser, R.: J. Electroanal. Chem. *117*, 257 (1981)
54. Pettinger, B., Philpott, M. R. P., Gordon, J. G.: J. Chem. Phys. *85*, 2746 (1981)
55. Pettinger, B., Wetzel, H.: in Ref. 4, p. 293
56. Plieth, W., Roy, B., Bruckner, H.: Ber. Bunsenges. Phys. Chem. *85*, 499 (1981)
57. Plieth, W., Roy, B., Bruckner, H.: ibid. *86*, 273 (1982)
58. Macomber, S. H., Furtak, T. E.: Chem. Phys. Lett. *90*, 59 (1982)
59. Moerl, L., Pettinger, B.: Sol. State Comm. *43*, 315 (1982)
60. Watanabe, T., Pettinger, B.: Chem. Phys. Lett. *89*, 501 (1982)
61. Murphy, D. V., von Raben, K. U., Chen, T. T., Owen, J. F., Chang, R. K.: Surf. Sci. *124*, 529 (1983)
62. Furtak, T. E., Roy, D.: Phys. Rev. Lett. *50*, 1301 (1983)
64. Watanabe, T., Kawanami, O., Honda, K., Pettinger, B.: Chem. Phys. Lett. *102*, 565 (1983)
65. Virdee, H. R., Hester, R. E.: J. Phys. Chem. *88*, 451 (1984)

66. Tadayyoni, M. A., Farquharson, S., Li, T. T., Weaver, M.: ibid. *88*, 470 (1984)
67. Loo, B. H., Lee, Y. G.: Appl. Surf. Sci. *18*, 345 (1984)
68. Lombardi, J. R., Birke, R. L., Sanchez, L. A., Bernhard, J., Sun, S. Ch.: Chem. Phys. Lett. *104*, 240 (1984)
69. Creighton, J. A., Blatchford, C. G., Albrecht, M. G.: J. Chem. Soc. Farad. Trans. II, *75*, 790 (1979)
70. Kerker, M., Siiman, O., Brumm, L. A., Wang, D.-S.: Appl. Opt. *19*, 3253 (1980)
71. Wetzel, H., Gerischer, H.: Chem. Phys. Lett. *76*, 460 (1980)
72. Abe, H., Manzel, K., Schulze, W.: J. Chem. Phys. *74*, 792 (1981)
73. Garrell, R. L., Shaw, K. D., Krimm, S.: ibid. *75*, 4155 (1981)
74. Von Raben, K. U., Chang, R. K.: Chem. Phys. Lett. *79*, 465 (1981)
75. Akins, D. L.: J. Coll. Interf. Sci. *90*, 373 (1982)
76. Creighton, J. A.: in Ref. 4, p. 315
77. Lee, P. C., Meisel, D.: J. Phys. Chem. *86*, 3391 (1982)
78. Wetzel, H., Gerischer, H., Pettinger, B.: Chem. Phys. Lett. *85*, 187 (1982)
79. Blatchford, C. G., Siiman, D., Kerker, M.: J. Phys. Chem. *87*, 2503 (1983)
80. Creighton, J. A.: Surf. Sci. *124*, 209 (1983)
81. Creighton, J. A., Alvarez, M. S., Weitz, D. A., Garoff, S., Kim, M. W.: J. Phys. Chem. *87*, 4793 (1983)
82. Garrell, R. L., Shaw, K. D., Krimm, S.: Surf. Sci. *124*, 613 (1983)
83. Heard, S. M., Grieser, F., Barraclough, C. G.: Chem. Phys. Lett. *95*, 154 (1983)
84. Siiman, O., Lepp, A., Kerker, M.: J. Phys. Chem. *87*, 5319 (1983)
85. Siiman, O., Lepp, A., Kerker, M.: Chem. Phys. Lett. *100*, 163 (1983)
86. Siiman, O., Bumm, L. A., Callaghan, R., Blatchford, C. B., Kerker, M.: J. Phys. Chem. *87*, 1014 (1983)
87. Kneipp, K., Fassler, D.: Chem. Phys. Lett. *106*, 498 (1984)
88. Kerker, M., Siiman, O., Wang, D.-S.: J. Phys. Chem. *88*, 3168 (1984)
89. Moskovits, M., Suh, J. S.: ibid. *88*, 1293 (1984)
90. Pettinger, B.: Chem. Phys. Lett. *110*, 576 (1984)
91. Pettinger, B., Gerolymatou, A.: Ber. Bunsenges. Phys. Chem. *88*, 359 (1984)
92. Weitz, D. A., Oliveria, M.: Phys. Rev. Lett. *52*, 1433 (1984)
93. Weitz, D. A., Lin, M. Y.: Surf. Sci., in press
94. Liao, P. F., Bergmann, J. G., Chemla, D. S., Wokaun, A., Melngailis, J., Hawryluk, A. M., Economou, N. P.: Chem. Phys. Lett. *82*, 355 (1981)
95. Liao, P. F., Stern, M. B.: Opt. Lett. *7*, 483 (1982)
96. Yamada, H., Yamamoto, Y.: Surf. Sci. *134*, 71 (1983)
97. Pockrand, I., Billmann, J., Otto, A.: J. Chem. Phys. *78*, 6384 (1983)
98. Ertürk, Ü., Pockrand, I., Otto, A.: Surf. Sci. *131*, 39 (1983)
99. Otto, A.: ibid. *75*, L392 (1978)
100. Manzel, K., Schulze, W., Moskovits, M.: Chem. Phys. Lett. *85*, 183 (1982)
101. Sanda, P. N., Warlaumot, J. M., Demuth, J. E., Tsang, J. C., Christman, K., Bradley, J. A.: Phys. Rev. Lett. *45*, 1519 (1980)
102. Seki, H.: Solid State Commun. *42*, 695 (1982)
103. Macomber, S. H., Furtak, T. E., Devine, T. M.: Chem. Phys. Lett. *90*, 439 (1982)
104. Horisberger, M.: Scanning Electron Microscopy *11*, 9 (1981)
105. Horisberger, M.: Trends in Biotechnology, 395 (1983)
106. Copeland, R. A., Foder, S. P. A., Spiro, T. S.: J. Am. Chem. Soc. *106*, 3872 (1984)
107. Tran, C. D.: Anal. Chem. *56*, 824 (1984)
108. Tran, C. D.: J. Chromatogr. *292*, 432 (1984)
109. Séquaris, J. M., Koglin, E.: Fresenius Z. Anal. Chem., *321*, 758 (1985)
110. Tang, J., Albrecht, A. C.: in: Raman Spectroscopy, Vol. 2, (Szymanski, H. A., Ed.), Plenum, New York 1977, p. 33
111. Furtak, T. E., Reyes, J.: Surf. Sci. *93*, 351 (1980)
112. Kerker, M., Wang, D. S., Chew, H.: Appl. Opt. *19*, 4159 (1980)
113. Gersten, J. I., Nitzan, A.: J. Chem. Phys. *73*, 3023 (1980)
114. Chen, Y. J., Chen, W. P., Burstein, E.: Phys. Rev. Lett. *36*, 1207 (1976)
115. Chen, W. P., Ritchie, G., Burstein, E.: ibid. *37*, 993 (1976)

116. Jha, S. S., Kirtley, J. R., Tsang, J. C.: Phys. Rev. *B22*, 3973 (1980)
117. Moskovits, M.: J. Chem. Phys. *69*, 4159 (1978)
118. Burstein, E., Chen, Y. J., Lundquist, S.: Bull. Am. Phys. Soc. *23*, 130 (1978)
119. McCall, S. L., Platzman, P. M., Wolff, P. A.: Phys. Lett. A *77*, 381 (1980)
120. Adrian, F. J.: Chem. Phys. Lett. *78*, 45 (1981)
121. Wang, D. S., Kerker, M.: Phys. Rev. *B24*, 1777 (1981)
122. Barber, P. W., Chang, R. K., Massoudi, H.: Phys. Rev. Lett. *50*, 997 (1983)
123. Barber, P. W., Chang, R. K., Massoudi, H.: Phys. Rev. B, *27*, 7251 (1983)
124. Chew, H., Wang, D. S., Kerker, M.: ibid. *28*, 4169 (1983)
125. Chew, H., Wang, D. S., Kerker, M.: J. Opt. Soc. Am. B., *1*, 56 (1984)
126. Wokaun, A.: ETH Habilitationsschrift, Eidgenössische Technische Hochschule, Zürich 1982
127. Liao, P. F., Bermann, J. G., Chemla, D. S., Wokaun, A., Melngailis, J., Hawryluk, A. M., Economou, N. P.: Chem. Phys. Lett. *82*, 355 (1981)
128. Kerker, M.: in: The Scattering of Light and other Electromagnetic Radiation, Academic Press, New York 1969
129. King, F. W., Van Duyne, R. P., Schatz, S. C.: J. Chem. Phys. *69*, 4172 (1978)
130. Ueba, H.: in Ref. 4, p. 173
131. Ueba, H.: Surf. Sci. *131*, 328 (1983)
132. Ueba, H.: ibid. *131*, 347 (1983)
133. Persson, B. N. J.: Chem. Phys. Lett. *82*, 561 (1981)
134. Otto, A., Billmann, J., Eickmans, J., Ertürk, U., Pettenhofer, C.: Surf. Sci. *138*, 319 (1984)
135. Burstein, E., Chen, Y. J., Chen, C. Y., Lundquist, S., Tosath, E.: Solid State Commun. *29*, 567 (1979)
136. Gadzuk, J. M., Holloway, S., Mariani, C., Horn, K.: Phys. Rev. Lett. *48*, 1288 (1982)
137. Burstein, E., Brotman, A., Apell, P.: J. Phys. (Paris) *C10*, 429 (1983)
138. Furtak, T. E., Roy, D.: Phys. Rev. Lett. *50*, 3101 (1983)
139. Roy, D., Furtak, T. E.: J. Chem. Phys. *81*, 4168 (1984)
140. Bötcher, C. J. F.: Theory of Electric Polarization, Vol. 1, Elsevier New York 1973, p. 13
141. Tsuboi, M., Takahashu, S., Honda, I., in: Physico-Chemical Properties of Nucleic Acids, Vol. 2, (Duchesne, I., Ed.), Academic, New York 1973, p. 31
142. Nishimura, Y., Tsuboi, M., Kato, S., Morakuma, K.: J. Am. Chem. Soc. *103*, 1354 (1981)
143. Nishimura, Y., Tsuboi, M., Kato, S., Morokuma, K.: in: Raman Spectroscopy-linear and nonlinear, (Lascombe, J., v. Huong, P., Eds.), J. Wiley, New York 1982, p. 703
144. Holcomb, D. N., Timasheff, S. N.: Biopolymers *6*, 513 (1968)
145. Valenta, P., Nürnberg, H. W.: Biophys. Struct. Mechanism *1*, 17 (1974)
146. Nürnberg, H. W., Valenta, P.: in: (Everett, D. H., Vincent, B., Eds.), Ions in Macromolecular and Biological Systems, Bristol, Scientechnica 1978, p. 201
147. Malfoy, B., Séquaris, J.-M., Valenta, P., Nürnberg, H. W.: Bioelectrochem. Bioenerg. *3*, 440 (1976)
148. Séquaris, J.-M., Malfoy, B., Valenta, P., Nürnberg, H. W.: ibid. *3*, 461 (1976)
149. Reynaud, J. A., Malfoy, B., Séquaris, J.-M., Sicard, P. J.: ibid. *4*, 380 (1977)
150. Brabec, V., Palecek, E.: Biophys. Chem. *4*, 79 (1976)
151. Miller, I. R.: J. Mol. Biol. *3*, 229 (1961)
152. Séquaris, J. M., Valenta, P., Nürnberg, H. W., Malfoy, B.: Bioelectrochem. Bioenerg. *5*, 483 (1978)
153. Séquaris, J. M., Valenta, P., Nürnberg, H. W.: Int. J. Radiat. Biol. *42*, 407 (1982)
154. Nürnberg, H. W.: in: Bioelectrochemistry I, (Milazzo, S., Blank, M., Eds.), Plenum Pub. Corp., New York 1983, p. 183
155. Peticolas, W. L.: Biochimie *57*, 417 (1975)
156. Thomas, G. J.: Jr. Spex Speaker *11* (1976)
157. Spiro, T. G., Loehr, T. M.: in: Advances in Infraned and Raman Spectroscopy, Vol. 4, (Clark, R. J. H., Hester, R. E., Ed.), London, Heyden 1975
158. Lawley, P. P.: in: Progress in nucleic acid research and molecular biology, Vol. 15, (Cohn, W. E., Ed.), Academic Press, New York 1975, p. 219
159. Séquaris, J. M.: in: Applications de la voltammétrie à l'étude des acides désoxyribonucléiques natifs et modifiés, Thèse Doctorat d'Etat, Univ. Orléans 1982
160. Séquaris, J.-M., Nürnberg, H. W., Valenta, P.: Toxicol. Environm. Chem., *10*, 83 (1985)

161. Strauss, B., Hill, T.: Biochim. Biophys. Acta *213*, 14 (1970)
162. Uhlenhopp, E. L., Krasna, A. I.: Biochemistry *10*, 3290 (1971)
163. Rosenberg, B., van Camp, L., Krigas, T.: Nature *205*, 698 (1965)
164. Howle, J. A., Gale, G. R.: Biochem. Pharmacol *19*, 2757 (1970)
165. Macquet, J. P., Butour, J. L.: Eur. J. Biochem. *83*, 375 (1978)
166. Lippard, S. J., Ushay, H. M., Merkel, C. M., Poirier, M. C.: Biochemistry *22*, 5165 (1983)
167. Malfoy, B., Hartman, B., Macquet, J. P., Leng, M.: Cancer Res. *41*, 4127 (1981)
168. Eastman, A.: Biochemistry *22*, 3927 (1983)
169. de Mul, F. F. M., van Weilie, A. G. M., Otto, C., Mud, J., Greve, J.: J. Raman Spectr. *15*, 268 (1984)
170. Dürbeck, H. W., Frischkorn, C. G. B.: Jahresbericht 1980/81 der Kernforschungsanlage Jülich, 1981, p. 67
171. Frischkorn, C. G. B., Smyth, M. R., Golimowski, J.: Fresenius Z. Anal. Chem. *300*, 407 (1980)
172. Smyth, M. R., Frischkorn, C. G. B.: ibid. *301*, 220 (1980)
173. McConnell, B., Hippel, P. H.: J. Mol. Biol. *50*, 297 (1970)
174. Fritzsche, H.: Biochim. Biophys. Acta *149*, 173 (1967)
175. Livramento, L., Thomas, Jr., G. J.: J. Am. Chem. Soc. *96*, 6529 (1974)
176. Thomas, Jr., G. J., Livramento, J.: Biochemistry *14*, 5210 (1975)
177. Chen, M. C., Lord, R. C., Mendelsohn, R.: Biochim. Biophys. Acta *328*, 252 (1973)
178. Chen, M. C., Lord, R. C., Mendelsohn, R.: J. Amer. Chem. Soc. *96*, 3038 (1974)
179. Kisters, B.: Doctor Thesis, Univ. Köln and KFA Jülich, in preparation
180. Bellocq, A. M., Lord, R. C., Mendelsohn, R.: Biochim. Biophys. Acta *257*, 280 (1972)
181. Stein, W. H., Moore, S.: J. Biol. Chem. *178*, 88 (1949)
182. Carey, P. R.: Resonance Raman Spectroscopy in Biochemistry and Biology, Quarterly Reviews of Biophysics *11*, 309 (1978)
183. Jeanmaire, D. L., Van Duyne, R. P.: J. Electroanal. Chem. *84*, 1 (1977)
184. Baranov, H. V., Babovich, Ya. S.: Opt. Spektrosk. *52*, 385 (1982)
185. Hildebrant, P., Stockburger, M.: J. Phys. Chem. *88*, 5935 (1984)
186. Cotton, T. M., Schultz, S. G., Van Duyne, R. R.: J. Am. Chem. Soc. *104*, 6528 (1982)
187. Tabashi, M., Kato, K., Itoh, K.: Chem. Phys. Lett. *97*, 528 (1983)
188. Alix, A. M. P., Bernard, L., Manfait (Eds).: Spectroscopy of Biomolecules, Wiley J. & Sons, 1985
a) Hildebrand, P., p. 25
b) Cotton, T. M., Holt, R., p. 38
c) Otto, C., Huiziga, A., De Mul, F. F. M., Greve, J., p. 141
d) Picquart, M., Lacrampe, G., Jaffrain, M., p. 190
e) Koglin, E., Séquaris, J.-M., p. 221
f) Séquaris, J.-M., Lewinsky, H. H., Koglin, E., p. 237
g) Nabiev, I. R., p. 348
189. Taniguchi, I., Iseki, M., Toyosawa, K., Yamaguchi, H., Yasukouchi, K.: J. Electroanal. Chem. *164*, 385 (1984)
190. McMahon, J. J., Melendres, C. A.: J. Phys. Chem., in press
191. Nabiev, I. R., Elfrem'ov, R. G., Chumanov, G. D., Kuryatav, A. B., Bystrov, V. F.: Biol. Membranes (Russian), 1985, V2
192. Prescott, B., Gamache, R., Livramento, J., Thomas, G. J.: Biopolymers *13*, 1821 (1974)
193. Bloomfield, V. A., Crothers, D. M., Tinoco, J.: Physical Chemistry of Nucleic Acids, Harper & Row, Publishers, New York, Evanston, San Francisco, London 1974
194. Fasman, G. D.: Handbook of Biochemistry and Molecular Biology, Vol. II, 3rd Edition, CRC press, Cleveland, Ohio 1976
195. White, A., Handler, P., Smith, E. L.: Principles of Biochemistry, McGraw-Hill Kogakusha, LTD 1973
196. Krznaric, D., Valenta, P., Nürnberg, H. W.: J. Electroanal. Chem. *65*, 863 (1975)
197. Valenta, P., Nürnberg, H. W., Krznaric, D.: Bioelectrochem. Bioenerg. *3*, 418 (1976)
198. Temerk, Y. M., Valenta, P., Nürnberg, H. W.: ibid. *7*, 705 (1980)
199. Temerk, Y. M., Valenta, P., Nürnberg, H. W.: J. Electroanal. Chem. *131*, 265 (1982)
200. Lord, R. C., Thomas, G. T.: Spectrochimica Acta *23a*, 2551 (1967)
201. Delabar, J. M.: J. Raman Spectrosc. *7*, 261 (1978)

Sampling and Sample Preparation of Environmental Material

Richard G. Melcher, Thomas L. Peters, and Herbert W. Emmel

Michigan Applied Science and Technology Laboratories, The Dow Chemical Company, Midland, Michigan, U.S.A.

Table of Contents

Topics in Current Chemistry, Vol. 134
© Springer-Verlag, Berlin Heidelberg 1986

1 Introduction

The area of environmental monitoring is a very broad and rapidly growing field, and no attempt will be made to cover the expanse of the technology in any detail in a single chapter. This chapter will not cover the analytical technology used to quantify specific substances but it will concentrate on summarizing the major concepts and techniques for collecting environmental samples and preparing them for analysis. Although this approach may appear to divide the problem, it is extremely important for a successful program to have good communication between the toxicologist who must assess the toxicity of substances, the field researcher taking the samples and the analytical chemist who must determine the concentration of the substance in the samples and the environment. The factors which affect the collection and determination of trace quantities can be quite complex, and each specialist involved in method development, sampling or analytical measurements must have a basic understanding of the total effort.

The value of any environmental survey is dependent on the quality of its sampling program. Analytical methods can be highly sensitive but the results of an analysis are only as good as the sampling and sample preservation methods used. Sampling is done for a specific purpose and the protocol followed should minimize changes in the sample and contamination which would interfere with the analytical procedures to be used.

Monitoring can be broken down into at least four types depending on the puspose of the study. Reconnaissance monitoring attempts to observe changes with time by periodic sampling; surveillance monitoring involves periodic sampling to ensure compliance with regulation; spot checking attempts to pinpoint a specific parameter in cases such as spills; and, objective monitoring provides data for the development of models and simulation. In the overall picture, environmental monitoring "can be considered as a means of determining whether existing controls are adequate and will continue to protect man and his environment." [1)]

The purpose of the monitoring project must be thoroughly understood, and careful planning is essential to ensure that the proper samples are taken and their integrity maintained. Analysis at the time of collection is seldom possible so the samples must be transported and stored so that they will reflect the original components and concentrations. Adsorption of desired components on the walls of the container or leaching of contaminants from the container can affect the integrity of a sample. Loss of desired components may occur from breakdown due to effects of heat, light, moisture, oxygen, or biological activity.

Each year new and improved analytical instruments and methods are introduced resulting in improved specificity and sensitivity of analyses. It has been observed that, "The number of these compounds detected in a sample of water is related to the sensitivity of the measurement technique: as the detection level decreases an order of magnitude, the number of compounds detected increases accordingly. Based on the number of compounds detected by current methods, one would expect to find every known compound at a concentration of 10^{-12} g/L or higher in a sample of treated drinking water." [2)]

As detection limits are pushed lower, it is easy to see that if stringent controls are not maintained over the various aspects of sampling, it is possible for "blank" contamination to be higher than the analyte in the actual sample. At other times a number of extraneous "peaks" will be observed which in many cases will have to be identified and quantitated. Environmental regulations may then require periodic determinations of these "impurities" — a waste of time, effort, and money. Much of this can be avoided if care is taken to insure that the proper equipment and procedures are used for sampling.

Air

Because of the physical nature of air, some special sampling problems are encountered. Except in situations where "whole-air" samples can be taken and returned to the lab for analysis, the most critical part of the analysis is the on-site sampling step using the proper technique and equipment and making careful measurements for flowrates and volumes. Sampling techniques vary greatly with the chemical and physical properties of the components of interest. In most situations the system must be defined and the collection and analytical methods selected and tested before the samples are taken. Unlike the liquid and solid sample matrice, the collection of gaseous samples is more closely related and dependent upon the technique which will be used for analysis, since it often requires concentration and separation of components from the gaseous matrix at the time of sampling.

The development of specific and highly sensitive gas chromatographic detectors, liquid chromatographic systems, ion chromatography and other new analytical instrumentation has enabled a greater flexibility in the collection parameters and choice of collection systems. Gas chromatography is the most widely used analytical technique for organic compounds because of its selectivity and sensitivity. Gas chromatographic procedures are abailable or can be developed for a wide range of compounds by the proper selection of columns and detectors. The range can be broadened by using chemical derivatives and gas chromatographic/mass spectrometric techniques. Liquid chromatography, infrared spectrometry, and other analytical techniques can be used when appropriate. For inorganic compounds element specific techniques such as atomic absorption spectroscopy and inductively coupled plasma optical emission spectroscopy are the two most utilized instrumental techniques. Polarography, neutron activation and other analytical techniques are used when appropriate.

Several reviews on personal monitoring [3–5] and ambient air monitoring [6–8] are available in the literature along with a number of books containing sampling and analytical methodology [9–14]. NIOSH has published a compilation of over 500 monitoring methods for 737 analytes in seven volumes (with a eighth volume in preparation), and they are presently availyble from National Technical Information Service (NTIS), Springfield, VA [15–21].

2 Gases and Vapors in Air

For our purpose in the discussion of sampling, a substance is considered to be a gas if this is its normal physical state at atmospheric pressure and room temperature.

A substance, which is normally a liquid or a solid under these conditions, may volatilize or sublime into the atmosphere because of its vapor pressure. In this volatilized state it is considered to be a vapor. Liquids and solids may exist in the atmosphere as both a vapor and as a particulate (mist or dust), and sampling methods must be used which can collect both phases, without bias, or selectively separate the two phases for independent determination.

There are three basic approaches to sampling gases and vapors. The first approach is to take a "whole-air" sample, which is to confine some segment of the atmosphere in a container and return it "unchanged" to the laboratory for analysis. The second approach is to concentrate by separation of the substances from air using techniques such as absorption, adsorption, condensation or chemical reaction. The concentrated sample is then returned to the laboratory where it is analyzed directly or recovered in a form which can be analyzed. The third approach is to measure the specific component on-site using direct reading and portable instrumentation or by observing a color change resulting from a controlled chemical reaction.

2.1 Whole-Air Samples

Whole-air samples are sometimes referred to as "grab samples" or "instantaneous samples"; however, various techniques for taking a whole-air sample over an extended period of time by using a low-flow pump or critical orifice leak device have been used. Whole-air samples are taken by pulling air into an evacuated glass bulb, can, tube, syringe, etc., or by pumping the gas into a container or plastic bag. This technique is valuable for samples where sample integrity can be maintained and where analytical sensitivity is adequate to preclude preconcentration. The collection devices are resealed after sampling and returned to the lab for analysis. Sensitive analytical techniques such as gas chromatography, infrared and mass spectrometry can be used for qualitative and quantitative analysis of the sample directly. Various concentration techniques can also be used in the lab to increase sensitivity [22,23)].

2.2.1 Sampling Bulbs and Containers

Various types of rigid samplers are shown in Fig. 1. Glass evacuated samplers (Fig. 1a) are heavy-walled containers, usually of 250 to 1000 milliliter capacity. Some special design samplers have also been investigated [22)]. Other containers such as metal cans [24] and small metal cylinders have been used. Glass sampling bulbs containing greased stopcocks or stopcocks made of TEFLON † resin may also be used if they are capable of holding a vacuum (Fig. 1b).

For preparing sealed glass evacuated samplers, air is removed using a heavy duty vacuum pump (1 to 15 mm of Hg) and the neck is heated with a torch and drawn out. A small scratch is made at the end of the neck so that it can be broken at the sampling site. After sampling, the neck is resealed using a wax filled cap and the pressure of the sample is taken as the barometric pressure reading at the site. An adaption of this technique has been described by Berg et al. [22)] where samplers were prepared by drawing out and evacuating 100 mL Pyrex test tubes.

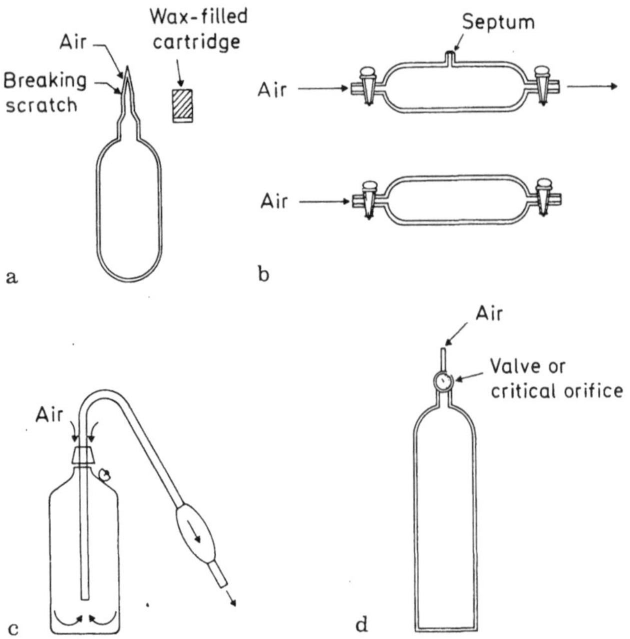

Fig. 1a–d. Rigid Whole-Air Samplers. **a** Evacuated Bulb; **b** Flow-Through Sample Bulb; **c** Displacement Sample Bottle; and **d** Evacuated Metal Cylinder

Evacuated samplers which are sealed with a valve or stopcock must be checked for leaks by evacuating to an absolute pressure of 25 mm Hg, or less. The valves are closed and the vacuum checked after one hour or more. Prior to sampling, the containers should be prepared in an uncontaminated atmosphere, and the evacuated pressure obtained should be measured with a mercury manometer. The volume of collected sample at barometric pressure is calculated as follows:

$$V_s = V_b \times [(P_1 - P_2)/P_1] \quad (1)$$

where:
V_s = volume of sample at barometric pressure,
V_b = volume of bulb
P_1 = barometric pressure at time of sampling
P_2 = pressure in evacuated bulb.

The evacuated sampling container has been widely used for sampling gases such as carbon dioxide, oxygen, methane, carbon monoxide, hydrogen and nitrogen. Many organic gases and vapors have also been sampled from workplace atmospheres and process vents and stacks. Otson et al.[25] used evacuated glass bulbs to determine dichloromethane in a work room using paint removers, and Berg et al.[22] used a special design bulb for trace quantities of a variety of solvents. Evacuated sampling containers are not generally suited for sampling hydrogen sulfide, oxides of nitrogen, sulfur dioxide, or other reactive gases or vapors.

A variation of the evacuated bulb can be used for sampling some reactive gases and vapors. An absorption or reaction liquid is placed in the bulb before it evacuated and sealed. When the sampler is opened, the sampled substance is absorbed in the liquid or reacted to a form that may be determined by chemical analysis. This technique is more closely related to impinger and absorber techniques which will be discussed in the next section.

Displacement is also an effective and simple means for collecting a whole-air sample. The most widely used device is a glass bulb with two stopcocks, (Fig. 1b). These are also available with a septum-sealed opening which makes it convenient for removing samples with a gas syringe for injection into a gas chromatograph. Samples are taken by attaching a pump to one end and drawing the sample through the bulb. The volume of sample pulled through the bulb should be at least ten times the volume of the bulb. Figure 1c shows another type of gas displacement sampling apparatus. Air in the bottle is pulled out using a one-way bulb, syringe or pump. Simple, small glass bottles have also been used for sampling. VAN Houten and Lee [26)] use 4-oz French square bottles sealed with a cap containing a rubber septum and lined with three layers of Saran[1] film. A number of solvents were held for 30 days and good recovery obtained. Harsch [24)] designed a container made from a stainless steel beaker and used it for sampling halocarbons and hydrocarbons in ambient and workplace atmospheres and in power plant stacks.

Syringes can also be used to take and transport samples to the laboratory. Glass syringes are simple to use and have similar retention characteristics as glass sampling bulbs. The plungers should fit tightly but should not be greased if organic compounds are to be collected. Lang and Freedman [27)] tested a variety of syringes for the collection of fixed gases and methane in mine atmospheres. They recommended 10-ml disposable plastic syringes with a butyl rubber plunger on the basis of efficiency and cost.

2.1.2 Plastic Bags

Whole-air samples can be taken conveniently for many gases and vapors using flexible plastic bags [28–41)]. Plastic bags are light, nonbreakable and are easily filled from a completely collapsed state with a one-way bulb, syringe or small pump. Samples can also be taken by placing an empty bag inside a sealed rigid container and slowly evacuating the air from the container [39)]. A self-filling bag has also been described by Curles and Hendricks [32)].

The sampling bags are commercially available in a variety of sizes and material; such as Saran, SCOTCHPACK, MYLAR, TEFLON, TEDLAR, KEL-F, polyethylene and polyester. Some of the materials are aluminized or laminated with aluminium to reduce permeability. Plastic bags must be cleaned by filling with clean air flushing several times before use. The bag should also be checked for leaks by filling and observing after 24 hours or by partially filling and alternately placing sections of the bag under water to observe bubbles.

The types of chemicals which can be collected using plastic bags varies with the bag material, concentration, temperature and storage duration. Some investi-

[1] Trademark of the Dow Chemical Company

gators recommend preconditioning the bags with the gas or vapor to be collected, and filling the bag several times at the sampling site before the final sample is taken. A number of references give storage data for various plastic bags for a number of gases and vapors. A detailed method for the determination of C_1 through C_5 hydrocarbons has been standardized by ASTM [40]. Nelson [36] and Schuette [35] summarize information sources on storage properties. Polasek and Bullin [37] have discussed storage properties for various bags when sampling low concentrations; however, some of their findings have been disputed [38].

Because of the various parameters affecting storage, it is a good practice to investigate the storage characteristics of the sampling bags for the components being collected. This can be done by filling the bags with air and injecting known amounts of the component. The bag can then be sampled and the component determined over a period of time (Fig. 2). To determine if any very rapid adsorption or reaction occurs, the contents of the storage test bag (once the curves have leveled out) can be squeezed into an identical empty bag. The curves should continue

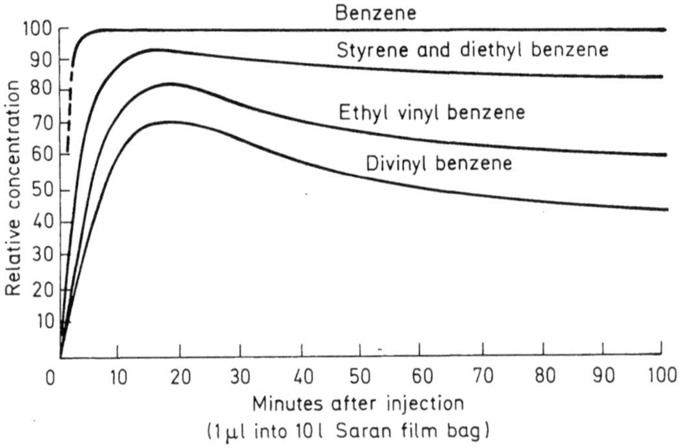

Fig. 2. Effect of Storage Time On Retention of Organic Vapors In A Sampling Bag Made Of SARAN Film. Am. Ind. Hyg. Assoc. J. *39* 325 (1978)

without a major drop in concentration if the bags are suitable for that compound. Sample bags should also be checked for memory affects from previous samples by flushing the bag, filling with air and analyzing after a storage period.

2.2 Sampling with Concentration

Whole-air samples, in general, collect a segment of the atmosphere and return it to the lab "unchanged" for analysis. When "sampling with concentration" techniques are used, the desired substances are separated from air by absorption in a liquid reaction to form a nonvolatile product, adsorption on solid sorbents or condensation.

Two things are accomplished using these techniques:

1) the sensitivity for the detection and determination of the desired compound is increased and,

2) a time-weighted-average concentration over the sampling period is obtained. The sampling duration is chosen with the sampling purpose and the limitations of the sampling technique in mind. Sampling periods may vary from 5–30 minutes for determining excursion concentrations or from 1 to 24 hours for integrated samples.

Since the separation and concentration of substances from air depends on the physical and chemical properties of the substance and the collection medium, it is essential that the procedures are planned and tested prior to sampling. Collection efficiency, recovery, affect of humidity, affect of other substances collected and storage of the sample are just some of the important parameters which need to be investigated. Table 1 gives an outline to an approach for

Table 1. Progressive Development and Validation steps

Suggested Procedure (Little Or No Experimental Work)
1. Chemical, physical, and toxicological properties listed.
2. Concentration range and required sensitivity estimated.
3. Collection system(s) extrapolated from similar compounds.
4. Analytical procedure suggested.
5. Possible interferences indicated.

Tentative Procedure (Limited Experimental Work)
1. Analytical procedure tested.
2. Collection efficiency determined.
3. % Recovery determined.
4. Preliminary breakthrough and bias study.
5. Preliminary field samples.
6. Effect of interferences, coadsorption and temperature (if indicated).

Validated Method (e.g. Systematic Study For Solid Sorbents)
1. Determination of breakthrough volume at concentrations of 2 times exposure guideline and relative humidity of 85%.
2. Five samples at each concentration, 0.1, 0.5, 1 and 2 times exposure guideline for relative humidities less than 50% and greater than 85%.
3. Six samples at the exposure guideline concentration (three collected at each humidity) and stored for at least 14 days.
4. Statistical evaluation of data.
5. Field validation by comparison to accepted method or by field spiking.
6. Collaborative studies with other laboratories.

developing an air sampling method for an untested gas or vapor. If some of the information is already available, several of the first steps may not be necessary. If a fully validated method from the literature is used, some testing in the laboratory is still necessary to confirm that the method is applicable for the intended use and that the analytical procedures and equipment can be used effectively.

Since all the sampling with concentration techniques require some type of pumping device to move the air into the sampling device, the selection and calibration of the sampling pump should be done with care. Various types and sizes of pumps are available from manufactures, and some discussions of pumps and pumping devices can be found in the literature [9-12]. Since the accuracy of the final result can be no better than the accuracy in knowing the sample volume, factors such as the affect of temperature, longterm stability and short-term variability of the flow rate should be known. When pumping through a liquid adsorbent, a protective trap should be used to protect the pump and rotometers. A liquid film can foul the pump and rotameters. Activated charcoal can be used for organic solvents and corrosive vapors, and silica gel is useful for water vapors. Frequent calibration under actual or simulated sampling conditions is strongly recommended.

2.2.1 Liquid Impingers and Bubblers

Impingers and bubblers containing a liquid have been used extensively for the collection of many gases and vapors. More recently, the use of impingers and bubblers has been replaced by solid sorbents for the collection of many substances; however, for many compounds (particularly reactive compounds, strong acids and strong bases) impingers and bubblers are still an effective and sometimes the only means for their collection. Several types of impingers and bubblers are shown in Fig. 3. Impingers, which were originally designed for particulate sampling, can be

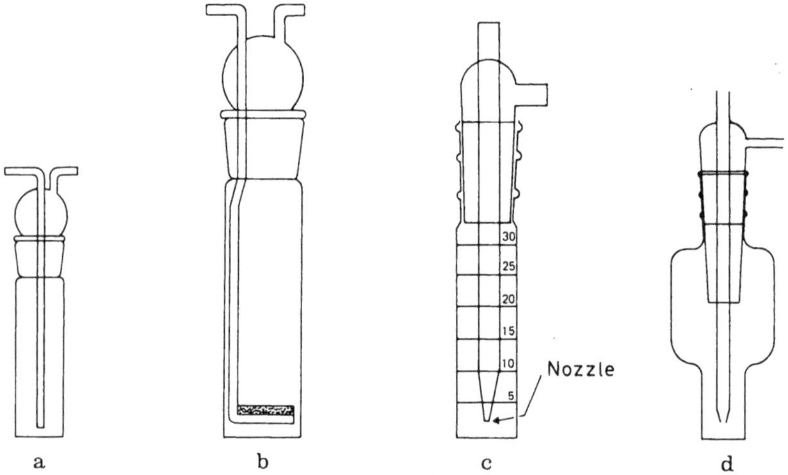

Fig. 3a–c. Liquid Bubblers And Impingers. **a** Simple Bubbler; **b** Bubbler With Frit; **c** Midget Impinger; and **d** Nonspill Impinger

used for vapors under certain conditions [42,43]. Bubblers have been designed to more efficiently scrub the gas or vapor from the air as it passes through the liquid. Midget impingers [42] and nonspill impingers and bubblers [44,45] can be used for personal samples as well as for area samples. Sampling trains [46] similar to the one described in U.S. Environmental Protection Agency Method # 5 can be used in combination with filters, various solutions and sometimes solid adsorbents for sampling particulates, vapors and gases in industrial stacks and vents.

The major factors which are involved in the collection of gases and vapors using impingers and bubblers are [47]:

a. Solubility of the contaminant in the collecting liquid.
b. Rate of diffusion of contaminant into the liquid.
c. Vapor pressure of contaminant at the sampling temperature.
d. Chemical reactivity of the contaminant with the reagent (including hydrogen bonding as in collecting acetone in chloroform).
e. Contact area (size of air bubble) and time of contact (flow rate) of the contaminated air through the liquid reagent.
f. Volatility of the collecting liquid.
g. Analytical techniques to be applied after the sample has been collected.

The simple bubbler and midget impinger can be used for a number of compounds as long as collecting efficiency is at least 90% under the condition of sampling. The impinger, which does not insure intimate mixing of the gas at it passes through the liquid column is suitable for gases and vapors which are strongly retained by some mechanism. Some of the mechanisms necessary for good collection efficiency are high solubility, low volatility, neutralization reactions, formation of precipitates and other chemical reactions. Although a chemical reaction is usually more efficient, gases and vapors which do not react can be collected in liquids if they are significantly soluble in the medium. Methanol and acetone can be collected in water for example. Methyl ethyl ketone, although water soluble, is more difficult to collect in water [48]

Collection efficiency can be estimated for nonreactive compounds [48,49], but it is highly recommended that actual measurement be carried out in the laboratory and/or possibly during field sampling. Two or three impingers can be connected in series for determining collection efficiency or for routine sampling to increase efficiency. The amount found in the first impinger is compared to the total amount found to determine a unit efficiency. If the amount found in the last impinger is greater than 10% of the total, the results may be questionable. If the efficiency is not acceptable, sampling may be carried out at a lower flow rate or at reduced temperature by immersing the absorber in an ice bath. The ice bath increases the collection efficiency and reduces loss of the collection solvent by volatilization.

Fritted bubblers are generally more efficient and are recommended when impinger efficiency drops below 90%. The frits break the air into a froth of small bubblers with a much higher contact area. The frits, usually glass, are available in fine, medium and coarse porosity. Plastic diffusers are also available to adapt impingers into a more efficient bubbler. If the gas is appreciably reactive or soluble, a coarse frit is usually suitable and a medium frit is recommended if gases and vapors are more difficult to collect. The flow rate must be adjusted to maintain discrete bubbles to obtain full efficiency. Fine frits create a much higher back pressure and generally do not offer much advantage over a medium frit since the bubbles tend to coalesce near the surface of the frit to increase their size and decrease the bubble population [49].

Although more efficient than impingers, bubblers have some disadvantages which must be considered. Much higher back pressures are produced by the frit, and since the back pressure may vary from bubbler to bubbler, careful flow calibration is necessary for each sampling train [50]. Bubblers are also more difficult to rinse out and are not recommended for the collection of substances which form precipitates with the reagent, e.g., H_2S with $CdCl_2$. If the air being sampled contains particulates which may clog the frit, a nonabsorbing pre-filter must be used [47]. A strongly alkaline solution should be poured into the bubblers just prior to sampling and removed promptly after collection since the solution may attack the glass frit and change the flow calibration.

Besides using glass frits, other modifications have been made to impingers to increase efficiency by increasing contact area. Impingers can be packed with glass wool or glass beads. Linch et al. [51] found that 3-mm glass beads packed to the 25-ml mark in a midget impinger will extend the surface area, act as baffles to increase contact time and promote mixing. A smaller volume of liquid is needed for packed impingers and some highly viscous liquids can be used more efficiently.

Many methods using impingers and bubbers are available in the literature. Neutralization reactions using caustic for acid vapors; HF, HCl, HNO_3, etc., and acidic solution for collection of basic gases; amines, ammonia, etc., are usually simple and very efficient. Organic acids can be collected, but they are difficult to analyze directly and several methods have been reported using derivatization after collection. Williams and Mazur [52] reported a method for acetic acid which is collected in impingers containing sodium carbonate, esterified and the headspace analyzed by GC. Maleic, fumaric and succinic acids were collected in impingers by Wathne [53], methylated using boron trifluoride and analyzed by GG. Traces of phenols in auto exhaust and tobacco smoke have been collected in 0.12% NaOH solution and determined by reversed-phase high-performance liquid chromatography after derivatization with p-nitrobenzenediazonium tetrafluoroborate.

Some compounds have low enough volatility and are soluble enough to be collected by absorption in a solvent. Vinyl acetate has been collected in toluene [54] and isooctane can be used for the collection of aromatics such as ethyl benzene, styrene [55] and pesticides. Ethylene glycol has also been used to collect pesticides. A colorimetric method was developed by Palassis [56] for tetramethyl and ethylene thiourea. Samples were collected in impingers containing water and derivatized with pentacyanoamineferrate to form a colored coordination complex.

Many compounds rely on a chemical reaction with the impinger solution to form a precipitate, complex or chemical derivative [57], e.g., hydrogen sulfide, carbon dioxide [61], formaldehyde, organo-lead [58,59] and mercury compounds [60], nickel carbonyl [61], nitrogen dioxide [62], ozone [63], phosphine [64], and sulfur dioxide [65]. Ruch [57] has published a book with abstracts impinger and bubbler methods for over 160 compounds. Several methods using 2,4-dinitrophenylhydrazine (NDPH) in impingers have been developed for aldehydes [66,67]. An interesting method was developed by Romano and Renner [68] where ethylene oxide is converted to ethylene glycol in an impinger containing dilute sulfuric acid.

The most difficult type compounds to determine in air is one which is highly unstable and whose products cannot be related byck to the original concentration. It is necessary in this case to form a derivative on contact during the collection step by placing the derivatizing reagent in the impinger. Developing methods for reactive compounds, which often must be determined at very low levels, can be a difficult and time consuming task. A classic example of the many stages of development for reactive isocyanates has been given in a recent review [5]. A variety of impinger/derivative methods are given in the literature for reactive compounds such as chloroacethyl chloride [69], bis (chloromethyl)ether [70,71], o-phenylenediamine [72], ethylenimine [73] and alkyl-2-cyanoacrylate [74].

2.2.2 Solid Sorbents-Solvent Desorption

Solid sorbents are being used extensively to sample contaminants in air. A small tube containing a solid sorbent is convenient to use, can concentrate trace contaminants and can be worn by a worker to determine breathing zone concentrations. Because solid sorbents are so convenient to use and transport, methods using solid sorbents are generally perferred over whole air and impinger methods for many compounds. There are two basic techniques for collection of substances in air using solid sorbents. The most widely used technique utilizes a small pump to draw the air sample through a bed of solid sorbent. The second technique, which is discussed in Section 2.2.4, utilizes diffusion of compounds into a chamber containing a solid sorbent. The compounds are recovered from the sorbents by desorption with a suitable solvent or by thermal desorption.

Solid sorbent tube/pump sampling followed by solvent desorption of collected compounds from solid sorbents is the most commonly used technique. The procedure is relatively simple; once the compound is desorbed, the extract can be analyzed by gas chromatography or other standard analytical techniques. Parts-per-million concentrations in air are usually determined, although parts-per-billion sensitivity can be obtained for some compounds by using large sample volumes and high-sensitivity detectors. Charcoal is the most widely used sorbent while silica gel, alumina, porous polymers and various gas chromatographic packings are used for specialized applications.

In selecting a sorbent for high collection efficiency, the recovery of the compound must also be considered. Often a mutual compromise may be necessary to obtain

Table 2. General Sorption-Desorption Systems for Organic Compounds

Sorbent	*Desorption Solvent*	*Types of Compounds*
Activated Carbon	Carbon disulfide, Methylene chloride, Ether (1% Methanol or 5% Isopropanol sometimes added)	Misc. volatile organics: Methyl chloride, vinyl chloride and other chlorinated aliphatics, aliphatic and aromatic solvents, acetates, ketones, alcohols etc.
Silica gel	Methanol, Ethanol Ether, Water	Polar compounds: alcohols, phenols, chlorophenols, chlorobenzenes, aliphatic and aromatic amines, etc.
Activated Alumina	Water, Ether Methanol	Polar compounds: alcohols, glycols, ketones, aldehydes, etc.
Porous Polymers	Ether, Hexane, Carbon Disulfide, Alcohols	Wide range of compounds: phenols, acidic and basic organics, multi-functional organics, pesticides, etc.
Chemically Bonded And Other GC Packings	Ether, Hexane, Methanol	Specialized: High boiling compounds pesticides, herbicides, polynuclear aromatics, etc.

an acceptable system. Table 2 lists some of the most used sorbents for the various types of compounds collected, although overlap allows some flexibility when sampling mixtures. Prior treatment and activation of the sorbent will affect efficiencies. For example, not all types of charcoal are the same and not all batches of the same type of charcoal necessarily have the same collection and recovery properties. Some sorbents, such as charcoal, have wide applicability while some sorbents are designed for a specific type of problem.

Collection tubes containing the most frequently used sorbents are commercially available in several sizes from suppliers. The tube generally contains a front section where the major amount of the contaminant is collected and a back section (1/4 to 1/2 the size of the front section) which is used to determine if excessive breakthrough has occurred. Tubes containing 150 mg and 600 mg of sorbent are commonly used for personal sampling; however, for long-term sampling of high concentrations and/or highly volatile compounds, tubes containing one gram or more may be necessary. Although many sorbents can be purchased from a supplier already packed and sealed in tubes, it may be necessary to prepare collection systems in the lab for special situations. The sorbents must be free from contaminants and properly activated. Coconut-shell charcoal should be heated to 600 °C for one hour before packing [75]. Silica gel and alumina can be activated in an oven overnight at 350 to 400 °C in a dry nitrogen atmosphere. Porous polymers can be cleaned before packing using Soxhlet extraction [76–78]. The cleaned sorbent must be stored in sealed containers away from any possible contamination, and a clean environment must be maintained while packing the tubes. Lab packed tubes and commercial tubes should be analyzed before taking samples to confirm that no interferences are present. Sorbents can be packed in straight tubes [79], u-tubes [9] or in other containers such as a midget impinger. Sorbents have also been used with plastic air sampling bags. One to ten grams of sorbent is placed in a bag and a "whole-air" sample is taken. The bag is then shaken to adsorb the contaminants on the sorbent.

Without getting too deeply in adsorption theory, two types of sorption processes may be considered when discussing collection of substances from air. Volumetric breakthrough usually occurs when sampling low concentrations on porous polymers, and therefore, it will be discussed in more detail in the next section under thermal desorption. The phenomenon which usually controls breakthrough of most organic compounds when using activated carbon is capacitive breakthrough. The compounds are strongly held by carbon and saturation (capacitive breakthrough) occurs before volumetric breakthrough for most compounds. This type of capacitive breakthrough is also observed for other sorbents and depends on the sorbent and volatility of the compound [80,81].

Figure 4 illustrates the distribution curve of a compound through the sorbent bed and the capacitive breakthrough curve of the compound in the effluent. At the start of collection the compound is distributed through a section of the sorbent as shown by curve 1. After continued collection this section becomes "saturated", that is an equilibrium is established with incoming concentration Ci where the vapor sorption and desorption rates are equal. This is shown by curve 2. The sorption front has moved through the front section of the collection tube (L 2/3) and is being collected on the backup section. If collection continues, the equilibrium zone lenghtens and the compound begins to break through the collection tube at time T_B, as shown by curve 3. The breakthrough curve 4 is generated by monitoring concentrations of the compound in the effluent, and when all the sorbent is "saturated" the effluent concentration approaches the input concentration Ci.

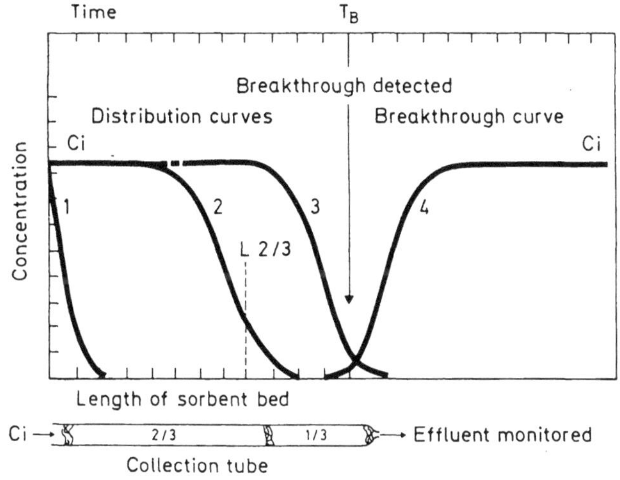

Fig. 4. Concentration Distribution In A Solid Sorbent Collection Tube. Am. Ind. Hyg. Assoc. J. *39* 350 (1978)

Breakthrough is defined as the detection of the compound in the effluent as a percentage of Ci. As a practical guide in air sampling, this is often set at 5%[82]. The breakthrough volume, which is more indicative of the collection efficiency, is the product of the sampling rate and the sampling time. A more detailed discussion of the collection mechanism can be found in the literature for sorbents such as charcoal[83–86], silica gel[87] and gas chromatographic packings[88]. A general guideline can be proposed for actual field samples. If less than 10% of the total amount collected is found on the 1/3 backup section, significant loss of the compound has probably not occurred, and if greater than 25% is detected, loss has probably occurred and results should be reported as "minimum amount present". More specific values can be obtained for this general statement by a detailed study of the breakthrough profiles for each specific sorbent and sorbate.

Figure 4 deals with the collection of one compound. When two or more compounds are collected, the compound most strongly held may displace the other compounds down the length of sorbent bed. This effect is very pronounced for silica gel since atmospheric water vapor, which is strongly adsorbed on silica gel, will displace compounds (especially nonpolar compounds) and promote premature breakthrough. Other factors must also be considered when using solid sorbent sampling. Various physical and environmental factors which affect collection and recovery are discussed in the literature[82,89–93]. Deteriorative effects on collection efficiency will be detected, after the fact, by high concentrations on the backup section. However, if the factors are recognized before or during sampling, a greater safety factor can be applied to the sample volume which will reduce the number of invalid samples and the need to resample. Factors which influence collection efficiency are discussed below.

1. *Size of Collection Tube.* In general, if the size (amount of sorbent) is doubled, then breakthrough volume (capacity) is doubled. Breakthrough volume is the volume of sample which can be pulled through the tube before the component of interest starts to elute.
2. *Flow Rate.* The effect of flow rate varies with the sorbent. If the flow rate is too high, a nonequilibrium condition occurs due to poor vapor contact, and poor collection efficiency will result. In most cases, once the equilibrium flow rate is reached, no increase in breakthrough volume is observed with reduction in flow rate. In some sorbents, such as silica gel, a high flow rate will cause a heating effect due to adsorbent water. This heating effect may decrease breakthrough volume.
3. *Concentration.* Breakthrough occurs sooner for higher concentrations. For charcoal, the empirical Freundlich isotherm appears to apply [86,94]. This equation takes the form:

$$\log T_B = \log a + b \log C \qquad (2)$$

   A straight line results if the log of the breakthrough time T_B is plotted against the log of the concentration, C. The line will have slope b and intercept of log a.
4. *Humidity.* In general, an increase in humidity will result in a decrease in breakthrough volume. The magnitude of this effect depends on the properties of the sorbent and sorbate. Although only a small amount of water is collected on charcoal, the high ratio of water molecules to the compound of interest affects the sorption-desorption equilibrium and can decrease breakthrough volume as much as 50%. This has greater affect with low concentrations of sorbate.
5. *Temperature.* An increase in temperature will result in a decrease in breakthrough volume. There is little specific information available for the various sorbents. A general guideline has been suggested for charcoal that for every 10 °C rise in temperature, the breakthrough volume will be reduced by 1–10%.

5\. *Coadsorption.* When two or more compounds are collected, the compound most strongly held will displace the other compounds, in order, down the length of sorbent bed. For a polar sorbent, compounds with the largest dielectric constant and dipole moment are most strongly held. For nonpolar sorbants, preferences are usually for the compounds of a larger molecular volume, and in general, the highest boiling point.

7\. *Migration.* A false indication of breakthrough may be caused by migration of the compounds collected on the front section to the backup section over an extended storage period. This can be reduced by refrigerating samples as soon as possible, or eliminated by using two tubes in series and separating them immediately after sampling.

Once the sample has been collected and returned to the laboratory, the collected compounds must be recovered from the sorbent for determination. Percent recovery is the percent of chemical recovered of the amount collected under actual sampling conditions. The major contributing factor is the desorption efficiency which is the partition at equilibrium of a chemical between a specific kind and volume of solvent and a specific batch and amount of solid sorbent. Recovery may also be influenced by other factors such as humidity, temperature and compound stability to oxidation.

$$\text{Recovery} = \text{Desorption Efficiency} \pm \text{other factors}\,. \tag{3}$$

Factors which cause changes in recovery are insidious, and unless these are understood and can be related to the chemical and physical properties of the compounds collected, errors can go undetected. The desorption efficiency is the most significant of the factors in defining the sorption-desorption system. Although desorption efficiency cannot always be isolated, it can be determined experimentally and is one of the first indicators of a potential problem in a suggested method.

1. *Desorption Efficiency*. The desorption efficiency is the most significant of the factors in defining the sorption-solvent desorption system. Once the desorption efficiency is determined, the effects of other factors can be examined by laboratory experimentation and field confirmation.
2. *Temperature*. The temperature effect on desorption efficiency can be significant due to a shift in the equilibrium. It is a common practice to cool the solvent before desorbing samples to reduce the heating effects. However, the equilibrium constant will change with temperature and the final desorption temperature before analysis of the solution may be critical.
3. *Humidity*. High humidity during collection may produce low recoveries for some compounds such as those which are easily hydrolyzed. If a large amount of water is collected, it may prevent good contact with a nonpolar desorption solvent, or change the equilibrium. However, high humidity may also improve desorption for some chemicals.
4. *Coadsorption*. Collection of other compounds can also affect recovery. The chemistry of all the compounds collected must be considered and the relative effects tested in the laboratory or in field spiking experiments.

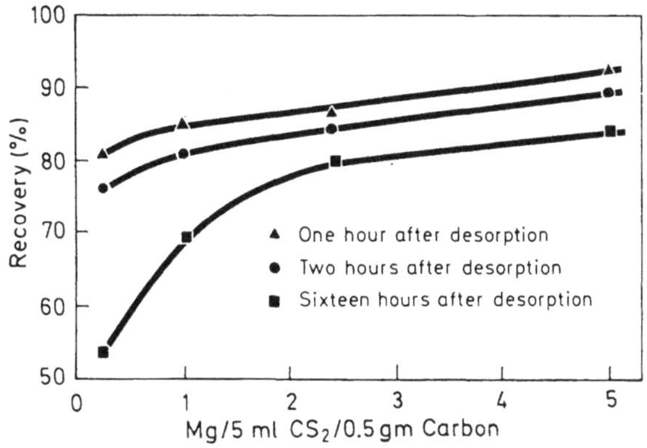

Fig. 5. Variation Of Desorption Efficiency With Concentration And Desorption Time. Am. Ind. Hyg. Assoc. J. *39* 355 (1978)

5. *Desorption Time.* One-half to one hour with good agitation is usually sufficient desorption time for most systems. Once optimum desorption has taken place, the system is generally stable; however, some exceptions have been observed [82]. Some compounds react or are readsorbed after an optimum desorption time as shown in Fig. 5. The active surface of the sorbent may act as a catalyst. Methanol has been shown to react with carbon disulfide in the presence of charcoal to form polysulfides, mercaptans and polyether-thioether compounds [82]. Decanting the solvent from the sorbent usually corrects this problem.
6. *Storage.* The period of time and the temperature at which the samples are stored prior to analysis may have a significant effect on recovery.
7. *Concentration.* When the desorption system is in equilibrium, the desorption efficiency should not vary with concentration. This is true for most compounds and a $\pm 5\%$ or less variation is observed over the concentration range of interest. However, some factors with affect recovery will have a greater percentage effect on lower concentrations. As a result, the recovery of some compounds decreases at lower concentrations (Fig. 5). The effects of concentration and desorption time should be identified early in the method development.

For the recovery of compounds from solid sorbents, the desorption efficiency is the most significant of the factors defining the sorption-solvent desorption system. The most common technique in determining desorption efficiency is to inject the compound or a solution of the compound directly into the solid sorbent [89,95–97]. The mixture is allowed to stand overnight and then desorbed and analyzed. Gases and highly volatile compounds are usually introduced as a mixture in air or nitrogen from a plastic bag or cylinder. The percent recovery can be determined in the same manner as the desorption efficiency except a known flow of air is pulled through the sorbent at the same time to determine the effect of the atmosphere. The closer the test atmosphere is to the actual air to be sampled the more accurate the recovery factor will be.

For many systems the desorption efficiency can be written in terms of an equilibrium constant; it is dependent on the ratio of solvent to sorbent for the distribution of the compound between the two phases. An equation has been derived by Dommer and Melcher [98] which relates the desorption efficiency to the volume of solvent and the amount of sorbent. The equation assumes the system is in equilibrium and can be approached from either direction. That is, the same desorption efficiency should be obtained when the compound is initially in the solvent or the solid phase. This has been shown to apply to most organic compounds in the concentration range of interest in industrial hygiene analyses. Desorption efficiency using the phase equilibrium method is similar to direct injection into the sorbent, only the test compund is prepared in the desorption solvent.

The phase equilibrium equations below can also be used to optimize the solid/liquid ratio when developing an analytical procedure.

$$\frac{1}{D} = K \frac{W_s}{W_l} + 1 \tag{4}$$

Where:
D = desorption efficiency (as a decimal fraction)

W_s = weight of solid phase
W_l = eight of liquid phase
K = constant for specific compound and sorbent.

Once K is determined, the desorption efficiency can be calculated for any solid and liquid ratio. Posner [99] further developed this concept and derived several other equations for calculating the desorption efficiency for any solid and liquid ratio and for determining the ratio necessary to obtain a desired desorption efficiency. Equation (5) is a modification of Eq. (5) and can be used to calculate the expected desorption efficiency when the volume is changed.

$$\frac{1}{D_n} = \frac{1}{n}\left(\frac{1}{D_1} - 1\right) + 1 \tag{5}$$

Where:

n = the ratio of solvent volumes $n = \frac{\text{new volume}}{\text{initial volume}}$
D_1 = initial desorption efficiency
D_n = desorption efficiency using new volume

Equation 6 can be used to select a volume to produce a desired desorption efficiency.

$$n_z = \left(\frac{1}{D_1} - 1\right)\frac{Z}{1 - Z} \tag{6}$$

Where n_z is the number of multiples of the original volume of desorbent needed to reach the desired desorption efficiency Z.

It should be noted that the partition ratio at equlibrium predicts the optimum desorption effiency attainable, and other experiments may be necessary to detect nonequlibrium situations. Desorption efficiency should not be taken as the recovery since other factors may have a significant effect. After a solvent/sorbent system is selected and tested using the phase equilibrium technique, direct injections of the test compound are made into collection tubes with and without air being pulled through. If the desorption efficiencies as determined by direct injection are considerably lower than phase equilibrium values, interaction or reaction on the sorbent surface is indicated. If the total recovery from the simulated air collection is lower than the direct injection efficiency (even through no breakthrough has occurred) hydrolysis, oxidation, or another reaction may be indicated.

A number of studies on desorption efficiency and recovery have been reported in the literature. Krajewski [97] compared three methods of determining desorption efficiencies to dynamically prepared standards and found the phase equilibrium data somewhat higher in most cases. Evans and Horstman [100] also showed that the recovery of styrene from dynamically sampled tubes was 18% lower than the direct spike method. They later showed that this was not due to a storage problem since they found no significant change in the recovery of styrene after six days [101]. Other researchers [89,102,103] have reported the effects of co-adsorbed compounds on the desorption efficiency. Posner and Okenfuss [92] studied the effects of the presence of other compounds on the desorption efficiency and reported no effect with nonpolar compound mixtures or when one polar compound was in the presence of non-polar compounds; however, a major effect was observed with mixtures of polar compounds. Pozzoli et al.[104] further expanded the concept of the phase equilibrium method by proposing a double elution technique to estimate the desorption efficiency directly on samples collected in the field by performing two successive elutions with the same volume of CS_2. The double elution technique was recommended to circumvent environmental conditions that may affect desorption efficiency during sampling and any effect of coadsorbed compounds.

Since charcoal is such a good sorbent and is readily available, the solution to some sampling problems is to find a way to increase the recovery of the desired compound from charcoal. One way is by increasing the solvent/sorbent ratio as discussed in the phase equilibrium section. Two other approaches are the use of mixed solvents and the two-phase solvent system. In general, polar compounds usually show low recoveries from charcoal. By adding several percent of a polar solvent to the carbon disulfide desorbent solvent, recovery is often improved by 10 to 20%. Methanol is the most frequently added polar solvent, and it is usually effective as long as it does not interfere with the gas chromatography. If the methanol/carbon disulfide system is used, the samples should be run within four hours since methanol reacts with carbon disulfide in the presence of charcoal[82]. In some cases ethanol, butanol, isopropanol, or acetone has been added to carbon disulfide to increase desorption efficiency. One or two percent acetone in carbon disulfide has been used to increase the recovery of acrylonitrile from charcoal; however, much larger amounts can be used if needed for other compounds since acetone is completely miscible with carbon disulfide. Posner[93] suggested using methylene chloride with 5% methanol to improve desorption efficiency and eliminate variability for polar compound mixtures, and Johansen and Wendelboe[105] suggested dimethylformamide which can be backflushed before it elutes from the GC column.

The mixed solvent technique has limited use for complex mixtures since it is more difficult to chromatograph, precludes determination of the polar solvent added, and may cause additional interference to other compounds present. A two-phase system has been developed by Langvardt and Melcher[106] which is capable of measuring both polar and nonpolar organic solvents present simultaneously in work environments. The charcoal collection tubes are desorbed with a 50/50 mixture of carbon disulfide and water. After desorption, the water and carbon sulfide layers are analyzed separately. The high recoveries of the polar compounds are attributed to their partitioning into the aqueous phase after desorption from charcoal by carbon disulfide. Not only does the partitioning eliminate interferences of some polar and nonpolar combinations, but the partition coefficients give additional qualitative information.

Silica gel is the second most widely used adsorbent. Many compounds which cannot be recovered from charcoal, such as highly polar compounds[107–109], phenols, amines[87,110,111], high boiling compounds and multifunctional compounds, often can be collected and recovered using silica gel. Polar and polarizable compounds are more strongly adsorbed on silica gel than nonpolar compounds because of its polar characteristics. The general order of strength of adsorption is water, alcohols, aldehydes, ketones, esters, aromatic compounds, olefins and paraffins. The biggest problem with silica gel is the adsorption of water which may cause desorption and loss of the collected compounds through frontal elution. The heating effect due to the heat of adsorption may cause polymerization or reaction of some compounds unless an inhibitor is added [112].

In spite of some of the disadvantages of silica gel, it is a very useful sorbent. Most of the early work with silica gel use a single U-tube or a train of two or more U-tubes. The U-tubes held at least 10 g of silica gel and sometimes one arm of the tube held a desiccant to reduce humidity effects [113]. The commercial tubes now available contain 150 mg to 1.5 g of silica gel sealed in glass tubes. Silica gel has been used for a wide range of organic solvents [114], halogenated hydrocarbons [115], and nitrogen dioxide [115]. Often chemicals collected on silica gel require analysis by HPLC [116,117] or derivatization prior to analysis.

Alternative sorbents for the collection of polar organic compounds which are sensitive to hydrolysis are porous polymers such as the Chromosorb porous polymer column packings, Porapak porous polymer column packings, Tenax-GC column packing, and Amberlite XAD sorbent products. XAD-2 resin has been used for a number of compounds [118–121] and, for example, has been shown valuable for the collection of reactive organo-thiophosphates [122]. Hydrolysis is observed for these compounds in atmospheres with high humidity, but once collection has occurred, the resin tends to stabilize the compounds and reproducible recoveries are obtained even after seven days of storage. Langhorst and Nestrick [123] developed a method for the collection of the chlorobenzene series on XAD-2 resin followed by analysis using a photoionization detector. In addition, XAD-7 has been used to sample epichlorohydrin and ethylene chlorohydrin [124] and XAD-4 has been used to collect 5,5,5-tributyl phosphorotrithioate and dibutyl disulfide [125].

Chromosorb 101 was used by Mann et al. [126] for determining 1,2-dibromo-3-chloropropane in air, Barnes et al. [127] collected 36 odor forming compounds on Chromosorb 103 and Tenax GC, Glaser and Woodfin [128] used Chromosorb 106 to collect 2-nitropropane, and Thomas et al. [129] collected chlordane with Chromosorb 102. The Porapak porous polymer packings are similar to Chromosorb porous polymer packings, and acetic anhydride was determined by Quazi and Vincent [130] in the presence of acetic acid by collecting on Porapak N sorbent. Although Tenax GC is widely used in thermal desorption, it has also been used in a number of solvent desorption methods [131,132] and in combination with polyurethane foam for pesticides and semivolatile organic compounds [134].

Alumina [134] has been used to collect alkanolamines and Giam et al. devised a method for collection and separation by selective elution of polychlorinated biphenyls and phthalates using Florisil [136]. Polyurethane foam has been used alone or in combination with filters or other sorbents for the collection of pesticides and other high boiling compounds [133,136,137]. A chemically bonded packing was also shown by Melcher et al. [138] to be excellent sorbents for pesticides and high boiling compounds. The recovery of these compounds is very poor from sorbent such as charcoal, alumina and silica gel. Gold et al. [139] found 13X molecular sieves to be a good sorbent for acrolein as well as for other aldehydes and alcohols. Suzuki and Imai [140] also use molecular sieves to collect acrolein and subsequently determined it by fluorimetry with o-aminobiphenyl. Another technique is to coat a solid sorbent with acid [87] or base [141,142] to collect basic and acidic compounds.

2.2.3 Solid Sorbent-Thermal Desorption

In the thermal desorption technique, samples are collected by pulling air through a tube containing a thermally stable sorbent bed. Instead of removing the sorbent and extracting with a solvent for analysis, the tube is heated and the absorbent compounds are purged directly into a gas chromatograph. Thermal desorption eliminates use of solvents and other handling operations, is more sensitive than solvent desorption techniques, and the collection tubes are reusable. The main advantage of this technique is the high sensitivity obtained since the total sample collected in 1–3 liters of air can be injected at one time. Sensitivity is in the low parts-per-billion range for most compounds. Another important advantage, especially for complex mixtures, is the absence of the solvent peak which is a major interference when low levels are being determined. One disadvantage of thermal desorption is the "one-shot" nature of the analysis. Multiple samples must be taken in order to run duplicate analyses and/or to examine by more than one technique. An unpredicted interference or instrumental miscue results in a lost sample. However, with the advancement of computer data handling and storage, this becomes less of a problem.

A number of factors must be considered when selecting a sorbent for use with thermal desorption:

1) suitable collection properties,
2) thermal stability with repeated use,
3) low background contaminants during desorption,
4) minimal decomposition or reaction during collection, storage or analysis.

A wide variety of sorbents have been evaluated which include: activated charcoal and synthetic carbons; porous polymers such as Tenax, Chromosorb series, Porapak series and XAD series; liquid phase coated GC packings and bonded GC packings. Although a wide variety of sorbents have been reported in the literature, the four listed below can be used to cover almost the entire range of compounds.

Tenax GC sorbent has a known upper temperature limit of 350 °C. It is a commonly used adsobent because of its high upper temperature limit and low background on desorption. Tenax is a porous polymer of 2,6-diphenyl phenol and has a packed density of approximately 0.22 g/mL (60/80 mesh). Chromosorb 106 is a cross-linked polystyrene porous polymer. It has a published upper temperature limit of 250 °C and a packed density of approximately 0.39 g/mL (60/80 mesh). Porapak N sorbent is a styrene/divinyl benzene porous polymer in wich vinyl pyrollidone is added to increase its polarity. The published upper temperature limit of Porapak N is 190 °C. Porapak N has a packed density of approximately 0.42 g/mL (60/80 mesh). Carbosieve B sorbent is a synthetic carbon molecular sieve and is one of the most retentive solid adsorbents available. It has an upper temperature limit of at least 400 °C and a packed density of approximately 0.22 g/mL (60/80 mesh).

Tenax is generally useful for compounds of the same or less volatility than benzene. Chromosorb 106 is useful for compounds of medium volatility and Porapak N is capable of collecting alcohols and other highly polar compounds of medium volatility. Carbosieve B is best suited for very volatile compounds. Although these sorbents are suitable for mixtures of compounds, mixtures with a wide range of volatility may require two or three sorbents connected in series. Tenax is used first to remove the compounds of low volatility and Chromosorb 106 (or Porapak N) and Carbosieve B follow to adsorb the more volatile compounds. It is important to thermally desorb with the purge gas flowing in the opposite direction of the sampled air. Another sorbent which has been found useful for high boiling compounds such as pesticides is coated GC packings such as 20% DC-200 silicone oil coated on Chrmosorb W HP support (100/120). Table 3 lists some conditions for thermal desorption analysis. The exact selection of the analytical column and conditions will depend on the compounds to be analyzed.

Table 3. GC Conditions for Thermal Desorption Analysis

	Increase in Boiling Point of Collected Compound →			
Sampling tube	4-in. Carbosieve B adsorbent, 100/120	4-in. Porapak N porous polymer 80/100	4-in. Tenax-GC porous polymer, 60/80	2-in. 20% DC-200 silicone oil on C.W., H.P. support 100/120
Sampling Tube Desorption	5 min at 270 °C	5 min. at 200 °C	5 min. at 260 °C	5 min. at 230 °C
Column	2 ft × 0.125 in. s.s., Carbosieve B adsorbent, 100/120	4 ft × 0.125 in. s.s., Porapak N porous polymer, 80/100	8 ft × 0.25 in. s.s., 10% OV-17 silicone oil in Gas Chrom Q support, 60/80	6 ft × 0.25 in. glass, 10% ov-17 silicone oil on Gas Chrom Q support, 100/120
Column Temperature	5 min. at 80 °C program 20 °C/min. to 290 °C and hold	5 min. at 60 °C program 15 °C/min to 200 °C and hold	5 min. at 60 °C program 15 °C/min. to 280 °C and hold	5 min. at 90 °C program 15 °C/min. to 260 °C and hold
Injection Port Temperature	80 °C	120 °C	220 °C	200 °C
Carrier Gas Flow (ml N_2/min.)	20	20	30	20

It is important to thoroughly condition each sampling slug before it is used by heating and purging with nitrogen. When determining trace quantities, the background pattern becomes quite important. Decomposition and oxidation products of the sorbent can interfere with the analysis and extra care is needed in conditioning and in choosing desorption temperature and rate. Tubes are usually conditioned by heating in a flow of N_2 for 12–24 hours [143–147].

Recommendations for obtaining the lowest background include a pretreatment of the sorbent, usually Soxhlet extraction with a solvent, before packing the sampling tubes [76,78]. The apparatus used for desorption of the sampling tube and interface to the gas chromatograph can be relatively simple or highly complex. The basic components of a simple system were described by Russell [145]. The collection tube, usually 4—6 inches long and 0.25 inches in diameter, is connected directly to the gas chromatographic column or through a heated valve. The tube is heated with a heating tape or clamp oven, and the desorbed compounds are purged into a cold gas chromatographic column. After desorption, the column is temperature-programmed to obtain the chromatogram. Other thermal desorption systems can be integrated with an on-site chromatograph where the sample is collected, thermally desorbed and analyzed in a 5- to 50-minute periodic cycle [23,148].

A majority of the investigators use special design, "homemade" desorption systems [76,144,145,149–152] but a number of commercial systems are now available. The systems designed for workplace atmospheres [76,144–147,152–157], which are usually monitoring for ppm levels, are relatively simple compared to the ambient air monitoring systems which are used for low levels of compounds in a complex mixture. These systems often utilize multiple desorption transfer, cryogenic focusing [158–163], packed [150,164–166] or capillary gas chromatographic columns [165,166] and mass spectrometry detection [167–170].

The parameters which are often used in evaluating the collection properties of sorbents are the retention volume (peak maxima) and the breakthrough volume (first detectable loss). There are three techniques which can be used for determining the retention volume or breakthrough volume:

1. *Temperature Extrapolation.* The sorbent to be tested is packed into a collection tube and connected inside a gas chromatograph similar to a GC column. A compound is injected onto the column and the GC retention volume is taken as the product of the flow rate and elution time. Retention volumes are determined at several temperatures and the log of the retention volume is plotted vs. the reciprocal of the temperature (1/°K). This plot is then extrapolated to determine the retention volume at ambient temperatures.
2. *Disappearances of Vapor During Purging.* Collection tubes are loaded with a measured quantity of a compound and then purged with known volumes of air. The tubes are then desorbed and the amount lost is determined by comparison to unpurged tubes.
3. *Measurement of Breakthrough.* The breakthrough of compounds under sampling conditions are monitored by analyzing the effluent from the tube directly using a GC detector or by attaching a backup tube which is changed periodically and analyzed.

The breakthrough volumes determined by all of these methods are generally in agreement. Evaluation of various sorbents for a wide number of compounds using one or more of the above methods are given in the literature [80,143,149,150,153,158]. Techniques 2 and 3, which are often used in evaluating solvent desorption methods, may be more precise when a method is being validated under simulated or actual sampling conditions, but require more time and are tedious especially when a number of sorbents are being tested for a range of compounds. The temperature extrapolation technique offers the most rapid means of comparing sorbents, enables one to work with hazardous compounds in a safer laboratory experiment, and potentially allows the evolution of a general correlation between the collection efficiency of a sorbent for a compound and the compound's boiling point or molar volume.

Collection efficiency is defined in the conventional manner as the inlet concentration minus the outlet concentration divided by the inlet concentration. For most sorbent sampling tubes, with enough effectiveness to be of interest, the initial collection efficiency is almost always greater than 90%. In the course of continued sampling, the capacity of the collection tube will be exceeded and breakthrough will occur. This may happen in two ways. For atmospheres containing high concentrations of organic vapors, the pores of the resin will become filled and capacitive (weight) breakthrough will occur due to sorbent "saturation" (see Fig. 4). For low organic concentration, the compound will progress through the collection tube by virtue of its equilibrium between the sorbent phase and the mobile air stream, as in a gas chromatographic experiment. This phenomenon, volumetric breakthrough, is related to GC retention volume (V_r). There appears to be a concentration (weight loading) for each compound on a specified sorbent at which the breakthrough changes from volumetric to capacitive [80]. Below this loading, the breakthrough volume is independent of the concentration and can be related to the retention volume of a single injected peak or in terms of the frontal elution of a continuous assault concentration. The sorbents used in thermal desorption are usually of lesser adsorptive strength than carbon and are used to collect much smaller amounts of chemicals. As a result, the temperature extrapolation is a useful tool for evaluating sorbents. The use of the temperature extrapolation technique has been described by a number of investigators [171]: The parameter usually calculated from the experiment is the specific volumetric capacity (V_g) in ml/g, which is calculated from the retention time, flow rate and resin quantity.

$$V_g = \frac{F \times T_r}{g} \tag{7}$$

Where:
T_r = retention time in seconds to peak maxima
F = carrier gas flow rate in ml/sec.
g = resin weight in grams.

After obtaining the retention volume at several temperatures, the log of retention volume is plotted vs. 1/°K and the curve extrapolated to 20 °C or calculated by least squares linear regression. The breakthrough volume, the point at which the compound is first detected, is dependent on the sensitivity of detection and the efficiency of the "column" (peak width), but the retention volume is independent of these factors. Taking into account the unknown effects of coadsorbed compounds under true atmospheric conditions, the maximum safe sampling volume (MSSV) can be estimated as being one-half the V_r.

Thermal desorption methods for workplace atmospheres generally are developed for a single compound or small groups of similar compounds. Russell [145] reported the use of four sorbents to cover a wide range of compounds. Dietrich et al. [144] studied Tenax and Porapak N sorbents for various compounds and devised a splitter system where only a portion of the sample was injected into the GC and the rest was saved for a duplicate run. Campbell and Moore [147] developed a method for acrylonitrile, acrolein, acetonitrile, and acetone using Porapak N. Tenax was used by Bowen [154] for a series of aromatic amines which were sampled from air or water, and Tenax was also used by Podolak et al. [152] for phenol which was thermally desorbed into an infrared cell for identification and quantitation. Activated charcoal has been used by Myeres et al. [155] for the determination of vinyl chloride and for a wide range of volatile compounds by Parks et al. [153]. Pellizzari [156] studied various polymer beads, carbons and liquids phase coated packings for the collection of groups of polar compounds. The high sensitivity of thermal desorption and specificity of mass spectrometry was used by Shadoff et al. [76] for the determination of bis(chloromethyl)-ether collected on Chromosorb 101. Ambient atmospheric analysis becomes more complex than workplace analysis since a large number of compounds at very trace levels are present [150, 151, 159, 160, 165, 172–176]. When monitoring a workplace, the compounds likely to be present are usually known. When analyzing ambient atmospheres the compounds must be identified, and the combination of thermal desorption, capillary GC and mass spectrometry is a very powerful technique for this purpose.

2.2.4 Chemical Dosimeters (Passive Monitors)

Although the portable pump/sorbent tube systems are being used extensively for monitoring industrial workplace atmospheres, chemical dosimeters (passive monitors, diffusional dosimeters, etc.) have more recently become available, and a major effort is underway to evaluate them for applications in the workplace. They are more convenient to use since they require no pump or tubing, and can be worn in the breathing zone with little interference to the worker. Dosimeters measure time-averaged concentrations by collection of the vapor present in the air according to physical principles of mass transport across a defined diffusion layer [177] or permeation through a membrane [178] as the rate limiting steps. A number of designs for the diffusional dosimeter and the permeation dosimeter have been reported in the literature and various types are commercially available. Because of the various designs, the following discussions will be general in nature and some comments may or may not apply to a specific dosimeter. The manufactures' instructions should be followed to obtain the best results.

The solid sorbent diffusional dosimeter usually consists of a small badge-like container which can be attached to a worker or placed in an area for sampling. It is basically composed of a diffusion space or a group of spaces with a defined length to cross sectional area ratio. A porous wind screen may be used to define the opening and the solid sorbent, usually bound in a pad, is placed at the opposite end of the space.

In the diffusional dosimeter, the steady-state mass transport of the vapors follows Fick's first Law of Diffusion from the defined aperature(s) on the front of the dosimeter, through the length of the diffusion space, to the collecting medium. A choice of flow rates, range, and sensitivity can be obtained by selecting design parameters. The relationship between the vapor concentration and the weight of material collected by the monitor is given by a simplified version of Fick's Law of Diffusion:

$$M = \frac{DACt}{L}. \tag{9}$$

Where:
M = total mass of contaminant collected (ng)
D = molecular diffusion coefficient (cm^2/sec)
A = diffusion path area (cm^2)
L = diffusion path length (cm)
C = environmental contaminant concentration ($mg/m^3 = ng/cm^3$)
t = sampling time (sec)

The assumption in this simplified equation is that an effective collection medium is used and the concentration of the analyte at the sorbent surface is zero. For solid sorbent samplers, this is not always true for the more volatile compounds and becomes a problem for the weakly retained species, when peak exposures are followed by no or low exposure or when samples are stored for a long period of time before analysis. A more exact Eq. substitutes the quantity ($C—C_0$) for C in Eq. (9). Where C_0 is the concentration at the surface of the adsorbing layer.

Since no pump is used to pull air into the sampler, the sampling rate is dependent on the diffusion coefficient for each compound collected. The sampling rate for a specific compound is expressed in the equation:

$$SR = \frac{DA}{L} = \frac{M}{(C-C_0)\,t}. \qquad (10)$$

Where SR is the sampling rate for a specific compound (cm^3/min).

The solid sorbents are desorbed with a suitable solvent in a similar manner as discussed for tube/pump sampling. The desorption efficiency (DE) must also be determined for each compound. Once the mass of the contaminant (M) is determined, its time-weighted-average concentration (C) in air can be calculated:

$$C(mg/m^3) = \frac{M(ng)}{SR(cm^3/min) \times t\ (min) \times DE}. \qquad (11)$$

An integrated concentration can also be expressed as a dosage in ppm-hrs accumulated over a given period of time. For example, an eight-hour time-weighted-average of 10 ppm is the same as an eight-hour dose of 80 ppm-hr.

A number of factors should be understood and considered before a dosimeter can be used effectively.

1. *Sampling Rate*. The equation relating sampling rate, SR, was discussed earlier. The sampling rate for each compound can be obtained from the manufacturer or by exposing the dosimeter to known concentrations in the laboratory. Sampling rates may also be estimated from diffusion coefficients, if the sampling rate of one substance is known, using the Eq. (12):

$$SR_2 = D_2 \frac{SR_1}{D_1}. \qquad (12)$$

2. *Orientation of Dosimeter*. Orientation of the dosimeter face with respect to the air velocity direction is not controllable in the field. The degree this factor may effect sampling is dependent on the diffusion path length/face are (L/A). Dosimeters are designed to minimize this effect.
3. *Face Velocity*. If the air movement at the face of the dosimeter is very low, a stagnant air layer will form because of the depletion of the contaminant in the immediate area. A minimum amount of air movement (greater than 5 ft/min) is necessary to maintain ambient concentrations of the contaminant at the face of the dosimeter. When placed on a worker, this minimum requirement is

usally met; however, if the dosimeter is used as an area monitor, its placement should be considered so that stagnant areas are avoided.

4. *Reciprocity.* The dose, ppm-hr, should be dependent only on the product of the concentration times the exposure time. The same mass of contaminant should be collected at a concentration of 80 ppm for one hour as collected with a concentration of 10 ppm for eight hours.
5. *Sorbent Capacity or Saturation Point.* After a certain amount of substance has been adsorbed by the dosimeter the ability of the sorbent to remove vapors from the diffusion space is reduced and the sampling rate begins to decrease. The saturation point for many chemicals can be obtained from the manufacture or determined experimentally in the lab. To determine the saturation point in the lab, the dosimeter is exposed to various doses and the response or sampling rate is plotted against the dose. The point at which an unacceptable deviation in linearity occurs is taken as the saturation point, Fig. 6. Some dosimeters are designed with a backup pad which is placed behind the primary pad to measure the overload and extend capacity.

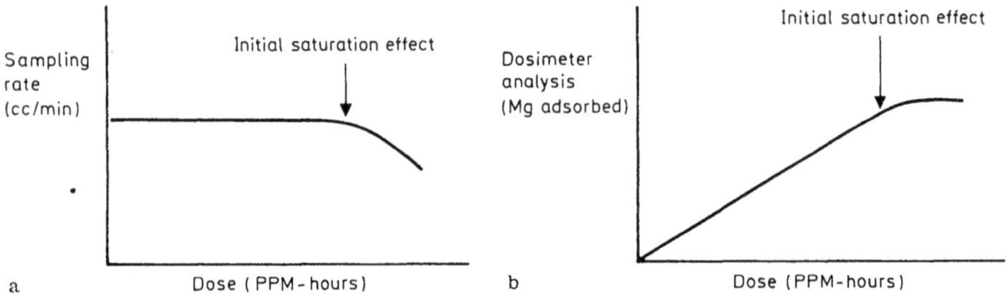

Fig. 6a and b. Saturation Effect In Solid Sorbent Chemical Dosimeters. **a** Effect On Sampling Rate; and **b** Effect On Total Amount Collected

6. *Competitive Coadsorption.* The saturation point is dependent on the sum of all components adsorbed. The combined weights of the multiple compounds collected should not exceed the capacity for the single contaminant with the lowest saturation point.
7. *Retention by Sorbent.* Some volatile compounds may not be held strongly by the sorbent. As a result, the exposure profile may have a considerable effect on the result. When exposed to a constant concentration, this effect is small; however, when exposed to a high concentration in the early part of the sampling period, the results may be low.
8. *Temperature.* Temperature is expected to have a minimal effect. A one percent increase in apparent concentration for each 10 °F above 77 °F and a one percent decrease for each 10 °F below 77 °F.
9. *Humidity.* Atmospheric water vapor can significantly reduce the adsorptive capacity of solid sorbents and dosimeters should be tested at the maximum relative humidity expected in field use if this information is not available from the manufacturer.

10. *Storage*. Samples should be run as soon as possible after collection. Storage of several weeks may be possible if the exposed dosimeters are refrigerated. The effect of storage should be determined for each contaminant.

A number of reviews on dosimeter monitoring devices [179–183] have been published. A recent review by Rose and Perkins [182] discusses the theory of operation, statistical considerations, and various sources of error in detail, and gives a historical development of the chemical dosimeters and their application to monitoring workplace atmosphere. Fowler [183] gives a good discussion of the theory, environmental factors, face velocity, and response time. Activated charcoal is the sorbent of choice for dosimeters for a wide range of organic compounds, and several manufacturers supply activated charcoal devices based on diffusion. A number of studies have compared one or more of these badges to charcoal tubes or to each other [178, 184–190]. In one study, Coutant [191] evaluated dosimeters for 24 hour ambient air monitoring at low levels. Although most examples for the charcoal dosimeter use gas chromatographic analysis, Baker [192] developed an infrared method for identification and quantitation of many organic compounds. Some specialized dosimeters have been developed for organic compounds, such as acrylonitrile [187], aniline [193], formaldehyde [194], phosgene [195], and benzene [196]. Several researchers have combined the advantages of the dosimeter and thermal desorption technique. Benson and Boyce [186, 187] designed and evaluated a badge for diffusional sampling of acrylonitrile followed by thermal desorption/gas chromatographic analysis. The badge contains a stainless steel gauge element packed with Porapak N sorbent, which is removed for analysis. A tube-shaped dosimeter containing a silicone membrane and a defined diffusion path was developed and evaluated by Brown, et al. [197], for benzene, acrylonitrile and styrene.

The permeation dosimeter operates based on the fact that the rate at which a given gas permeates a given membrane is a fixed value, and that the total mass of the gas that is transported through the membrane becomes a function of the concentration of that gas in the ambient atmosphere and the time of exposure. The collecting mechanism for transported gases can be an adsorption medium, such as activated charcoal or silica gel, or it can be an absorption system involving a solution that captures and stabilizes the permeated species. The quantity of analyte collected (M) over the time period (t) is given by Eq. (13):

$$M = kCt \tag{13}$$

Where k is the calibration constant which is characteristic of each membrane and analyte, and is determined by exposing the membrane device to an atmosphere containing a known concentration of the analyte [178]. For sampling organic compounds, activated charcoal is used to fill the space behind the membrane. After sampling, the charcoal is removed and analyzed. The dosimeter can be filled and reused many times before the membrane needs to be changed. Dosimeters based on permeation membranes have been developed for a variety of inorganic chemicals, such as hydrogen fluoride by Ryan and West [198], hydrogen cyanide by Hardy and West [199], hydrogen sulfide by Hardy, et al. [200], and chlorine by Hardy, et al. [201].

A number of other dosimeters have also been designed for the collection of specific inorganic chemicals. These usually contain a reactant chemical, either impregnated into a solid support or in solution. The first quantitative device reported in the literature [Palmes and Gunnison [177]] was for the determination of sulfur dioxide (SO_2). Since then, dosimeters of three different designs — impregnated charcoal [202], permeation [203], and liquid contained in a sealed pouch containing a diffusion barrier [204] — have all been successful for the determination of SO_2. Woebkenberg [205] studied three passive monitors for nitrogen dioxide.

2.3 Detector Tubes

There are many situations where rapid results are needed at the time of sampling. Although portable instruments can be set up on-site, in many cases this is not feasible or practical. Detector tubes are rapid, convenient, and are universally used for the detection and estimation of many gases and vapors in air. There are a number of manufacturers who produce various types of detector tubes, and there are tubes available for over two-hundred gases and vapors.

Detector tubes consist of a glass tube containing an inert granular material impregnated with chemicals which react with the gas or vapor of interest producing a color change. The color change can be related to concentration by one of three procedures. The most widely used procedure is to compare the length of stain to a calibration chart or to read the concentration directly from a scale printed on the tube. A second procedure, which is sometimes used, is to measure the amount of air required to produce a detectable color change. The third procedure, which is more difficult, is to compare the shade or intensity of the color change to a set of standards.

The complex interrelationships between the factors affecting the kinetics of indicator tube reactions have been studied and presented elsewhere [206]. Saltzman [206] has developed an equation relating the length of stain to the sample volume and concentration of the gas in air.

$$L/H = \ln (CV) + \ln (K/H) \tag{14}$$

Where: L = the length of stain in centimeters
C = the gas concentration in parts per million
V = the air sample volume in cubic centimeters
K = a constant for a given type of indicator tube and test gas
H = a mass transfer proportionality factor having the dimensions of centimeters, and known as the height of a mass transfer unit.

A linear plot of L versus the logarithm of (CV) for a constant flowrate should yield a straight line with a slope of H.

Different manufacturers may use different chemical reactions for the same gas or vapor and it is important to follow the manufacturers instructions very carefully. The instruction sheets supplied by the manufacturer give the principal chemical reaction and the procedure for obtaining quantitative information. The instruction sheet also gives other important information such as storage conditions, shelf life, chemical interferences and corrections for temperature, humidity and atmospheric pressure. It is important to point out that detector tubes, in general, are not highly specific for one gas or vapor. A careful interpretation of the results must include a knowledge of the area sampled and an understanding of the limitations of the detector tube used [207]. Detector tubes are widely used for short-term "grab" samples of one to ten minute duration; however, long-term tubes for one to eight hour sampling have been designed for some chemicals. A number of studies for the calibration and evaluation of short-term detector tubes have been published [208-212]. Other studies have examined the effects of flow rate [213,214], temperature [215,216], humidity [215,216], and pressure [214,215]. Various publications [208-212,217-220] and reviews [12,206,221,222] have shown wide application of short-term detector tubes.

To use the tubes, the sealed ends are broken and a given volume of air is pulled through the tube by a mechanical pump. Two recommended types of pumps are commercially available;

1) bellows-type pumps with limiting orifices and,
2) precision piston pumps with limiting orifices.

The pumps generally have a capacity of 100 ml for a full pump stroke. The sample volume taken can be controlled by the number of pump strokes taken for each tube. Pumps must be properly maintained and procedures for leak testing and for measuring the volume and flow rate can be obtained from the manufacturers. The volume of the pump should be accurate to $\pm 5\%$ of the value stated. Detector tubes made by one manufacturer should not be used with a pump made by a different manufacturer since the pumps have different flow characteristics and could cause different lengths of stain. Each lot of detector tubes is calibrated by the manufacturer using his specific pump design.

Some accessories are available to extend the use of detector tubes for special situations. For remote sampling of dangerous or inaccessible areas, the detector tube can be connected to the pump with a long rubber tube. The detector tube is then placed in the area to be sampled and the pump operated remotely. A sample should never be drawn through rubber tubing before entering the detector tube. When sampling hot vent or flu gases, a cooling tube can be used in front of the detector tube. A four foot length of metal tube is usually capable of cooling the gas sufficiently so that the indicator in the detector tube will not be destroyed [206]. The dead volume should be negligible with respect to the sample volume and caution should be used since loss of some compounds could occur due to condensation or adsorption on the tube walls. Another accessory, the hot wire pyrolzyer, is available to thermally convert some compounds into more detectable species. This can also be done chemically for some compounds by using specially designed reactor tubes containing a reactive chemical which converts the unreactive compound into a detectable substance.

Although the detector tube was designed initially for short-term sampling some researchers attempted to use them for longer periods with limited success [223,224]. In the attempt to use the tubes for longer periods the flow rate was reduced so that a comparable volume of air was sampled. This low flow appeared to affect the detector tube reagent systems and cause secondary reactions [225]. Because of the special requirements necessary for long-term sampling [226] detector tubes have been specifically designed for that purpose for a limited number of compounds.

Long-term detector tubes are used in a similar manner to short-term tubes except a sample is pulled through the detector tube at a slow, constant flow rate by an electrical pump. The pump should have a stable low flow rate of 2–50 ml/min for periods up to 8 hours. The recommended flow rate and other precautions are given by the manufacturers.

Long-term detector tubes would have an advantage over other methods such as charcoal tubes since they could be used to give quantitative information immediately after sampling and would not require further shipping, storage or analysis. Studies are still underway to more thoroughly test and evaluate the accuracy of long-term detector tubes [227].

3 Particulates in Air

The three main types of particulates of concern in air are dust, mist and fume. Airbone dust can be composed of hard, rock-like materials; small solid particles from plants or animals; or carbonacious material and ash from combustion sources. Mist is formed when materials, which are normally liquids at room temperature, are made airborne by splashing or spraying or by condensation of vapors in air. Fumes are formed from materials which are solid at room temperature and are airborne through condensation of vapor as, for example, found above molten metal and in welding operations.

Sampling of particulates may be directed at determining the size, size distribution, total mass and/or specific chemical identification. The sampling train usually consists of a probe or inlet, a particulate collector and pump. The pump may be calibrated for flow or a flow measuring device may be included in the train. The particulate collector may consist of one or a combination of devices such as a filter impinger, cyclone or impactor.

3.1 Filters

Filters are the most common means of collecting particulates. Filters are available in many different sizes and porosity and are made of materials such as cellulose fibers, glass fibers, ceramic fibers and polymeric fibers and membranes.

Cellulose fiber filters are inexpensive and have high tensile strength, however, they are hygroscopic in nature and careful drying and weighing is necessary to minimize weighing errors. Glass fiber filters are relatively friable, and some are available with binders to increase their mechanical strength. Filters with binders should not be used if the binders interfere with analysis. Polystyrene fiber filters have low flow resistance while polymeric membrane filters have much higher flow resistance than cellulose fiber filters. Membrane filters are made by the precipitation of resins, such as polyvinyl chloride, acrylonitrile and cellulose esters, under conditions to produce a uniform and narrow range of pore sizes. A recent review discusses a wide range of applications for membrane filters and future trends [228].

Filters are available in disposable plastic holders which can be used "open-faced" or "closed-face" [229], or can be used with a variety of filter holders. Filter holders should hold the filters without leaking around the edge or without tearing the filter. A back-up support screen is necessary with membrane, glass fiber and polystyrene fiber filters to prevent rupture during use. It is important to insure that connections and joints to and within the filter assembly are tight to prevent air leakage. Each filter assembly should be checked for leaks by applying a vacuum leak test [230].

Filters are used in various ways to quantitate particulates. The concentration of of particulates in air can be determined by direct weighing and by chemical analysis (mass concentration) or by counting particulates by microscopic examination or other counting techniques (number concentration).

When determining mass concentration, total particulates can be determined [231] or some pre-separation of larger particle sizes can be accomplished prior to filter collection. For "respirable" dust sampling [232-234] a device such as a cyclone or elutriator is used to remove larger particles [235], and filters are used to collect the fine particles [236]. Some separation of chemical fractions has also been obtained by selective dissolution of the particulate using a series of solvents of increasing polarity [237].

Many types of particulates are sampled and determined gravimetrically as a nuisance particulate TLV (10 mg/m^3) [238]. The adsorption of moisture on the filters is a general concern [239] and methods have been tried to eliminate or quantify adsorbed water weight gain by control filters, matched filters [240] and controlling the humidity [241,142]. A recent report indicates moisture can affect all types of filters to some degree [243].

There are many examples in the literature for the collection of particulates with filters followed by chemical analysis using gas chromatography [244-246], liquid chromatography [247,248], thin layer chromatography [249], x-ray [250,251], nuclear magnetic resonance [252], atomic absorption [253], neutron activation analysis [254,255] and colorimetric [256] methods. In some cases, when particulates and vapor may be present at the same time filters are followed by a solid adsorbent [257].

Membrane filters are often used for collection of particulates for examination under the microscope. When the membrane is immersed in a liquid which has the same refractive index, it becomes transparent and the particles may be counted under the microscope. This method is widely used for the determination of asbestos fibers [258-259].

The sampling train design recommended by EPA Method #5 has become a standard for measuring particulates in power generating facilities, incinerators and industrial vents [46]. The filter element is held in a heated housing to prevent condensation of volatile substances and followed by a series of impingers. Since particulates can vary greatly in size, care must be taken when sampling a dynamic gas stream to eliminate bias due to particulate size (mass). Isokinetic techniques are used to minimize this effect by matching the velocity of the gas pulled into the tip of the sampling probe to the linear velocity in the pipe. The flow of the particles in the pipe or vent may also be nonuniform and traverse sampling points may be necessary to obtain a representative sample.

The high volume air sampler has been used extensively over the past twenty years for measuring ambient concentrations of total suspended particulate. The original instrument used a pleated filter made from cellulose fibers which had to be tare and post weighed inside an oven. The unit was improved by an adapter for flat sheets, filters and a shelter. Recently a new blower motor has been suggested [260]. Air is drawn into the covered housing and through the glass fiber filter by means of a high volume flow rate blower at 1.1 to 1.7 cubic meters per minute. The filters are carefully removed and weighed for the gravimetric determination of particulate [261, 262] or analyzed for specific compounds [263–265].

3.2 Impingers

Although impingers are still being used for the collection of mineral dust, most methods for particulates have been replaced by dry filter techniques. Impinger methods are generally used only when dry filtration methods are not feasible. Impingers were used extensively for collecting samples for the determination of "respirable" particles using microscopic counting techniques on the particles which settled to the bottom of a counting cell. The exposure guideline for mineral dust was largely based on this type of data collected by the U.S. Public Health Service between 1925 and 1940 [42]. Impingers have also been used to collect particulates which are determined by chemical analysis (see Sect. 2.2.1). When air is drawn through the glass jet of the impinger, a high impingement velocity causes particles to impact on the bottom plate and become suspended in the collection liquid. Several types of impingers have been used. Greenburg-Smith impingers are the largest and sample at a flow rate of one cubic foot/minute into 100 ml of liquid. The Wilson impinger samples at a rate of 5 liters/minute into 10 mL of liquid, and the commonly used midget impinger originally designed by the Bureau of Mines, samples at a rate of 2.8 liters/minute into 10 mL of liquid. A micro impinger has also been suggested [50].

The distance from the tip of the impinger to the flask bottom is critical and is standardized for the midget impinger at 5 mm $\pm$ 0.5 mm [266]. The selection of the collection liquid may also be critical, and coal dust was found to collect better in isopropyl alcohol than in water or ethyl alcohol [267]. Efficiency can be increased by using a reagent which will react with and dissolve the particulate. Good efficiency is observed for mists such as sulfuric acid mists [268]. Impingers are generally efficient for particulates greater than one micron in size but for smaller particle size filters are recommended.

3.3 Cyclones and Elutriators

Collection of "respirable" dust is usually accomplished using a two-stage sampler [232]. The first stage, which is often a cyclone or an elutriator, removes the high mass "nonrespirable" particles and the second stage, a high efficiency filter collects all the particles which penetrate the first stage.

Several types of miniature cyclones, 10 mm to 50 mm are, available. The shape of the cyclone is either cylindrical or an inverted cone with the air entering tangent to the side. Dust entering the cyclone swirls at a high rate of speed and the particles of higher mass are thrown to the side due to centrifugal force and collect at the base. Cyclones can be operated in any orientation so long as they are not turned upside down.

The particle range collected by the cyclone depends on the size of the cyclone and the flow rate which controls the velocity inside the cyclone. Various studies have been made to determine the collection characteristics [269-271], and a flowrate of 1.7 L/min has been recommended for the 10 mm cyclone [272]. Various types of cyclones have similar size-efficiency performance curves; however, each design must be calibrated since a slight variation will cause a change in efficiency. Cyclones tend to be smaller than elutriators for the same efficiency because particles rotate several times under a high centrifugal force.

Elutriators can be horizontal or vertical. The horizontal elutriator is usually composed of several thin rectangular ducts connected in parallel [273]. Particles passing through the element will fall under gravity. Depending on the flowrate, higher mass particles fall to the floor of the element and are captured. In a vertical elutriator air is pulled upward through an inverted cone and particles are separated depending on their terminal velocity [274, 275].

Pumps used to pull air through cyclones and elutriators should be steady and free from pulsed flow [276]. A pulsed flow tends to collect a higher mass of "respirable" dust. Pulsation dampers are available which reduce the pulsation to an acceptable level.

3.4 Impactors

Impingement on a flat plate held close to a jet of air containing particulates has been used for many years and the theory is discussed in the literature [277, 278]. The single plate was improved with the development of the cascade impactor. The cascade impactor has a number of stages. Each stage collects a different particle size range which is controlled by the impingement jet above each stage.

Some investigators have used adhesive coated impaction surfaces [279-282] to reduce problems of loss of particles due to bounce and blow-off [283-285].

Some new developments in impactor design include a parallel stage impactor [286], a micro-orifice impactor for sub-micron aerosol size classification [287] and an eight stage, low pressure impactor [281, 282].

Water and Solids

Chromatography coupled with a variety of detectors is the most common technique for the determination of trace level organics in environmental samples. Gas chromatography is used more frequently than liquid chromatography undoubtedly due to the ease of coupling gas chromatography and mass spectrometry for identification purposes. For many of these analytical schemes, a means of isolating/concentrating the organic compounds from the sample matrix into a suitable solvent is necessary. A brief synopsis of some of the various techniques to achieve this purpose is given on the following pages.

Trace levels of inorganic elements (metals) are most frequently determined using atomic absorption spectroscopy, flame, graphite furnace or hydride generation.

Recently, inductively coupled plasma emission spectroscopy, a multielement/simultaneous analysis system, has made significant contributions to environmental surveys.

4 Preparation of Water Samples for Analyses [288–291]

4.1 Liquid-Liquid Extraction (LLE)

The batch LLE is perhaps the simplest and most widely used technique for the extraction of organic contaminants from water. The technique, which consists of mixing the water sample with an immiscible organic solvent, is quick and fairly well characterized. The principle used is that the organic contaminants will be more soluble in the organic solvent than in the water and will preferentially partition into the solvent. An important parameter for LLE procedures is the choice of solvent. It must a) be immiscible with water, b) not contain species that would interfere with the analysis, c) extract the organics of interest from the sample, and d) be compatible with the proposed analytical procedure.

The LLE can actually be accomplished in a variety of ways. The most common procedure is by mixing the sample and solvent in a separatory funnel. The phases are allowed to separate and the organic layer removed. Usually several extractions of the water, each time with fresh solvent, are required for good recoveries. The various solvent extracts are combined, concentrated, and analyzed. Other means of mixing, such as rolling, sonication, and stirring can also be utilized.

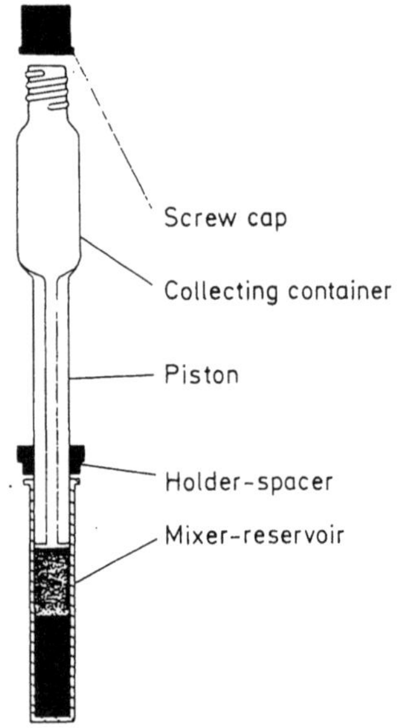

Fig. 7. Mixxor Extraction Device

The main advantage of the technique lies in its simplicity and minimum equipment required. The extraction can even be done in the sample bottle if there is enough headspace for adequate mixing after adding the solvent.

One of the more recent devices introduced specifically for rapid liquid-liquid extractions is the MIXXOR® device [292, 293] (Fig. 7). These devices come in various sizes to handle sample volumes up to 20 mL. The mixing is accomplished by forcing the liquid from one chamber to another through a small orifice. A ground glass plunger with a small diameter longitudinal pasage is pushed into a matched close fitting vial containing the sample and extraction solvent. The sample/solvent mixture is forced through the passage in the plunger and sprayed into a closed glass chamber attached to the plunger. As the plunger is withrawn from the vial, the the mixture is sucked back into the vial. Several "pumps" of this unique device are sufficient for extraction.

The advantage of this system is that small volumes of a water sample can be rapidly extracted with very small volumes of solvent. In the smallest MIXXOR (2 mL) it is relatively simple to extract 2 mL of water with 100 μL of hexane and recover approximately 75% of the hexane for analysis.

The main disadvantage of this device is the ease with which emulsions are generated.

4.2 Continuous Liquid-Liquid Extraction (CLLE)

Continuous extractors offer some advantages for difficult to extract species and for samples that readily form emulsions. A basic common design distills the solvent to a chamber which release it as fine droplets through a frit either down or up (depending on solvent density) through a water-sample [294]. The solvent then cycles back to the distillation pot where the extracted organics are concentrated. Because the sample is continuously extracted with fresh distilled solvent, an overnight extraction will concentrate even marginally soluble species. Occasionally even this gentle mixing with some samples can result in the formation of an emulsion. In these cases a flow-under or flow-over extractor is required [295]. Mixing of the phases does not take place in these extractors. The organic phase floats over or flows under the aqueous phase. The partitioning of contaminants into the organic phase takes place at the organic-water interface. A slow turning mixer provides sufficient agitation of the sample so that quantitative extraction can occur. Generally even the most emulsion prone samples yield to this extraction device.

4.3 Sorbent Column Extraction

A column filled with sorbent material, through which an aqueous sample is passed, provides another means of isolating certain organic compounds from water [296-298]. The adsorbent materials used are varied; activated carbon, XAD resins, Tenax-GC, bonded organic phases on silica and polyurethane foam to name a few [299-303].

An advantage of this type of extractor is that sampling and extraction can be done in the field simultaneously. This means that very large volumes of water can be sampled for high sensitivity since only the sorbent column has to be transported back to the laboratory for extraction and analysis.

The organics are commonly removed by solvent elution or, in some cases, thermal desorption [304]. Difficulty with recovery of organics are possible especially when using activated carbon adsorbent [305].

While the aforementioned resins are suitable for accumulation of non-polar organics, the concentration of low molecular weight polar and ionic species requires use of ion exchange resins [306, 307]. Since the resins are based on a hydrocarbon polymer, some amount of hydrophobic adsorption will also occur.

Unfortunately, particulates in the usual environmental water samples tend to restrict and eventually block the flow of sample through the resin columns. Use is most common with groundwater and drinking water where particulates are not usually a problem and high concentration factors are required.

4.4 Lyophilization (Freeze-Drying) [308]

For the isolation of non-volatile water soluble compounds or biological materials from water, freeze drying is an effective technique. In this technique the water sample is frozen in a vial and the resulting ice sublimed away under vacuum. Organics are then solubilized in an organic solvent to separate them from the precipitated inorganic salts.

Although very effective for heat sensitive biological materials and other non-volatile organics, the process is very time consuming.

4.5 Gas Sparging

Both purge/trap (PaT)[309–311] and closed loop stripping (CLS) [312–315] are variations of this procedure. The basic principle of these techniques is that volatile organics are sparged from an aqueous sample using an inert gas and collected on an adsorbent trap. The organics are then either solvent extracted or thermally desorbed from the adsorbent for analysis.

Nearly all thermal desorption traps used contain some portion or are entirely Tenax-GC. Care should be exercised when heating this material. While the manufacturer claims stability up to 350 °C, at least one laboratory has found some breakdown occurring above 250 °C with benzene as the major breakdown product [316]. PaT analyses are generally done using 10 mL or less of sample. In general, a flow of 30 to 40 mL/min for 10 to 15 minutes provides the optimum compromise between purging efficiency for "heavier" organics and adsorbent trap breakthrough time for the "light" organics. In this technique the entire contents of the the adsorbent trap are thermally desorbed onto the front of a gas chromatographic column. Analysis proceeds by temperature programming the column to elute and separate the components. The apparatus for this procedure is available from a variety of commercial suppliers including automated versions that handle a number of samples without operator intervention. This technique is used extensively for the determination of halogenated volatile organics in water.

For the CLS procedure a few changes are made. A much larger volume of sample is used, typically one liter or more. A stainless steel bellows pump is used to recirculate approximately 50 mL of gas through the sample and adsorbent trap (hence, "closed loop"). The trap consists of from one to five mg of carbon supported between two stainless steel screens. After sparging (three to eight hours typically) the carbon trap is desorbed by passing 10 μL of carbon disulfide through the trap and into a specially designed reservoir from which an aliquot can be withdrawn for analysis. Since the system is a closed loop, it can be sparged for much longer times without concern for breakthrough. This greatly extends the volatility range for which the procedure is useful. Excellent recoveries can be obtained for compounds thought to be relatively non-volatile, i.e. PCBs [317]. The CLS system yields perhaps the highest concentration factor ($\times$ 100,000) with the least sample manipulation of any current technique. The major problem that will be encountered with any sparging technique is sample foaming. For some cases a slower purge flow or a foam trap will alleviate the situation. For severly foaming samples a situation analogous to the flow-over-extractor will have to be created. This is done by placing a stir bar into a suitable purge vessel with the sample and adjusting the speed such that a deep stable vortex is formed. The purge gas is then introduced from the top of the vessel through a piece of 1/16″ stainless steel tubing that extends down into the vortex without touching the water. The remainder of the purging and analysis is carried out as before. The organics will migrate from the surface of the water into the purge gas and no foam will be generated. Depending on the PaT system being used slight modifications to the equipment may be necessary.

4.6 Static Headspace

This technique is performed by analyzing the closed atmosphere above a sample [318–320]. Frequently the sample is heated in a thermostated bath to force more of the volatiles into the headspace to increase sensitivity. The procedure is simple, straightforward, rapid, and requires a minimum of equipment. Repeated equilibrations/analyses with fresh headspace gas using the same sample can provide limited identity information. The procedure is, however, limited to quite volatile water insoluble organics. As either water solubility increases or volatility decreases, the headspace concentration and, necessarily, the sensitivity decreases dramatically. For most environmental analytical applications, this procedure is used only if for some reason the PaT procedure cannot be employed.

4.7 Distillation Concentration/Extraction

Many of the organics that are normally extracted from aqueous samples using LLE techniques can be extracted and concentrated more easily using steam distillation techniques. In some respects it can be thought of as a heated gas sparging technique. One apparatus particularly well-suited for the isolation of water insoluble neutral organics from aqueous samples is the steam distillation extractor (SDE) [321].

This extractor continuously cycles the sample steam distillate through an immiscible lighter-than-water solvent such as hexane. Routinely, large volumes of sample (4000 mL) can be distilled/extracted in a 5 mL volume of solvent. Emulsions and interferences that are commonly observed in an extraction are reduced or eliminated entirely. Normally, species that can be steam distilled can also be gas-chromatographed. This results in a "cleaner" extract and reduces the build-up of residue in the injector of the gas chromatograph. A prediction of whether or not a particular compound will steam strip from water can be made on the basis of its "relative volatility to water" [322].

The small volumes of solvent normally used in steam distillation techniques facilitates solvent concentration and minimizes interferences due to solvent impurities and/or preservatives. Temperature stability of each analyte to be steam distilled must be demonstrated in the matrix. Extreme care must be exercised to be certain the species is neither formed nor destroyed during the several hour distillation/extraction.

A more general purpose steam distillation/extraction apparatus is the steam codistillation extractor (SCDE) [323-325]. This unit allows simultaneous condensation of a steam distillate and an immiscible extraction solvent. The steam condensate mixes with solvent condensate on the condenser walls. The phases are then separated and each returns to their respective distillation pots (steam condensate to sample chamber and solvent to solvent chamber). Fresh solvent continuously contacts the steam condensate so marginally distilled/extracted species are concentrated in the solvent chamber. The SCDE also has an advantage in that either heavier- or lighter-than-water solvents can be used. The same precautions noted for using the SDE also apply to the SCDE.

4.8 Azeotropic Distillation/Concentration

Distillation has been used extensively for the concentration of various water soluble organics. When combined with a headspace technique or a specially designed refluxing still, detection limits down to the part-perbillion (ppb) level can be obtained using gas chromatography [326-328]. As a rule, a water soluble organic can be concentrated by this procedure if it forms an azeotrope with water which has a boiling point of less than 99 °C. Compounds that do not azeotrope with water, such as methanol and acetone, can still be concentrated provided their boiling point is substantially less than 100 °C.

The advantages of distillation techniques over direct injection of aqueous solutions includes concentration and elimination of dissolved solids. Injection of samples containing dissolved solids can rapidly plug the gas chromatographic injection port with salts and have deleterious effects on both the column and subsequent samples.

As with all distillation techniques, boiling a sample to achieve concentration can be a problem with reactive materials. Sufficient experiments should be done to insure that compounds of interest are neither formed nor destroyed during the process.

4.9 Dissolved Metals

For the determination of dissolved metals the sample needs to be filtered through a 0.45 μ cellulose membrane filter as soon after collection as possible. An initial portion of the sample is used to rinse the filter apparatus and then discarded. After the sample has been filtered the filtrate must be acidified with high quality nitric acid to a pH of <2. Normally 3 mL/liter is sufficient to preserve the integrity of the sample. The metals of interest can be determined using the appropriate and/or available instrumentation.

4.10 Suspended Metals

For the determination of suspended metals a representative volume of unpreserved sample must be filtered through a 0.45 μ cellulose membrane filter. The filter containing the insoluble material is transferred to a beaker and cautiously digested with concentrated nitric acid until complete. The solution is evaporated to near dryness and either dilute hydrochloric acid or nitric acid is added depending on the instrumental technique used and/or the metals determined. The solution should be filtered and diluted to a specified volume.

4.11 Total Metals

For the determination of total metals the sample is acidified with nitric acid to a pH of <2 at the time of collection. The sample is not filtered. A representative well mixed sample is transferred to a beaker and cautiously digested with nitric acid until complete. The solution is evaporated to near dryness and either dilute hydrochloric acid or nitric acid is added depending on the instrumental technique used and/or the metals determined. The solution should be filtered and diluted to a specified volume.

For the determination of total arsenic and selenium utilizing hydride atomic absorption techniques it is important to carefully digest the sample with sulfuric and nitric acids, maintaining oxidizing conditions at all times.

The cold vapor technique for determining mercury is the most widely accepted method for achieving sub ppm concentrations. The sample is mildly digested with sulfuric and nitric acid in the presence of potassium permanganate and potassium persulfate in order to convert all forms of mercury to the ionic form.

5 Preparation of Solid Samples for Analysis (Soil, Sediment, etc.)

5.1 Soxhlet Extraction

The most common means for exhaustive extraction of solid material is via a soxhlet extraction apparatus. These devices, are analogous to the continuous extractors for water. The finely divided sample is held in a chamber and solvent (either heavier or lighter then water) is distilled up into it. When full, the solvent siphons (cycles) back into the distillation pot. The number of cycles required are dependent on the desired analyte and the particular matrix but at least twenty cycles are usually required for quantitative extraction.

5.2 Steam Distillation

The same apparatus (SDE and SCDE) as described for the extraction of water can be used for solids. The sample is placed in the apparatus with reagent water, typically up to 5% solid sample in the water [327)]. The rest of the extraction proceeds exactly as with water extraction. The same safeguards should be observed as regards analyte stability, etc.

5.3 Analysis for Volatiles

Neither soxhlet extraction nor steam distillation is designed to isolate volatiles from solids for subsequent determination. Slurrying the solids in water and then applying the PaT procedure has been reported [310)]. A vacuum extractor with cryogenic concentration has been applied to both fish and sediment samples for determination of volatile priority pollutants [329)]. PaT, LLE, and static headspace techniques have all been applied to the determination of volatiles in sludges from municipal waste treatment plants [330)].

6 Treatment of Water and Solid Sample Extracts

6.1 Sample Extract Cleanup

Often sample extract fractionation or "cleanup" is necessary to separate the analyte of interest from co-extracted interferences prior to extracts analysis. Usually these fractionations are accomplished using fluorosil, silica, or alumina although media as exotic as carbon on polyurethane foam and gel permeation chromatography have been reported [331)]. One of the most elaborate and extensive fractionation schemes is that reported for isolation of various chlorinated dioxins [332)].

6.2 Sample Extract Concentration

In order to achieve the desired sensitivity most environmental analytical techniques employ some form of solvent extract concentration.

1. Rotary Evaporation. Extract concentration by means of rotary evaporation involves a vacuum distillation from a rotating flask. Although it is relatively rapid, it is possible to contaminate the sample with impurities from the vacuum

source if an efficient trap is not used. For this reason, a water aspirator is usually the "cleanest" vacuum source available for this procedure. The speed of evaporation is difficult to control and frequently "bumping" can cause significant losses as well as contamination of the apparatus. Usually this concentration technique is used for relatively non-volatile analytes.

2. Kuderna-Danish (K-D) Evaporative Distillation. The majority of extract concentrations done in environmental analyses are accomplished via K-D distillations. The technique introduces no impurities, is relatively rapid, and can easily concentrate extracts to a final volume of 1 mL with commercially available equipment. Solvent exchanges (i.e., from methylene chloride to hexane) can also be accomplished during the concentration process. This is particularly necessary if a halogen sensitive detector will be used for the analysis.
3. Evaporation Under Flowing Gas Stream (Blow-down). For solvent volumes of less than 20 mL, evaporation under a flowing stream of a pure inert gas such as nitrogen is a relatively fast and easy means of achieving concentration. One important parameter to watch is the purity of the gas. Special filters are usually necessary to avoid introducing contamination from the blow-down gas during the concentration [333].

One factor that must always be checked before using any of these concentration techniques is the recovery of the analyte of interest from the solvent being used. In general, the K-D techniques will give the highest recovery, especially when small volumes (less than 10 mL) are being concentrated.

7 Sampling Water and Solids

Since everything that comes in contact with an environmental sample (including light and air) has the potential to alter the sample, careful attention must be given to every aspect of sample handling. Due to the intimacy and time of contact, the materials of construction of the sample container and cap should be closely examined.

Collection bottles must be appropriate for the sample and species to be determined. For collection of water for determination of organic and inorganic impurities, properly cleaned glass bottles are usually the best choice. The bottle cap liners are also important. Cardboad, plastic, and foil liners should be avoided if at all possible. A liner of Teflon resin has been found to be the best choice [334].

The cleaning of sampling containers and equipment is extremely important when determining trace level components in environmental samples. To minimize sample cross contamination in sampling equipment and to eliminate interferences due to glassware obtained directly from the manufacturer, the sample containers and other associated equipment should be washed with soap and hot water and rinsed thoroughly to remove all organic and inorganic residues. Prior to sampling all sample containers, caps, and cap liners must be inspected and flawed items discarded. Each item is then cleaned with a 2% solution of RBS-35 (a surfactant available from Pierce Chemical Company, Rockford, IL) or equivalent. An ultrasonic bath should be used to insure complete cleaning. Each item is then rinsed with distilled water, methanol, acetone, and finally reagent grade methylene chloride.

The sample containers are then air dried in an organic and dust free environment. After drying, containers should be sealed with the clean caps and liners and stored in a clean area to prevent re-contamination before they are used. For trace metal analysis the sample bottle should be thoroughly washed with detergent and tap water; rinsed with 1:1 nitric acid, tap water, 1:1 hydrochloric acid, tap water and finally deionized water [290].

7.1 Surface Water Sampling

For our purposes surface water consists of any body of water exposed to the atmosphere. Examples are lakes, streams, sewers, rivers, ponds, etc.

7.1.1 Sampling for Water Miscible and Semi-Volatile, (b.p. 150 °C) Organics

Since water quality varies from point to point in most water systems, sampling sites appropriate for the study must be selected [335–339]. No specific guidelines can be given as to the exact locations for sampling; however, some factors influencing the selection of sampling sites are:

1. Objectives of the stdy — each site must contribute some data toward the objective of the study.
2. Accessibility — a sampling site should be accessible without extraordinary effort or danger.
3. Representative sample — one of the most difficult sampling problems can be obtaining a representative sample. To be representative the sample taken must reflect the overall composition of the entire body. If the effects of a certain source are of interest, the sample must be taken at a point where total mixing with the carrier stream has occurred. In situations such as this, heterogeneous samples can invalidate an entire study.
4. Available facilities — sources of power for electrically driven apparatus, ice for cooling the samples, and a means to promptly transport the samples to the laboratory must be considered.

The actual procedure used to collect the sample can be either the "grab" or the "composite" technique. The grab sample is a discrete sample collected over a period of time not to exceed 15 minutes. It can be collected manually or by using some other suitable device.

For collection of a manual grab sample the clean sample bottle should remain closed until the bottle is under water and at the desired depth. This is necessary to avoid contamination of the sample with any "film" of organic contamination that may be floating on the surface. If not specified in the protocol of the study, 1/2 depth of the water is a reasonable sample collection point. When the desired depth is reached, the sample bottle is opened, allowed to fill, closed, and retrieved. If the analytical scheme to be followed involves analyses of aliquots of the sample, prerinsing of the bottle with sample may be necessary to passivate any adsorptive sites in the glassware [299].

Another type of grab sample is the depth integrated sample. Many of the organic compounds found in the environment are only slightly soluble in water and are often found adsorbed on the particulates in water. Since particulates will be more concentrated toward the bottom of the stream, a representative sample of a following stream requires that water be collected throughout the vertical profile of the stream. One way of approximating this ideal is to lower a weighted open bottle to the bottom of the stream and raise it to the surface at an overall uniform rate such that the bottle will be just filled on reaching the surface [342].

When the sampling is completed, the bottle should be sealed with a cap lined with Teflon and transported to the laboratory for analysis as soon as possible.

The composite sample is formed by mixing discrete samples at periodic time internals or as a continuous proportion of the flow. Composite sampling can be accomplished by manual or automatic techniques. Manual compositing can be done in a variety of ways.

1. Taking a constant volume sample with a constant time interval between samples.
2. Taking a constant volume sample with the time interval between the samples being proportional to the flow.
3. Taking sample volumes that are proportional to the total stream flow volume since the last sample at constant time intervals.
4. Taking sample volumes proportional to the total stream flow rate at the time of sampling at constant time intervals.

Automatic compositing is typically done in two ways:

1. Continuous pumping rate.
2. Sample pumping rate proportional to the stream flow.

Before any samples are collected using an automatic sampler, a blank sample should be generated on-site by pulling reagent water through the system in the same manner as samples will be collected. This blank should be taken to the laboratory with the samples and processed as a sample. When using automatic samplers every effort should be made to insure that the sample contacts only inert, non-contaminating materials such as glass and Teflon. Recent studies have shown the importance of using only tubing made of Teflon in continuous samplers for water collection [334]. Various plastics are available for many samplers but can significantly affect the sample through both adsorption and contamination. To achieve flexibility some manufacturers add large amounts (up to 40%) of plasticisers to the tubing. The absorption characteristics of various plastic tubings is not surprising when you consider that XAD-2, a resin used widely for isolation of organics from water, is a plastic (polystyrene). A blank sample provides one indication of how successful you have been in avoiding contamination in the sampling/transport process. Since the composite covers a length of time and varying concentrations, no prerinsing to passivate the active sites in the system is possible. This can be partially overcome by using a large reservoir container and higher pumping rates so that the volume collected approaches the capacity of the container. By using a high volume/inner surface area ratio container, the effect on results of adsorption on the sample container walls is minimized. Provision should also be made to keep the sample refrigerated/preserved during the time it is in the sampler storage reservoir as well as during transport to the laboratory. Again the samples should be shipped in glass bottles with caps lined with Teflon. Generally, the best all-purpose preservation scheme for the sample is to refrigerate at 4 °C and store in the dark. The sooner the sample can be analyzed, the more reliable the results. There is no universal preservation procedure to maintain sample integrity. Techniques used to preserve one parameter can change or interfere in the determination of another. The answer to this problem is to split the sample at the time of collection and preserve each aliquot as required for a specific analysis [341]. A list of a wide variety of preservation techniques and the parameters that they preserve has been published [349]. In some cases, the addition of 2 mL of concentrated sulfuric acid per liter of sample combined with storage at 4 °C preserved stability for up to 4 weeks. A correlation was found between organic loss and microbiological activity suggesting that biological activity governs sample stability [342]. Microbial activity was also found responsible for degradation of various hydrocarbons in water [343]. For trace metal analysis the most appropriate preservation technique is to acidify the sample with 3 mL of concentrated nitric acid per liter and store at 4 °C.

7.1.2 Sampling for Volatile (Purgeable) Organics

In sampling for volatile organics such as trihalomethanes, a number of parameters are different when compared to the procedures for semi-volatiles.

In most cases these compounds are determined either by a purge/trap (PaT) procedure [309–311], a direct aqueous injection gas chromatographic procedure (DAIGC) [344, 345], or by a specialized version of liquid-liquid extraction (LLE) [346]. In any case the amount of sample that is necessary is much smaller, on the order of 40 to 125 mL depending on how the analysis will be done. For the PaT procedure, a 40-mL glass vial with a septum screw cap lined with Teflon is used. A 125-mL hypo vial with septum crimp cap lined with Teflon is ideal for the LLE procedure. Either volume is more than adequate for the DAIGC procedure.

Cleaning of the sample containers is also different in that no organic solvents are used. The septa and vials are cleaned in hot detergent water and rinsed repeatedly with hot distilled water. They are then dried in a clean oven at 100 °C for one hour. The screw caps with septa are then placed on the vials while still warm. The empty vials are then sealed in clean wide-mouth jars over a layer of activated carbon and transported to the sampling site. The crimp top vials are handled in an analogous manner but the tops are not crimped down.

Due to the volatility of purgeable organics only grab samples should be collected. Attempts to generate composite samples will result in losses of some materials. Samples should be taken upstream of any aeration and not in a turbulent area of the sample stream. The conventional glass grab sampling apparatus is adequate for sample collection if the sample cannot be collected directly into the vial. Immediately after a large grab sample is obtained it should be poured with minimum agitation into the vial until it is overflowing. The septum cap is then applied such that no air bubbles are present. The filled vials are then returned to the wide-mouth jars with the layer of adsorbent (activated carbon) on the bottom to decrease chances of any cross-contamination [347]. The samples should be refrigerated at 4 °C and transported to the laboratory for immediate analysis. For preservation, various scavengers (i.e., citric acid, sodium thiosulfate) can be added to destroy any residual free chlorine and prevent changes in the sample [348].

7.1.3 Documentation of Sampling Conditions

At the time of sampling all conditions concerning how, where, and when the samples were taken should be recorded. Of particular importance to determine the total pollution "load" is the flow rate where applicable. The means of measurement can range from a graduated container and stopwatch to accoustic flow meters. An excellent compilation of flow measurement techniques was recently published [349].

7.2 Groundwater Sampling

Groundwater, water found in an underground aquifer, presents some difficult sampling problems. The soil subsurface is an extremely complex and relatively inaccessible environment. Large differences can be noted in physical, chemical and biological characteristics within small vertical and horizontal distances. The only practical way in which this underground environment can be sampled is by means of a monitoring well, an expensive answer [350].

Since aquifers are used extensively as a source of drinking water, analyses are usually aimed at very low levels of organic contamination. Extreme care must be taken not be contaminate the aquifer through the act of installing a monitoring well. Since a monitoring well samples only a very small part of an aquifer horizontally and, in many cases, vertically, a thorough knowledge of the hydrogeological makeup of the area should be gained before selection of sampling points.

Material and method of well construction are both critical. Double cased monitoring wells using casing made of Teflon should be used whenever possible, and the intake part of the well should be made depth discrete [351-357]. Other requirements of monitoring wells have been described in a recent comprehensive study [358].

After installation of a well it should be pumped or bailed continuously with periodic backflushing until the water is free of any turbidity. Before any sample collection, the well should be again flushed to remove the stagnant water in the well casing. A common procedure is to pump or bail the well until a minimum of 4 to 10 bore volumes have been removed.

Collection of water from a monitoring well can be done in a variety of ways. The method chosen will depend on circumstances and the organics that are to be determined.

The bailer is the simplest and oldest means of collecting water from a well. It is basically a container that is lowered into the well using a cable or chain and then pulled out with the sample. The advantage of this well sampling procedure are:

1. No electrical power or heavy equipment is needed.
2. The system is portable and can easily be cleaned after each use.
3. Bailers can be constructed of inert materials such as glass or Teflon.
4. Minimal disturbance of the water during sampling reduces losses of volatile organics.

One precaution that must be taken when using bailers is to use a metal cable or chain rather than a rope. Ropes are virtually impossible to clean and will contaminate the samples. This is especially true of plastic ropes.

Although bailers can be used in most situations for all classes of organic materials, they do have one major disadvantage. When a large volume of water has to be removed (i.e., flushing a well), use of a bailer can be very time-consuming and physically exhausting.

In certain circumstances, a suction lift sampler can be used. The samplers are portable, can be operated by hand or battery, and have pumping rates in excess of 5 gallon/minute. The major disadvantages are that they tend to degas the sample causing losses of volatiles and are limited to relatively shallow wells, less than 25 feet deep.

For very deep wells portable submersible pumps may be the only choice. Powered by line electricity or a portable generator, these pumps can bring up water from several hundred feet deep. When choosing a pump of this type attention must be paid to possible contamination from materials of construction, connection lines, etc. They do churn up the water substantially so losses of volatiles will occur.

Pressure lift samplers are a fairly non-contaminating means of obtaining samples from a well. Gas pressure, preferably nitrogen, is applied to the well in such a manner as to force the water up. If oxidation is not a concern, a small air compressor can be used to pressurize the system. In other cases a cylinder of compressed nitrogen will have to be transported to the site. All tubing used for connectors and to apply pressure to the well must be clean and made of non-contaminating material such as Teflon. It should also be structurally strong since the depth to which this procedure can be used is governed by how much pressure can safely be applied to the well. The major disadvantage of this system for organics sampling is that gas stripping of volatile organics can occur.

A number of variations on these basic designs have been developed as well as some fairly sophisticated devices designed solely for well water sampling. Many are described in detail in a recent publication [358]. Once the samples have been obtained from the well it should be put into an appropriate sample container cleaned using the previously mentioned procedures, preserved and shipped to the laboratory.

7.3 Unsaturated Zone Water Sampling

The soil area above the water table is known as the unsaturated zone. In the study of migration of pollutants through the soil to the groundwater, it is desirable to sample the water in the unsaturated zone. Typically this is done with a type of suction lysimeter but recently a hollow fiber membrane approach was attempted. However, the cellulose acetate fibers were found to be unsuitable due to degradation and inability to withstand repeated, prolonged exposures to the vacuum required for sampling [359]. A later study indicated hollow fibers could be used in place of lysimeters [360]. At present, the most reliable procedure for determining volatile organics in soil water is a suction lysimeter connected in series with a purging apparatus and an adsorbent trap [361]. Water is sucked from the soil into the purging chamber by applying vacuum to the lysimeter through the purging chamber and the adsorbent trap. The vacuum is turned off, appropriate valves switched and the volatiles remaining in the water are sparged with nitrogen onto the trap. The trap is then removed from the system and returned to the laboratory for analysis.

7.4 Sampling of Soil [362–364]

7.4.1 Surface Soil

For sampling purposes we shall describe surface soil as the loose surface layer of earth consisting primarily of humus, clay, sand and small size gravel, but excluding vegetation. When choosing a sampling site the past history of the area should be considered. Generally soil that has been recently disturbed by plowing or digging is to be avoided. Once a site has been found that meets the study objectives, a grid pattern should be established. Ten equal size subsamples will be taken randomly over the sampling area and combined to form a composite sample. Due to the natural heterogeneity of soil, a composite sample is more representative of a locale than a single grab sample [365]. Ten subsamples represent a compromise for obtaining a representative sample in an efficient manner. Although each subsample is taken randomly within the gird area, they should be taken from locations at least 1.5 meters and not greater than 15 meters apart. With subsamples taken within the required distances, each sampling area is greater than 9.3 sq. meters and less than 930 sq. meters.

To collect a soil subsample, carefully scrape aside all vegetation and debris. Collect the soil with a clean stainless steel utensil, making sure not to exceed 3 cm in excavated depth. The subsamples should be placed in a clean glass wide-mouth bottle with a cap lined with Teflon. The bottle should be of sufficient size such that when all 10 subsamples are collected it is approximately 1/2 full. The extra volume is needed so that the soil can be homogenized before any subsamples are withdrawn for analysis. After collection the samples are stored in the dark at 4 °C to retard compositional changes due to biological activity.

7.4.2 Depth Sampling of Soil

When a study of the vertical migration of organics in soil is needed, samples will have to be obtained from various known depths. Sampling techniques to accomplish this include manual excavation of a pit or trench, various types of hand or motor driven core sampling devices, or sampling thieves. In a study of this type, the sampling technique should provide an accurate measurement of the depth of the sample below the original surface. It should also minimize any contamination of the sample with soil from either above or below the layer sampled.

Manual excavation is suitable for nearly all soil types. All digging tools should be clean and free of oil, grease or any other contaminants. When digging the pit or trench, all soil removed must be piled on one side so that the original surface is preserved for sampling purposes. When the excavation is large enough to sample the desired stratum, a 3-cm thick section should be scraped away before taking the sample. Samples may be taken with a clean stainless steel utensil and placed in a clean glass jar with a lid lined with Teflon. The samples are then refrigerated at 4 °C while protected from light and transported to the laboratory.

Core sampling, in its simplest form, can be practiced by driving an open pipe into the ground. After pulling the pipe from the ground the soil core is pushed out and the appropriate layer taken for analysis. Commercial core samplers operate on the same basic principle but have features to make them easier to use. Specially designed ends allow them to penetrate the soil more easily, and removable liners allow easier removal of the soil core while minimizing chances of cross-contamination between samples.

When using a core sampler the depth to which the sampler penetrates should be compared with the core sample length. Soils which exhibit a compression of greater then 25% should be sampled by another technique or a differently designed core sampler.

Cross-contamination will occur along the periphery of the soil core as the sampler moves down through the soil strata. When the core is removed for analysis, the outside centimeter should be scraped away and the sample taken from the center of the core. If the sample of the core is to be stored or transported, it must be placed in a clean glass jar with a lid lined with Teflon and kept at 4 °C and away from light. If the entire core is to be stored or transported, it should be kept sealed in the liner or sampler and in a vertical position.

7.5 Sampling of Sediments

Sediments are those solid materials deposited by water action and found beneath the surface of stagnant or moving water [366)]

Sediments may consist of sand, salt, gravel, organic materials, trash, and living organisms as well as various proportions of water.

Grab samples of this material are usually taken either by hand (shallow water) or by using a small dredge (deep or inaccessible water). A dredge consits of two spring loaded steel jaws. It is lowered by hand using a rope, chain, or cable to the sediment and then the jaws are triggered to close and trap a sample of the sediment. The device must be clean and free of debris from previous samples before use.

The contents of the dredge should be placed in a clean holding container from which an appropriate sized sample can be taken. The sample should be placed in a clean glass wide-mouth bottle and sealed with a cap lined with Teflon. Organics in the sediment can be altered by drying and oxidation so the material must not be dried out or exposed to the atmosphere unnecessarily. Store the samples out of the light at 4 °C for transport to the laboratory.

7.6 Sampling of Sludge

Sludge is here defined as that solid or semi-solid biologically active material used in wastewater treatment plants to break down organic matter. The material to be sampled may be obtained from relatively stationary points within the plant, from a pumpable slurry return line, or from the dewatered filter cake.

Sludge samples may contain relatively large quantities of biologically active organisms and should be considered biologically hazardous. Handling procedures should be designed to prevent exposure of persons handling these materials.

Samples should be placed in clean wide-mouth glass jars and sealed with a lid lined with Teflon. Slurry samples must be deactivated to reduce biological activity while maintaining the integrity of the sample. This can be accomplished by dropwise addition of reagent grade concentrated hydrochloric acid with stirring of the sample to a pH of 1–2. Depending on the source and composition of the sludge, foaming and gas evolution can take place when acidifying. Wait until all reaction has ceased before sealing the container. While this is adequate if only semi-volatile organics are to be determined, losses of volatiles will occur. If volatile organics are to be determined, the only preservation that can be used is storing the sample at 4 °C. If possible the sample should be analyzed within 8 hours.

For the determination of semi-volatiles the steam distillation procedures should be considered as well as the flow over/under continuous extractors since sludges tend to emulsify easily during liquid-liquid extractions. When PaT analyses are to be performed, the samples usually can be diluted with reagent water to minimize the foaming problems that can be experienced. Headspace analysis of the neat sample is also an alternative. Previous work indicated the most reproducible results were obtained using an adaptation of Henderson's LLE technique [330, 346)]. Sludges were diluted with reagent water and extracted with cyclohexane. Determinations were made by gas chromatography with an electron capture detector.

8 References

1. Principles for Evaluating Chemicals in the Environment, Washington, D.C., National Academy of Sciences 1975
2. Donaldson, W. T.: Trace Organics in Water, Environ. Sci. and Technol. *11*, 348 (1977)
3. Wallace, L. A., Ott, W. R.: Personal Monitors: A State-of-the-Art Survey, J. Air Pollut. Control Assoc. *32*, 601 (1982)
4. Lutz, G. A.: Literature Review of Personal Air Monitors for Potential Use in Ambient Air Monitoring of Organic Compounds, EPA-600/482-048, NTIS order no. PB82-228917 (1982)
5. Melcher, R. G.: Industrial Hygiene, Anal. Chem. *55*, 40R (1983)
6. Saltzman, B. E., Burg, W. R.: Air Pollution, Anal. Chem. *49*, 1R (1977)
7. Katz, M.: Advances in the Analysis of Air Contaminants: A Critical Review, J. Air Pollut. Control Assoc. *30*, 528 (1980)
8. Fox, D. L., Jeffries, H. E.: Air Pollution, Anal. Chem. *53*, 1R (1981)
9. Industrial Environment — Its Evaluation and Control, NIOSH, Washington, D.C., U.S. Government Printing Office 1973
10. Walters, D. B. (ed.): Safe Handling of Chemical Carcinogens, Mutagens, Teratogens and Highly Toxic Substances, Vol. 1 and Vol. 2, Ann Arbor, MI, Ann Arbor Science 1980
11. Choudhary, G. (ed.): Chemical Hazards in the Workplace — Measurement and Control, ACS Symp. Series 149, Washington, D.C., American Chem. Soc. 1981
12. Linch, A. L.: Evaluation of Ambient Air Quality by Personnel Monitoring, Vol. 1 and Vol. 2, Cleveland, OH, CRC Press 1981[2]
13. Annual Book of ASTM Standards — Atmospheric Analysis; Occupational Health and Safety, Vol. 11.03, Philadelphia, PA, American Soc. for Testing and Materials 1983
14. Fishbein, L.: Chromatography of Environmental Hazards, Vol. I–III, Amsterdam—Oxford—New York, Elsevier 1975
15. Taylor, D. G. (ed.): NIOSH Manual of Analytical Methods, Vol. 1, National Technical Information Service, Springfield, VA, NTIS order no. PB274-845 (1977)
16. Ibid.; Vol. 2, NTIS order no. PB276-624 (1977)
17. Ibid.; Vol. 3, NTIS order no. PB276-838 (1977)

18. Ibid.; Vol. 4, NTIS order no. PB83-105439 (1978)
19. Ibid.; Vol. 5, NTIS order no. PB83-105445 (1979)
20. Ibid.; Vol. 6, NTIS order no. PB82-157728 (1980)
21. Ibid.; Vol. 7, NTIS order no. PB83-015452 (1981)
22. Berg, S., Jacobsson, S., Nilsson, B.: Evaluation of an Evacuated Glass Sampler for the Analysis of Volatile Organic Compounds in Ambient Air, J. Chromatogr. Sci. *18*, 171 (1980)
23. Melcher, R. G., Caldecourt, V. J.: Delayed Injection-Preconcentration Gas Chromatographic Technique for Parts-Per-Billion Determination of Organic Compounds in Air and Water, Anal. Chem. *52*, 875 (1980)
24. Harsch, D. E.: Evaluation of a Versatile Gas Sampling Container Design, Atmos. Environ. *14*, 1105 (1980)
25. Orson, R., Williams, D. T., Bothwell, P. D.: Dichloromethane Levels in Air After Application of Paint Removers, Am. Ind. Hyg. Assoc. J. *42*, 56 (1981)
26. Van Houten, R., Lee, G.: A Method for the Collection of Air Samples for Analysis by Gas Chromatography, Am. Ind. Hyg. Assoc. J. *30*, 465 (1969)
27. Lang, H. W., Freedman, R. W.: The Use of Disposable Hypodermic Syringes for Collection of Mine Atmosphere Samples, Am. Ind. Hyg. Assoc. J. *30*, 523 (1969)
28. Boettner, E. A., Dallos, F. C.: Analysis of Air and Breath for Chlorinated Hydrocarbons by Infrared and Gas Chromatographic Techniques, Am. Ind. Hyg. Assoc. J. *26*, 289 (1965)
29. Clemons, C. A., Altshuller, A. P.: Plastic Containers for Sampling and Storage of Atmospheric Hydrocarbons Prior to Gas Chromatographic Analysis, J. Air Pollut. Control. Assoc. *14*, 407 (1964)
30. Confer, R. G., Brief, R. S.: Mylar Bags Used to Collect Air Samples in the Field for Laboratory Analysis, Air Engng. *7*, 34 (1965)
31. Vanderkolk, A. L., Van Farowe, D. E.: Use of Mylar Bags for Air Sampling, Am. Ind. Hyg. Assoc. J. *26*, 321 (1965)
32. Curtis, E. H., Hendricks, R. H.: Large Self-Filling Sample Bags, Am. Ind. Hyg. Assoc. J. *30*, 93 (1969)
33. Smith, B. S., Pierce, J. O.: The Use of Plastic Bags for Industrial Air Sampling, Am. Ind. Hyg. Assoc. J. *32*, 343 (1970)
34. Apol., A. G., Cook, W. A., Lawrence, E. F.: Plastic Bags for Calibration of Air Sampling Devices, Am. Ind. Hyg. Assoc. J. *27*, 149 (1966)
35. Schuette, F. J.: Plastic Bags for Collection of Gas Samples, Atmos. Environ. *1*, 515 (1967)
36. Nelson, G. O.: Controlled Test Atmospheres, Principles and Techniques, Ann Arbor, MI, Ann Arbor Science 1971
37. Polasek, J. C., Bullin, J. A.: Evaluation of Bag Sequential Sampling Technique for Ambient Air Analysis, Environ. Sci. Technol. *12*, 708 (1978)
38. Comments on: Evaluation of Bag Sequential Sampling Technique for Ambient Air Analysis, Environ. Sci. Technol. *13*, 609 (1979)
39. Schuetzle, D., Prater, T. J., Ruddell, S. R.: Sampling and Analysis of Emissions from Stationary Sources, 1. Odor and Total Hydrocarbons, J. Air Pollut. Control Assoc. *25*, 925 (1975)
40. Standard Test Method for C_1 Through C_5 Hydrocarbons in the Atmosphere by Gas Chromatography, D2820, in: Annual Book of ASTM Standards, Vol. 11.03, Philadelphia, PA, American Society for Testing and Materials 1983
41. Knoll, J. E., Penny, W. H., Rodney, M.: The Use of Tedlar Bags to Contain Gaseous Benzene Samples at Source-Level Concentrations, NTIS order no. PB-291569 (1978)
42. Lippmann, M. (ed.): Air Sampling Instruments for Evaluation of Atmospheric Contaminants, ACGIH, Cincinnati, OH 1972[4]
43. Roberts, L. R., McKee, H. C.: Evaluation of Adsorption Sampling Devices, J. Air Pollut. Control Assoc. *9*, 51 (1959)
44. Linch, A. L.: The Spill-Proof Microimpinger, Am. Ind. Hyg. Assoc. J. *28*, 497 (1967)
45. Heitbrink, W. A., Doemeny, L. J.: A Modified Impinger for Personal Sampling, Am. Ind. Hyg. Assoc. J. *40*, 354 (1979)
46. Standard Test Method for Particulates Independently or for Particulates and Collected Residue

Simultaneously in Stack Gases, D3685, in: Annual Book of ASTM Standards, Vol. 11.03, Philadelphia, PA, American Society for Testing and Materials 1983
47. Standard Recommended Practice for Sampling Atmospheres for Analysis of Gases and Vapors, D16050, in: Annual Book of ASTM Standards, Vol. 11.03, Philadelphia, PA, American Society for Testing and Materials 1983
48. Elkins, H. B.: The Chemistry of Toxicology, New York, John Wiley and Sons 1959[2]
49. Calvert, S., Workman, W.: The Efficiency of Small Gas Absorbers, Am. Ind. Hyg. Assoc. J. *22*, 318 (1961)
50. Linch, A. L., Corn, M.: The Standard Midget Impinger — Design Improvement and Miniaturization, Am. Ind. Hyg. Assoc. J. *26*, 601 (1965)
51. Linch, A. L., Charsha, R. C.: Development of a Freeze-Out Technique and Constant Sampling Rate for the Portable Uni-Jet Air Sampler, Am. Ind. Hyg. Assoc. J. *21*, 325 (1960)
52. Williams, K., Mazur, J. F.: Gas Chromatographic Analysis of Acetic Acid in Air, Am. Ind. Hyg. Assoc. J. *41*, 1 (1980)
53. Wathne, B. M.: Analysis of Maleic, Fumaric, and Succinic Acids in Air by Use of Gas Chromatography, Analyst (London) *105*, 400 (1980).
54. Deese, D. E., Joyner, R. E.: Vinyl Acetate: A Study of Chronic Human Exposure, Am. Ind. Hyg. Assoc. J. *30*, 449 (1969)
55. Yamamoto, R. K., Cook, W. A.: Determination of Ethyl Benzene and Styrene in Air, Am. Ind. Hyg. Assoc. J. *29*, 238 (1968)
56. Palassis, J.: The Sampling and Determination of Azelaic Acid in Air, Am. Ind. Hyg. Assoc. J. *39*, 731 (1978)
57. Ruch, W. E.: Quantitative Analysis of Gaseous Pollutants, Ann Arbor, MI, Ann Arbor — Humphrey Science Publishers 1970
58. Analytical Guide on Lead — Organic Tetramethyl and Tetraethyl Lead, Analytical Guides Committee, Am. Ind. Hyg. Assoc. J. *30*, 193 (1969)
59. Linch, A. L., Wiest, E. G., Carter, M. D.: Evaluation of Tetraalkyl Lead Exposure by Personnel Monitor Surveys, Am. Ind. Hyg. Assoc. J. *31*, 170 (1970)
60. Analytical Guide on Mercury — Monomethyl and Monoethyl Mercury Salts, Dimethyl and Diethyl Mercury, Analytical Guides Committee, Am. Ind. Hyg. Assoc. J. *30*, 194 (1969)
61. Brief, R. A., Venable, F. S., Ajemian, R. S.: Nickel Carbonyl: Its Detection and Potential Formation, Am. Ind. Hyg. Assoc. J. *27*, 72 (1965)
62. Analytical Guide — Nitrogen Dioxide, Analytical Guides Committee, Am. Ind. Hyg. Assoc. J. *31*, 653 (1970)
63. Byers, D. H., Saltzman, B. E.: Determination of Ozone in Air by Neutral and Alkaline Iodide Procedures, Am. Ind. Hyg. Assoc. J. *19*, 251 (1958)
64. Dechant, R., Sanders, G., Graul, R.: Determination of Phosphine in Air, Am. Ind. Hyg. Assoc. J. *27*, 75 (1966)
65. Analytical Guide — Sulfur Dioxide, Analytical Guides Committee, Am. Ind. Hyg. Assoc. J. *31*, 120 (1970)
66. Fung, K., Grosjean, D.: Determination of Nanogram Amounts of Carbonyls as 2,4-Dinitrophenylhydrazones by High-Performance Liquid Chromatography, Anal. Chem. *53*, 168 (1981)
67. Kuntz, R., Lonneman, W., Namie, G., Hull, L. A.: Rapid Determination of Aldehydes in Air Analyses, Anal. Lett. *13(A16)*, 1409 (1980)
68. Romano, S. J., Renner, J. A.: Analysis of Ethylene Oxide — Worker Exposure, Am. Ind. Hyg. Assoc. J. *40*, 742 (1979)
69. Laugvardt, P. W., Nestrick, T. J., Hermann, E. A., Braun, W. H.: Derivatization Procedure for the Determination of Chloroacetyl Chloride in Air by Electron Capture Gas Chromatography, J. Chromatogr. *153*, 433 (1978)
70. Solomon, R. A., Kallos, G. J.: Determination of Chloromethyl Methyl Ether and Bis-Chloromethyl Ether in Air at the Part-per-Billion Level by Gas-Liquid Chromatography, Anal. Chem. *47*, 955 (1975)
71. Tou, J. C., Kallos, G. J.: Possible Formation of Bis(chloromethyl) Ether from the Reactions of Formaldehyde and Chloride Ion, Anal. Chem. *48*, 958 (1976)
72. Burg, W. R., Winner, P. C., Saltzman, B. E., Elia, V. J.: The Development of an Air Sampling and Analytic Method for o-Pehnylenediamine in an Industrial Environment, Am. Ind. Hyg. Assoc. J. *41*, 557 (1980)

73. Morales, P., Stampfer, J. F., Hermes, R. E.: Air Sampling and Liquid Chromatographic Determination of Ethyleneimine, Anal. Chem. *54*, 1340 (1982)
74. Walker, R. F., Guiver, R.: Determination of Alkyl-2-cyanoacrylate Concentrations in Air, Am. Ind. Hyg. Assoc. J. *42*, 559 (1981)
75. Standard Practice for Sampling Atmospheres to Collect Organic Compound Vapors (Activated Charcoal Adsorption Method), D3686, in: Annual Book of ASTM Standards, Vol. 11.03, Philadelphia, PA, American Society for Testing and Materials 1983
76. Shadoff, L., Kallos, G., Woods, J.: Determination of Bis(chloromethyl) Ether in Air by Gas Chromatography-Mass Spectrometry, Anal. Chem. *45*, 2341 (1973)
77. Hubbard, S. A., Russwurm, G. M., Walburn, S. G.: A Method for Reducing and Evaluating Blanks in Tenax Air Sampling Cartridges, Atmos. Environ. *15*, 905 (1981)
78. Hunt, G., Pangaro, N.: Potential Contamination from the Use of Synthetic Adsorbents in Air Sampling Procedures, Anal. Chem. *54*, 369 (1982)
79. Campbell, E. E., Ide, H. M.: Air Sampling and Analysis with Micro Columns of Silica Gel, Am. Ind. Hyg. Assoc. J. *27*, 323 (1966)
80. Adams, J., Menzies, K., Levins, P.: Selection and Evaluation of Sorbent Resins for the Collection of Organic Compounds, EPA-600/7-77-044, NTIS order no. PB-268 559 (1977)
81. Bertoni, G., Bruner, F., Liberti, A., Perrino, C.: Some Critical Parameters in Collection, Recovery and Gas Chromatographic Analysis of Organic Pollutants in Ambient Air Using Light Adsorbents, J. of Chromatogr. *203*, 263 (1981)
82. Melcher, R. G., Langner, R. R., Kagel, R. O.: Criteria for the Evaluation of Methods for the Collection of Organic Pollutants in Air Using Solid Sorbents, Am. Ind. Hyg. Assoc. J. *39*, 349 (1978)
83. MSA Research Corporation: Package Sorption Device Systems Study, EPA-R2-73-202, NTIS order no. PB-221 138 (1973)
84. Jonas, L. A., Rehrmann, J. A.: Predictive Equations in Gas Adsorption Kinetics, Carbon *11*, 59 (1973)
85. Jonas, L. A., Rehrmann, J. A.: The Rate of Gas Adsorption by Activated Carbon, Carbon *12*, 95 (1974)
86. Nelson, G. O., Harder, C. A.: Respirator Cartridge Efficiency Studies: VI; Effect of Concentration, Am. Ind. Hyg. Assoc. J. *37*, 205 (1976)
87. Wood, G. O., Anderson, R. G.: Personal Sampling for Vapors of Aniline Compounds, Am. Ind. Hyg. Assoc. J. *36*, 538 (1975)
88. Novak, J., Vasak, V., Janak, J.: Chromatographic Method for the Concentration of Trace Impurities in the Atmosphere and Other Gases, Anal. Chem. *37*, 660 (1965)
89. Mueller, F. X., Miller, J. A.: Determination of Organic Vapor Mixtures Using Charcoal Tubes, Am. Ind. Hyg. Assoc. J. *40*, 380 (1979)
90. Shotwell, H. P., Caporossi, J. C., McCollum, R. W., Mellor, J. F.: A Validation Procedure for Air Sampling-Analysis Systems, Am. Ind. Hyg. Assoc. J. *40*, 737 (1979)
91. Severs, L. W., Melcher, R. G., Kocsis, M. J.: Dynamic U-Tube System for Solid Adsorbent Air Sampling Method Development, Am. Ind. Hyg. Assoc. J. *39*, 321 (1978)
92. Posner, J. C., Okenfuss, J. R.: Desorption of Organic Analytes from Activated Carbon, I: Factors Affecting the Process, Am. Ind. Hyg. Assoc. J. *42*, 643 (1981)
93. Posner, J. C.: Desorption of Organic Analytes from Activated Charcoal II: Dealing with the Problems, Am. Ind. Hyg. Assoc. J. *42*, 647 (1981)
94. Hill, Jr., R. H., McCammon, C. S., Sallwaechter, A. T., Teass, A. W., Woodfin, W. J.: Gas Chromatographic Determination of Vinyl Chloride in Air Samples Collected in Charcoal, Anal. Chem. *48*, 1395 (1976)
95. Gagnon, Y. T., Posner, J. C.: Recovery of Acrylonitrile from Charcoal Tubes and Low Levels, Am. Ind. Hyg. Assoc. J. *40*, 923 (1979)
96. White, L. D., Taylor, D. G., Mauer, P. A., Kupel, R. E.: A Convenient Optimized Method for the Analysis of Selected Solvent Vapors in the Industrial Environment, Am. Ind. Hyg. Assoc. J. *31*, 225 (1970)
97. Krajewski, J., Gromiec, J., Dobecki, M.: Comparison of Methods for Determination of Desorption Efficiencies, Am. Ind. Hyg. Assoc. J. *41*, 531 (1980)
98. Dommer, R. A., Melcher, R. G.: Phase Equilibrium Method of Determination of Desorption Efficiencies, Am. Ind. Hyg. Assoc. J. *39*, 240 (1978)

99. Posner, J. C.: Comments on "Phase Equilibrium Method for Determination of Desorption Efficiencies" and Some Extensions in Use in Methods Development, Am. Ind. Hyg. Assoc. J. *41*, 63 (1980)
100. Evans, P. R., Horstman, S. W.: Desorption Efficiency Determination Methods for Styrene Using Charcoal Tubes and Passive Monitors, Am. Ind. Hyg. Assoc. J. *42*, 471 (1981)
101. Evans, P. R. Horstman, S. W.: Field Study of Styrene Decay on Charcoal, Am. Ind. Hyg. Assoc. J. *42*, 403 (1981)
102. Fracchia, M., Pierce, L., Graul, R., Stanley, R.: Desorption of Organic Solvents from Charcoal Collection Tubes, Am. Ind. Hyg. Assoc. J. *38*, 144 (1977)
103. Lorincz, M.: Test Method for Activated Charcoal Air Sampling Tubes Based on Liquid Chromatographic Measurements, J. Chromatogr. *166*, 141 (1978)
104. Pozzoli, L., Cottica, D., Ghittori, S.: Use of the Double Elution Technique to Estimate Desorption Efficiencies, Am. Ind. Hyg. Assoc. J. *43*, 292 (1982)
105. Johansen, I., Wendelboe, J. F.: Dimethylformamide and Carbon Disulfide Desorption Efficiencies for Organic Vapors on Gas-Sampling Charcoal Tube Analysis with a Gas Chromatographic Backflush Technique, J. Chromatogr. *217*, 317 (1981)
106. Langvardt, P. W., Melcher, R. G.: Simultaneous Determination of Polar and Non-polar Solvents in Air Using a Two-Phase Desorption from Charcoal, Am. Ind. Hyg. Assoc. J. *40*, 1006 (1979)
107. Bosserman, M. W., Ketcham, N. H.: An Air Sampling and Analysis Method for Monitoring Personal Exposure to Vapors of Acrylate Monomers, Am. Ind. Hyg. Assoc. J. *41*, 20 (1980)
108. Gilland, Jr., J. C., Bright, A. P.: Determination of Dimethyl and Diethylsulfate in Air by Gas Chromatography, Am. Ind. Hyg. Assoc. J. *41*, 459 (1980)
109. Hunt, R. J., Neubauer, N. R., Picone, R. F.: An Improved Procedure for Sampling and Analysis of Dinitrotoluene Vapor Concentration in Workplace Air, Am. Ind. Hyg. Assoc. J. *41*, 592 (1980)
110. Becher, G.: Glass Capillary Columns in the Gas Chromatographic Separation of Aromatic Amines; II. Application to Samples from Workplace Atmospheres Using Nitrogen-Selective Detection, J. Chromatogr. *103*, 211 (1981)
111. Vincent, W. J., Kahn, K. J., Ketcham, N. H.: Monitoring Personal Exposure to Ethylenediamine in the Occupational Environment, Am. Ind. Hyg. Assoc. J. *40*, 512 (1979)
112. Vincent, W. J., Guient, Jr., V.: Acrylic Acid — The Development of an Air Sampling and Analytical Methodology for Determining Occupational Exposure, Am. Ind. Hyg. Assoc. J. *43*, 499 (1982)
113. Whitman, N. E., Johnston, A. E.: Sampling and Analysis of Aromatic Hydrocarbon Vapors in Air: A Gas-Liquid Chromatographic Method, Am. Ind. Hyg. Assoc. J. *25*, 464 (1964)
114. Sherwood, R. J.: The Monitoring of Benzene Exposure by Air Sympling, Am. Ind. Hyg. Assoc. J. *32*, 840 (1971)
115. Feldstein, M., Balestrieri, S., Levaggi, D. A.: The Use of Silica Gel in Source Testing, Am. Ind. Hyg. Assoc. J. *28*, 381 (1967)
116. Morales, R., Rappaport, S. M., Hermes, R. E.: Air Sampling and Analytical Procedures for Benzidine, 3,3-Dichlorobenzidine and Their Salts, Am. Ind. Hyg. Assoc. J. *40*, 970 (1979)
117. Rappaport, S. M., Morales, R.: Air Sampling and Analytical Method for 4,4'-Methylenebis-(2-chloroaniline), Anal. Chem. *51*, 19 (1979)
118. Farwell, S. O., Bowes, F. W., Adams, D. F.: Evaluation of XAD-2-as a Collection Sorbent for 2,4-D Herbicides in Air, J. Environ. Sci. Health *B12*, 71 (1977)
119. Jackson, J. W., Thomas, T. C.: A Simple and Inexpensive Method for Sampling 2,4-D and 2,4-T Herbicides in Air, J. Air Poll. Control Assoc. *28*, 1145 (1978)
120. Langhorst, M. L.: Solid Adsorbent Collection and Gas Chromatographic Determination of the Propylene Glycol Butyl Ether Esters of 2,4,5-T in Air, Am. Ind. Hyg. Assoc. J. *41*, 238 (1980)
121. Gluck, S. J., Melcher, R. G.: Concentration and Determination of the Propylene Glycol Butyl Ether Esters of 2,4-Dichlorophenoxyacetic Acid (PGBE 2,4-D) in Air, Am. Ind. Hyg. Assoc. J. *41*, 932 (1980)
122. Kaminski, F., Melcher, R. G.: Collection and Determination of Trace Amounts of Organo-Thiophosphates in Air Using XAD-2 Resin, Am. Ind. Hyg. Assoc. J. *39*, 678 (1978)

123. Langhorst, M. L., Nestrick, T. J.: Determination of Chlorobenzene in Air and Biological Samples by Gas Chromatography, Anal. Chem. *51*, 2018 (1980)
124. Andersson, K., Levin, J. O., Lindahl, R., Nilsson, C. A.: Sampling of Epichlorohydrin and Ethylene Chlorohydrin in Workroom Air Using Amberlite XAD-7 Resin, Chemosphere *10*, 143 (1981)
125. Hermann, B. W., Seiber, J. N.: Sampling and Determination of 5,5,5′-Tributyl Phosphorotrithioate, Dibutyl Disulfide, and Butyl Mercaptan in Field Air, Anal. Chem. *53*, 1077 (1981)
126. Mann, J. B., Freal, J. J., Enos, H. F., Danauskas, J. X.: Development and Application of Methodology for Determining 1,2-Dibromo-3-Chloropropane (DBCP) in Ambient Air, J. Environ. Sci. Health, Part B *B15(5)*, 519 (1980)
127. Barns, R. D., Law, L. M., MacLeod, A. J.: Comparison of Some Porous Polymers as Adsorbents for Collection of Odor Samples and the Application of the Technique to an Environmental Malodor, Analyst *106*, 412 (1981)
128. Glaser, R. A., Woodfin, W. J.: A Method for Sampling and Analysis of 2-Nitropropane in Air, Am. Ind. Hyg. Assoc. J. *42*, 18 (1981)
129. Thomas, T. C., Jackson, J. W., Nishioka, Y. A.: Chlordane Sampling Efficiency with Chromosorb 102 and Ethylene Glycol, Am. Ind. Hyg. Assoc. J. *41*, 599 (1980)
130. Quazi, A. H., Vincent, W. J.: Sampling and Analysis of Acetic Anhydride in Air, Am. Ind. Hyg. Assoc. J. *40*, 803 (1979)
131. Stampfer, J. F., Hermes, R. E.: Development of Sampling and Analytical Method for Styrene Oxide, Am. Ind. Hyg. Assoc. J. *42*, 699 (1981)
132. Bishop, R. W., Ayers, T. A., Rinehart, D. S.: The Use of Solid Sorbent as a Collection Medium for TNT and RDX Vapors, Am. Ind. Hyg. Assoc. J. *42*, 586 (1981)
133. MacLeod, K. E., Lewis, R. G.: Portable Sampler for Pesticides and Semi-Volatile Industrial Organic Chemicals in Air, Anal. Chem. *54*, 310 (1982)
134. Langvardt, P. W., Melcher, R. G.: Determination of Ethanol- and Isopropanolamines in Air at Parts-per-Billion Levels, Anal. Chem. *52*, 669 (1980)
135. Giam, C. S., Chan, H. S., Neff, G. S.: Rapid and Inexpensive Method for Detection of Polychlorinated Biphenyls and Phthalates in Air, Anal. Chem. *47*, 2319 (1975)
136. Lewis, R. G., Brown, A. R., Jackson, M. D.: Evaluation of Polyurethane Foam for Sampling of Pesticides, Polychlorinated Biphenyls, and Polychlorinated Naphthalene in Ambient Air, Anal. Chem. *49*, 1668, (1977)
137. Erickson, M. D., Michael, L. C., Zweidinger, R. A., Pellizzari, E. D.: Development of Methods for Sampling and Analysis of Polychlorinated Naphthalenes in Ambient Air, Environ. Sci. Technol. *12*, 927 (1978)
138. Melcher, R. G., Garner, W. L., Severs, L. W., Vaccaro, J. R.: Collection of Chlorpyrifos and Other Pesticides in Air on Chemically Bonded Sorbents, Anal. Chem. *50*, 251 (1978)
139. Gold, A., Dubé, C. D., Perni, R. B.: Solid Sorbent for Sampling Acrolein in Air, Anal. Chem. *50*, 1839 (1978)
140. Suzuki, Y., Imai, S.: Determination of Traces of Gaseous Acrolein by Collection on Molecular Sieves and Fluorimetry, Anal. Chim. Acta. *136*, 155 (1982)
141. Hoshika, Y.: Gas Chromatographic Determination of Lower Fatty Acids in Air at Parts-Per-Trillion Levels, Anal. Chem. *54*, 2433 (1982)
142. Williams, K. E., Esposito, G. G., Rinehart, D. S.: Sampling Tubes for the Collection of Selected Acid Vapors in Air, Am. Ind. Hyg. Assoc. J. *42*, 476 (1981)
143. Sydor, R., Pietrzyk, D.: Comparison of Porous Copolymers and Related Adsorbents for the Stripping of Low Molecular Weight Compounds from a Flowing Air Stream, Anal. Chem. *50*, 1842 (1978)
144. Dietrich, M. W., Chapman, L. M., Mieure, J. P.: Sampling for Organic Chemicals in Workplace Atmospheres with Porous Polymer Beads, Am. Ind. Hyg. Assoc. J. *39*, 385 (1978)
145. Russell, J. W.: Analysis of Air Pollutants Using Sampling Tubes and Gas Chromatography, Environ. Sci. Technol. *9*, 1175 (1975)
146. Johansson, I.: Determination of Organic Compounds in Indoor Air with Potential References to Air Quality, Atmos. Environ. *12*, 1372 (1978)
147. Campbell, D. N., Moore, R. H.: The Quantitative Determination of Acrylonitrile, Acrolein, Acetonitrile, and Acetone in Workplace Air, Am. Ind. Hyg. Assoc. J. *40*, 904 (1979)

148. Frankel, L. S., Black, R. F.: Automatic Gas Chromatographic Monitor for the Determination of Parts-Per-Billion Levels of Bis(chloromethyl) Ether, Anal. Chem. *48*, 732 (1976)
149. Ciccoli, P., Bertoni, G., Brancaleoni, E., Fratarcangeli, R., Bruner, F.: Evaluation of Organic Pollutants in the Open Air and Atmosphere in Industrial Sites Using Graphitized Carbon Black Traps and GC/MS Analysis with Specific Detectors, J. Chromatogr. *126*, 757 (1976)
150. Brooks, B. I., Jickells, S. M., Nicolson, R. S.: Atmospheric Sampling for Public Health Investigations Using Adsorption Tubes with Quantitative GC of GC/MS Analysis, J. Assoc. of Public Anal. *16*, 101 (1978)
151. Pellizzari, E. D., Carpenter, B. H., Bunch, J. E., Sawicki, E.: Collection and Analysis of Trace Organic Vapor Pollutants in Ambient Atmospheres — Thermal Desorption of Organic Vapors from Sorbent Media, Environ. Sci. Techn. *9*, 556 (1975)
152. Podolak, G. E., McKenzie, R. M., Rinehart, D. S., Mazur, J. F.: A Rapid Technique for Collection and Analysis of Phenol Vapors, Am. Ind. Hyg. Assoc. J. *42*, 738 (1981)
153. Parks, D. G., Ganz, C. R., Polinsky, A., Schulze, J.: A Simple Gas Chromatographic Method for the Analysis of Trace Organics in Ambient Air, Am. Ind. Hyg. Assoc. J. *26*, 165 (1975)
154. Bowen, B. E.: Determination of Aromatic Amines by an Adsorption Technique with Flame Ionization Gas Chromatography, Anal. Chem. *48*, 1584 (1976)
155. Myers, S. A., Quinn, H. J., Zook, W. C.: Determination of Vinyl Chloride Monomer at the Sub-ppm Level Using a Personal Monitor, Am. Ind. Hyg. Assoc. J. *26*, 332 (1975)
156. Pellizzari, E. D., Bunch, J. E., Carpenter, B. H., Sawicki, E.: Collection and Analysis of Trace Organic Vapor Pollutants in Ambient Atmospheres — Techniques for Evaluating Concentrations of Vapors by Sorbent Media, Environ. Sci. Techn. *9*, 552 (1975)
157. Brookes, B. I.: Gas Analysis Using an Internal Standard in Adsorption Tubes, Analyst *104*, 698 (1979)
158. Pellizzari, E. D., Bunch, J. E., Berkley, R. E., McRae, J.: Collection and Analysis of Trace Organic Vapor Pollutants in Ambient Atmospheres. The Performance of a Tenax-GC Cartridge Sampler for Hazardous Vapors, Anal. Letters, *9*, 45 (1976)
159. Pellizzari, E. D., Bunch, J. E., Berkley, R. E., McRae, J.: Determination of Trace Hazardous Organic Vapor Pollutants in Ambient Atmosphere by Gas Chromatography/Mass Spec./Computer, Anal. Chem. *48*, 803 (1976)
160. Krost, K. J., Pellizzari, E. D., Walburn, S. G., Hubbard, S. A.: Collection and Analysis of Hazardous Organic Emissions, Anal. Chem. *54*, 810 (1982)
161. Pellizzari, E. D.: Analysis for Organic Vapor Emissions Near Industrial and Chemical Waste Disposal Sites, Environ. Sci. Technol. *16*, 781 (1982)
162. Pankow, J. F., Isabelle, L. M., Kristensen, T. J.: Tenax-GC Cartridge for Interfacing Capillary Column Gas Chromatography with Adsorption/Thermal Desorption for Determination of Trace Organics, Anal. Chem. *54*, 1815 (1982)
163. Cox, R. D., Earp, R. F.: Determination of Trace Level Organics in Ambient Air by High-Resolution Gas Chromatography with Simultaneous Photoionization and Flame Ionization Detection, Anal. Chem. *54*, 2265 (1982)
164. Rudolph, J., Ehhalt, D. H., Khedim, A., Jebsen, C.: Determination of C_2–C_5 Hydrocarbons in the Atmosphere at Low ppb to High ppt Levels, J. Chromatogr. *217*, 301 (1981)
165. Russell, J. W., Shadoff, L. A.: The Sampling and Determination of Halocarbons in Ambient Air Using Concentration on Porous Polymer, Environ. Sci. Tech. *9*, 1175 (1975)
166. Tyson, B. J.: Chlorinated Hydrocarbons in the Atmosphere — Analysis at the Parts-per-Billion Level by GC-Ms, Analytical Letters *8*, 807 (1975)
167. Holzer, G., Shanfield, H., Zlatkis, A., Bertch, W., Juarez, P., Mayfield, H., Liebich, H. M.: Collection and Analysis of Trace Organic Emissions from Natural Sources, J. Chromatogr. *142*, 755 (1977)
168. Billings, W. N., Bidleman, T. F.: Field Comparison of Polyurethane Foam and Tenax-GC Resin for High-Volume Air Sampling of Chlorinated Hydrocarbons, Environ. Sci. Technol. *14*, 679 (1980)
169. Murray, E. K.: Concentration of Headspace, Airborne and Aqueous Volatiles on Chromosorb 105 for Examination by Gas Chromatography and GC/MS, J. Chromatogr. *135*, 49 (1977)
170. Bursey, J. T., Smith, D., Bunch, J. E., Williams, R. N., Berkley, R. E., Pellizzari, E. D.:

Application of Capillary GC/MS/Computer Techniques to Identification and Quantitation of Organic Components in Environmental Samples, Am. Lab., December, 35, (1977)
171. Senum, G. I.: Theoretical Collection Efficiencies of Adsorbent Samplers, Environ. Sci. Technol. *15*, 1073 (1981)
172. Billings, W. N., Bidleman, T. F.: Field Comparison of Polyurethane Foam and Tenax-GC Resin for High-Volume Air Sampling of Chlorinated Hydrocarbons, Environ. Sci. Technol. *14*, 679 (1980)
173. Tyson, B. J.: Chlorinated Hydrocarbons in the Atmosphere — Analysis at the Parts-Per-Billion Level by GC-MS, Analytical Letters *8*, 807 (1975)
174. Helzer, G., Shanfield, H., Zlatkis, A., Bertch, W., Juarez, P., Mayfield, H., Liebich, H. M.: Collection and Analysis of Trace Organic Emissions from Natural Sources, J. Chromatogr. *142*, 755 (1977)
175. Ioffe, B. V., Isidorou, V. A., Zenkevich, I. G.: Gas Chromatographic-Mass Spectrometric Determination of Volatile Organic Compounds in an Urban Atmosphere, J. Chromatogr. *142*, 787 (1977)
176. Louw, C. W., Richards, J. F.: The Determination of Volatile Organic Compounds in City Air by Gas Chromatography, Atmospheric Environment *11*, 703 (1977)
177. Palmes, E. D., Gunnison, A. F.: Personal Monitoring Devices for Gaseous Contaminants, Am. Ind. Hyg. Assoc. J. *34*, 78 (1973)
178. West, P. W., Reiszner, K. D.: Field Tests of a Permeation-Type-Personal Monitor for Vinyl Chloride, Am. Ind. Hyg. Assoc. J. *39*, 645 (1978)
179. Orofine, T. A., Usmani, A. M.: Passive Dosimetry, Am. Lab *12(7)*, 96 (1980)
180. West, P. W.: Passive Monitoring of Personal Exposures to Gaseous Toxins, Am. Lab *12(7)*, 35 (1980)
181. Merino, M.: Personal Monitoring, Am. Lab *13(8)*, 92 (1981)
182. Rose, V. E., Perkins, J. L.: Passive Dosimetry — State of the Art Review, Am. Ind. Hyg. Assoc. J. *43*, 605 (1982)
183. Fowler, W. K.: Fundamentals of Passive Vapor Sampling, Amer. Lab. *14(12)*, 80 (1982)
184. Hickey, J. L. S., Bishop, C. C.: Field Comparison of Charcoal Tubes and Passive Vapor Monitors with Mixed Organic Vapors, Am. Ind. Hyg. Assoc. J. *42*, 264 (1981)
185. Mazur, J. F., Rinehart, D. S., Esposito, G. G., Podolak, G. E.: Evaluation of Passive Dosimeters for Assessing Vapor Degreaser Emissions, Am. Ind. Hyg. Assoc. J. *42*, 752 (1981)
186. Benson, G. B., Boyce, G. E.: A Thermally-Desorbable Passive Dosimeter for Personal Monitoring of Acrylonitrile, Ann. Occup. Hyg. *24*, 55 (1981)
187. Benson, G. B., Boyce, G. E., Haile, D. M.: Industrial Hygiene Measurements for Organic Pollutants (Acrylonitrile) Using Passive Dosimeters and Automated Thermal Desorption, Ann. Occup. Hyg. *24*, 367 (1981)
188. Voelte, D. R., Weir, F. W.: A Dynamic Flow Chamber Comparison of Three Passive Organic Vapor Monitors with Charcoal Tubes Under Single and Multiple Solvent Exposure Conditions, Am. Ind. Hyg. Assoc. J. *42*, 845 (1981)
189. Purnell, C. J., Wright, M. D., Brown, R. H.: Performance of the Porton Down Charcoal Cloth Diffusive Sampler, Analyst (London) *106*, 590 (1982)
190. Feigley, C. E., Chastain, J. B.: An Experimental Comparison of Three Diffusion Samplers Exposed to Concentration Profiles of Organic Vapors, Am. Ind. Hyg. Assoc. J. *43*, 227 (1982)
191. Coutant, R. W.: Applicability of Passive Dosimeters for Ambient Air Monitoring of Toxic Organic Compounds, Environ. Sci. Technol. *16*, 410 (1982)
192. Baker, Jr., B. B.: Infrared Spectral Examination of Air-Monitoring Badges, Am. Ind. Hyg. Assoc. J. *43*, 98 (1982)
193. Campbell, J. E., Konzen, R. B.: The Development of a Passive Dosimeter for Aniline Vapors, Am. Ind. Hyg. Assoc. J. *41*, 180 (1980)
194. Kring, E. V., Thornley, G. D., Dessenberger, C., Lautenberger, W. J., Ansul, G. R.: A New Passive Colorimetric Air Monitoring Badge for Sampling Formaldeyhde in Air, Am. Ind. Hyg. Assoc. J. *43*, 786 (1982)
195. Matherne, R. N., Lubs, P. L., Kerfoot, E. J.: The Development of a Passive Dosimeter for Immediate Assessment of Phosgene Exposures, Am. Ind. Hyg. Assoc. J. *42*, 681 (1981)

196. Sefton, M. V., Mastracci, E. L., Mann, J. L.: Rubber Disc Passive Monitor for Benzene Dosimeter, Anal. Chem. *53*, 458 (1981)
197. Brown, R. H., Charlton, J., Saunders, K. J.: The Development of an Improved Diffusive Sampler, Am. Ind. Hyg. Assoc. J. *42*, 865 (1981)
198. Ryan, R. L., West, P. W.: A Hydrogen Fluoride Personal Monitor Using Permeation Sampling, Am. Ind. Hyg. Assoc. J. *43*, 650 (1982)
199. Hardy, J. K. and West, P. W.: A Personal Monitor for Hydrogen Cyanide Employing Permeation Sampling, J. Environ. Sci. Health, Part A *A16*, 201 (1981)
200. Hardy, J. K., Strecker, D. T., Savariar, C. P., West, P. W.: A Method for the Personal Monitoring of Hydrogen Sulfide Utilizing Permeation Sampling, Am. Ind. Hyg. Assoc. J. *42*, 836 (1981)
201. Hardy, J. K., Dasgupta, P. K., Reiszner, K. D., West, P. W.: A Personal Chlorine Monitor Utilizing Permeation Sampling, Environ. Sci. Technol. *13*, 1090 (1979)
202. Tomkins, F. C., Goldsmith, R. L.: A New Personal Dosimeter for Monitoring of Industrial Pollutants, Am. Ind. Hyg. Assoc. J. *38*, 371 (1977)
203. McDermott, D. L., Reiszner, K. D., West, P. W.: Development of Long-Term Sulfur Dioxide Monitor Using Permeation Sampling, Environ. Sci. Technol. *13*, 1087 (1979)
204. Kring, E. V., Lautenberger, W. J., Baker, W. B., Douglas, J. J.: A New Passive Colorimetric Air Monitoring Badge System for Ammonia, Sulfur Dioxide, and Nitrogen Dioxide, Am. Ind. Hyg. Assoc. J. *42*, 373 (1981)
205. Woebkenberg, M. L.: A Comparison of Three Passive Personal Sampling Methods for Nitrogen Dioxide, Am. Ind. Hyg. Assoc. J. *43*, 553 (1982)
206. Saltzman, B. E.: Direct Reading Colorimetric Indicators in Air Sampling Instruments, Cincinnati, OH, Industrial Conference of Governmental Industrial Hygienists 1972[4]
207. Carlson, D. H., Osborne, M. D., Johnson, J. H.: The Development and Application to Detector Tubes of Occupational Diesel Pollutant Concentration Measurements, Am. Ind. Hyg. Assoc. J. *43*, 275 (1982)
208. Morgenstern, A. S., Ash, R. M., Lynch, J. R.: The Evaluation of Gas Detector Tube Systems, I. Carbon Monoxide, Am. Ind. Hyg. Assoc. J. *31*, 630 (1970)
209. Roper, C. P.: An Evaluation of Perchloroethylene Detector Tubes, Am. Ind. Hyg. Assoc. J. *32*, 847 (1971)
210. Ash, R. M., Lynch, J. R.: The Evaluation of Gas Detector Tube Systems: Benzene, Am. Ind. Hyg. Assoc. J. *32*, 410 (1971)
211. Ash, R. M., Lynch, J. R.: The Evaluation of Gas Detector Tube Systems: Carbon Tetrachloride, Am. Ind. Hyg. Assoc. J. *32*, 552 (1971)
212. Ash, R. M., Lynch, J. R.: The Evaluation of Gas Detector Tube Systems: Sulfur Dioxide, Am. Ind. Hyg. Assoc. J. *32*, 490 (1971)
213. Kusnetz, H. L., Saltzman, B. E., LaNier, M. E.: Calibration and Evaluation of Gas Detecting Tubes, Am. Ind. Hyg. Assoc. J. *21*, 361 (1960)
214. Saltzman, B. E.: Basic Theory of Gas Indicator Tube Calibration, Am. Ind. Hyg. Assoc. J. *23*, 112 (1962)
215. Leichnitz, K.: Use of Detector Tubes Under Extreme Conditions (Humidity, Pressure, Temperature), Am. Ind. Hyg. Assoc. J. *38*, 701 (1977)
216. McCammon, C. S.: The Effect of Extreme Humidity and Temperature on Gas Detector Tube Performance, Am. Ind. Hyg. Assoc. J. *43*, 18 (1982)
217. Linch, A. L.: Oxygen in Air Analysis — Evaluation of a Length of Stain Detector, Am. Ind. Hyg. Assoc. J. *26*, 645 (1965)
218. Hay, E. B.: Exposure to Aromatic Hydrocarbons in a Coke Oven By-Product Plant, Am. Ind. Hyg. Assoc. J. *25*, 386 (1964)
219. McKarns, J. S., Hill, F. N., Bolton, P. R.: Monostyrene Vapor Concentrations From Plastic Concrete, Am. Ind. Hyg. Assoc. J. *28*, 414 (1967)
220. Larsen, L. B., Hendricks, H.: An Evaluation of Certain Direct Reading Devices for the Determination of Ozone, Am. Ind. Hyg. Assoc. J. *30*, 620 (1969)
221. Ketcham, N. H.: Practical Experience with Routine Use of Field Indicators, Am. Ind. Hyg. Assoc. J. *23*, 127 (1962)
222. Direct Reading Colorimetric Indicator Tubes Manual, Akron, OH, American Industrial Hygiene Assoc. 1976

223. Ingram, W. T.: Personal Air-Pollution Monitoring Devices, Am. Ind. Hyg. Assoc. J. *25*, 298 (1964)
224. Linch, A. L., Pfaff, H.: Carbon Monoxide — Evaluation of Exposure Potential by Personnel Monitor Surveys, Am. Ind. Hyg. Assoc. J. *32*, 745 (1971)
225. Leichnitz, K. R.: Das Prüfröhrchenverfahren und seine Entwicklungstendenzen, Chemiker Zeitung *97*, 638 (1973)
226. Leichnitz, K. R.: Detector Tubes and Prolonged Air Sampling, National Safety News, April, 59 (1977)
227. Jentzsch, D., Fraser, D. A.: A Laboratory Evaluation of Long-Term Detector Tubes: Benzene, Toluene, Trichloroethylene, Am. Ind. Hyg. Assoc. J. *42*, 810 (1981)
228. Gelman, C., Meltzer, T. H.: Membrane Filters in Air Analysis, Anal. Chem. *51*, 22A (1979)
229. Beaulieu, H. J., Fidino, A. V., Kim, M. S., Arlington, L. B., Buchan, R. M.: A Comparison of Aerosol Sampling Techniques: "Open" Versus "Closed-Face" Filter Cassettes, Am. Ind. Hyg. Assoc. J. *41*, 758 (1980)
230. Gussman, R. A., Dennis, R., Silverman, L.: Notes on the Design and Leak Testing of Sampling Filter Holders, Am. Ind. Hyg. Assoc. J. *23*, 480 (1962)
231. Malanchuk, M.: Evaluation of Two Filter Material Types for Sampling Test Atmospheres, Amer. Lab. *Dec*, 92 (1982)
232. Roach, S. A., Baier, E. J., Ayer, H. E., Harris, R. L.: Testing Compliance with Threshold Limit Values for Respirable Dusts', Amer. Ind. Hyg. Assoc. J. *28*, 543 (1967)
233. Task Group on Lung Dynamics: Deposition and Retention Models for Internal Dosimetry of the Human Respiratory Tract, Health Phys. *8*, 155 (1962)
234. Lazarus, R.: Respirable Dust from Lignite Coal in the Victorian Power Industry, Amer. Ind. Hyg. Assoc. J. *44*, 276 (1983)
235. Aerosol Technology Committee: Guide for Respirable Mass Sampling, Am. Ind. Hyg. Assoc. J. *31*, 133 (1970)
236. Lippman, R.: Respirable Dust Sampling, Am. Ind. Hyg. Assoc. J. *31*, 138 (1970)
237. Schwartz, G. P., Daisey, J. M., Lioy, P. J.: Effect of Sampling Duration on the Concentration of Particulate Organics Collected on Glass Fiber Filters, Am. Ind. Hyg. Assoc. J. *42*, 258 (1981)
238. Threshold Limits Committee: Threshold Limit, Values of Airbone Contaminants, Cincinnati, OH, American Conference of Governmental Industrial Hygienists (published annually)
239. Hawley, R. E., Charell, P. R.: Moisture Uptake an Air Sampling Filters, Am. Lab. *12*, 69 (1980)
240. Millipore Corporation: Technical Service Brief TS 030 MA (1978)
241. Williams, C. J., Hawley, R. E.: An Industrial Hazard — Silica Dust, Am. Lab. *7*, 17 (1975)
242. Duvall, P. M., Bourke, R. C.: Personal and High Volume Air Sampling Correlation Particulates, Environ. Sci. & Techn. *8*, 765 (1974)
243. Charell, P. R., Hawley, R. E.: Characteristics of Water Adsorption on Air Sampling Filters, Am. Ind. Hyg. Assoc. J. *42*, 353 (1981)
244. Bove, J. L., Dalven, P.: A GC/MS Method of Determining Airbone Di-n-butyl- and Bis-(2-Ethylhexyl) Phthalates, Int. J. Environ. Anal. Chem. *10*, 189 (1981)
245. Palassis, J., Posner, J. C., Slick, E., Schulte, K.: Air Sampling and Analysis of Trimellitic Anhydride, Am. Ind. Hyg. Assoc. J. *42*, 785 (1981)
246. Palassis, J.: The Sampling and Determination of Azelaic Acid in Air, Am. Ind. Hyg. Assoc. J. *39*, 731 (1978)
247. Blinky, B. R.: Determination of Thiabendazole by Ion-Pair High-Performance Liquid Chromatography, J. Chromatogr. *238*, 506 (1982)
248. Seymor, M. J.: Determination of 2,4,7-Trinitro-9-fluorenone in Workplace Environmental Samples Using High-Performance Liquid Chromatography, J. Chromatogr. *236*, 530 (1982)
249. Vukusic, I.: TLC Determination of Airbone Carbonfuran and Quinalphos for Industrial Hygiene Purposes, HRC & CC, J. High Resolut. Chromatogr. Chromatogr. Commun *4*, 659 (1981)
250. Goynes, W. R., Berni, R. J., Tripp, V. W.: Identification of Biological Dusts by Elemental Analysis, Am. Ind. Hyg. Assoc. J. *41*, 469 (1980)

251. Lange, B. A., Haartz, J. C., Hornung, R. W.: Determination of Synthetic Amorphous Silica in Industrial Air Samples, Anal. Chem. *53*, 1479 (1981)
252. Lee, M. L. Novotny, M., Bartel, K. D.: Gas Chromatography/Mass Spectrometric and Nuclear Magnetic Resonance Determination of Polynuclear Aromatic Hydrocarbons in Airborne Particulates, Anal. Chem. *48*, 1566 (1976)
253. Gutknecht, W. R., Ranade, M. B., Grohse, P. M., Damle, A. S.: Development of a Method for Sampling and Analysis of Metal Fumes in: Chemical Hazards in the Workplace, (ed.) Choudhary, G., Washington, D. C., ACS Symp. Series 149, ACS 1981
254. Lambert, J. P. F., Wilshire, F. W.: Neutron Activation Analysis for Simultaneous Determination of Trace Elements in Ambient Air Collected on Glass-Fiber Filters, Anal. Chem. *51*, 1346 (1979)
255. Non-Destructive Neutron Activation Analysis of Air Pollution Particulates in: Methods of Air Sampling and Analysis, (ed.) M. Katz, Washington, D.C., American Public Health Association 1977
256. Bhargava, O. P., Bumsted, H. E., Grunder, F. I., Hunt, B. L., Manning, G. E., Riemann, R. A., Samuels, J. K., Tatone, V., Waldschmidt, S. J., Hernandez, P.: Study of an Analytical Method for Hexavalent Chromium, Am. Ind. Hyg. Assoc. J. *44*, 433 (1983)
257. Gunderson, E. C.: Sampling Methods for Airborne Pesticides in: Chemical Hazards in the Workplace, (ed.) Choudhary, G., ACS Symp. Series 149, Washington, D.C., ACS 1981
258. Pruett, J. G., Winslow, S. G.: Asbestos in Air. A Bibliography with Abstracts, 1964–1980, Report (D3REP3] 1980, NLM/TIRC-80/2, Avail. NTIS. From Energy Res. Abstr. 5(21) Abstr. No. 34126 (1980)
259. Standard Test Method for Airborne Asbestos Concentrations in Workplace Atmosphere, D4240, in: Annual Book of ASTM Standards, Vol. 11.03, Philadelphia, PA, American Society for Testing and Materials 1983
260. Gussman, R. A., Thorpe, M. J., Tisch, Jr., W. P., Spooner, C. M., Turner, W., McMahon, N. M.: Further Development of the High Volume Air Sampler for High Resistance Filter Media, Am. Ind. Hyg. Assoc. J. *44*, 704 (1983)
261. Standard Practice for Application of the Hi-Vol (High-Volume) Sampler Method for Collection and Mass Determination of Airborne Particulate Matter, D4096, in: Annual Book of ASTM Standards, Vol. 11.03, Philadelphia, PA, American Society for Testing and Materials (1983)
262. U.S. Environmental Protection Agency: Appendix B — Reference Method for the Determination of Suspended Particulate Matter in the Atmosphere (High Volume Method), Fed. Regis. 47(10), 2363—2375 (Jan. 15, 1982)
263. Knights, R. L.: Analysis of Particulate Organic Air Pollutants by High Resolution Mass Spectrometry, Adv. Environ. Sci. Technol. *9*, 237 (1980)
264. Grosjean, D., Van Cauwenberghe, K., Schmid, J. P., Kelley, P. E., Pitts, Jr., J. N.: Identification of C_3–C_{10} Aliphatic Dicarboxylic Acids in Airborne Particulate Matter, Environ. Sci. Technol. *12*, 313 (1978)
265. Karasek, F. W., Denney, D. W., Chan, K. W., Clement, R. E.: Analysis of Complex Organic Mixtures on Airborne Particulate Matter, Anal. Chem. *50*, 82 (1978)
266. Dowling, T., Davis, R. B., Linch, A. L.: Lead in Air Analyzer, Am. Ind. Hyg. Assoc. J. *19*, 330 (1958)
267. Jacobson, M., Terry, S. L., Ambrosia, D. A.: Evaluation of Some Parameters Affecting the Collection and Analysis of Midget Impinger Samples, Am. Ind. Hyg. Assoc. J. *31*, 442 (1970)
268. Kerrigan, J. V., Smajberk, K., Anderson, E. S.: Collection of Sulfuric Acid Mist in the Presence of a Higher Sulfur Dioxide Background, Anal. Chem. *32*, 1168 (1960)
269. Knuth, R. H.: Recalibration of Size-Selective Samplers, Am. Ind. Hyg. Assoc. J. *30*, 379 (1969)
270. Roesler, J. F., Stevenson, H. J. R. and Nader, J. S.: Size Distribution of Sulfate Aerosols in the Ambient Air, J. Air Pollut. Control Assoc., *15*, 576 (1965)
271. Blachman, M. W., Lippman, M.: Performance Characteristics of the Multi-Cyclone Aerosol Sampler, Am. Ind. Hyg. Assoc. J. *35*, 311 (1974)
272. AIHA Aerosol Technology Committee, Guide for Respirable Mass Sampling, Am. Ind. Hyg. Assoc. J. *31*, 133 (1970)
273. Walton, W. H.: The Theory of Size-Classification of Airborne Dust Clouds by Elutriation, J. of Phy. D: Applied Phys. *3*, 529 (1954)

274. Thomas, J. W. and Knuth, R.: Settling Velocity and Density of Monodisperse Aerosols, Am. Ind. Hyg. Assoc. J. *28*, 173 (1967)
275. Hughs, S. E., Smith, D. W., Urquhart, N. S.: Methodology for Cotton Gin Dust Sampling, Am. Ind. Hyg. Assoc. J. *42*, 407 (1981)
276. Bartley, D. L., Breuer, G. M., Baron, P. A., Bowman, J. D.: Pump Fluctuations and Their Effect on Cyclone Performance, Am. Ind. Hyg. Assoc. J. *45*, 10 (1984)
277. Marple, V. A., Liu, B. Y. H.: Characteristics of Laminar Jet Impactors, Environ. Sci. Technol. *8*, 648 (1974)
278. Mercer, T. T., Stafford, R. G.: Impaction from Round Jets, Ann. Occup. Hyg. *12*, 41 (1969)
279. Lundgren, D. A.: An Aerosol Sampler for Determination of Particle Concentration as a Function of Size and Time, J. Air. Poll. Control Assoc. *17*, 225 (1967)
280. Dzubay, T. G., Hines, L. E., Stevens, R. K.: Particle Bounce Errors in Cascade Impactors, Atm. Environ. *10*, 229 (1976)
281. Hering, S. V., Flagan, R. C., Friedlander, S. K.: Design and Evaluation of a New Low-Pressure Impactor, 1. Environ. Sci. Technol. *12*, 667 (1978)
282. Hering, S. V., Friedlander, S. K., Collins, J. J., Richards, L. W.: Design and Evaluation of a New Low-Pressure Impactor, 2. Environ. Sci. Technol. *13*, 184 (1979)
283. Rao, A. K., Whitby, K. T.: Non-Ideal Collection Characteristics of Inertial Impactors — II. Cascade Impactors, J. Aerosol Sci. *9*, 87 (1978)
284. Esmen, N. A., Ziegler, P., Whitfield, R.: The Adhesion of Particles Upon Impaction, J. Aerosol Sci. *9*, 547 (1978)
285. Esmen, N. N., Lee, T. C.: Distortion of Cascade Impactor Measured Size Distribution Due to Bounce and Blow-Off, Am. Ind. Hyg. Assoc. J. *41*, 410 (1980)
286. Lee, T. C., Esmen, N. A.: Design, Calibration and Testing of a Parallel Stage Impactor, Am. Ind. Hyg. Assoc. J. *41*, 24 (1980)
287. Kuhlmey, G. C., Liu, B. Y. H., Marple, V. A.: A Micro-Orifice Impactor for Sub-Micron Aerosol Size Classification, Am. Ind. Hyg. Assoc. J. *42*, 790 (1981)
288. Jolley, R. A.: Concentrating Organics in Water for Biological Testing, Environ. Sci. Technol. *15*, 874 (1981)
289. Poole, C. F., Schuette, S. A.: Isolation and Concentration Techniques for Capillary Column Gas Chromatographic Analysis, HRC & CC *6*, 526 (1983)
290. Kopp, J. F., McKee, G. D.: Manual-Methods for Chemical Analysis of Water and Wastes — 1978, U.S. Environmental Protection Agency Report, No. EPA-600/4-79-020, NTIS order no. PB-297 686 (1979)
291. Standard Methods for the Examination of Water and Wastewater, (ed.) Franson, M. A. H., Washington, D.C., American Public Health Association, 1980[15]
292. Cais, Shimoni, M.: A Feasible Solvent Separation System for Immunoassays, Ann. Clin. Biochem. *18*, 317 (1981)
293. Cais, M., Shimoni, M.: A Novel System for Mass Transport Through Selective Barriers in Non-Centrifugation Immunoassay, Ann. Clin. Biochem. *18*, 324 (1981)
294. Goldberg, M. C., DeLong, L., Sinclair, M.: Extraction and Concentration of Organic Solutes from Water, Anal. Chem. *45*, 89 (1973)
295. Peters, T. L.: Comparison of Continuous Extractors for the Extraction and Concentration of Trace Organics from Water, Anal. Chem. *54*, 1913 (1982)
296. Huibregtse, K., Harkin, J. M.: Rapid Analysis of Organic Pollutants in Surface Waters by High Pressure Liquid Chromatography, NTIS order no. PB81-116881 (1980)
297. Derenbach, J. B., Ehrhardt, M., Osterroht, C., Petrick, G.: Sampling of Dissolved Organic Material from Seawater with Reversed-Phase Techniques, Marine Chemistry *6*, 351 (1978)
298. Wolkoff, A. W., Creed, C.: Use of Sep-Pak C_{18} Cartridges for the Collection and Concentration of Environmental Samples, J. of Liquid Chromatogr. *4*, 1459 (1981)
299. Smith, S. R., Tanaka, J., Futoma, D. J., Smith, T. E.: Sampling and Preconcentration Methods for the Analysis of Polycyclic Aromatic Hydrocarbons in Water Systems, CRC Crit. Rev. Anal. Chem. *10*, 375 (1981)
300. Mangani, F., Crescentini, G., Bruner, F.: Sample Enrichment for Determination of Chlorinated Pesticides in Water and Soil by Chromatographic Extraction, Anal. Chem. *53*, 1627 (1981)

301. Junk, G. A., Richard, J. J., Grieser, M. D., Witiak, D., Witiak, J. L., Arguello, M. D., Vick, R., Svec, H. J., Fritz, J. S., Calder, G. V.: Use of Macroreticular Resins in the Analysis of Water for Trace Organic Contaminants, J. of Chromatogr. *99*, 745 (1974)
302. Cheh, A. H.: Artifacts and Losses in the Sampling of Chlorinated Water by XAD Adsorption, NTIS order no. PB 83-208843, 1983
303. Gesser, H. D., Chow, A., Davis, F. C., Uthe, J. F., Reinke, J.: The Extraction and Recovery of Polychlorinated Biphenyls (PCB) Using Porous Polyurethane Foam, Anal. Lett. *4*, 883 (1971)
304. Pankow, J. F., Isabelle, L. M.: Adsorption-Thermal Desorption as a Method for the Determination of Low Levels of Aqueous Organics, J. of Chromatogr. *237*, 25 (1982)
305. Chriswell, C. D., Ericson, R. L., Junk, G. A., Lee, K. W., Fritz, J. S., Svec, H. J.: Comparison of Macroreticular Resin and Activated Carbon as Sorbents, J. Amer. Water Works Assoc. *69*, 669 (1977)
306. Evans, S., Maalman, T. F. J.: Removal of Organic Acids from Rhine River Water with Weak Base Resins, Environ. Sci. Technol. *13*, 741 (1979)
307. Bickford, B., Bursey, J., Michael, L., Pellizzari, E., Porch, R., Rosenthal, D., Sheldon, L., Sparacino, C., Tomer, K., Wiseman, R., Yung, S., Gebhart, J., Rando, L., Perry, D., Ryan, J.: Master Scheme for the Analysis of Organic Compounds in Water. Part III: Experimental Development and Results, United States Environmental Protection Agency, Contract No. 68-03-2704, January 1980
308. Kepner, R. E., van Straten, S., Weurman, C.: Freeze Concentration of Volatile Components in Dilute Aqueous Solutions, J. Agric. Food Chem. *17*, 1123 (1969)
309. Bellar, T. A., Lichtenberg, J. J.: Determining Volatile Organics at Microgram-Per-Litre Levels by Gas Chromatography, J. of AWWA *66*, 739 (1974)
310. Ramstad, T., Nestrick, T. J., Peters, T. L.: Applications of the Purge-and-Trap Technique, American Laboratory, July, 65 (1981)
311. Dressman, R. C., McFarren, E. F.: A Sample-Bottle Purging Method for the Determination of Vinyl Chloride in Water at Sub-Microgram per Liter Levels, J. of Chromatogr. Sci. *15*, 69 (1977)
312. Grob, K.: Organic Substances in Potable Water and in its Precursor. Part I. Methods for Their Determination by Gas-Liquid Chromatography, J. of Chromatogr. *84*, 255 (1973)
313. Grob. K., Grob, Jr., K., Grob, G.: Organic Substances in Potable Water and in its Precursor. Part III. The Closed-Loop Stripping Procedure Compared with Rapid Liquid Extraction, J. of Chromatogr. *109*, 299 (1975)
314. Coleman, W. E., Melton, R. G., Slater, R. W., Kopfler, F. C., Voto, S. J., Allen, W. K., Aurand, T. A.: Determination of Organic Contaminants by the Grob Closed-Loop-Stripping Technique, J. of AWWA *73*, 119 (1981)
315. Grob, K., Zurcher, F.: Stripping of Trace Organic Substances from Water. Equipment and Procedure, J. Chromatogr. *117*, 285 (1976)
316. Martin, C. L., Lackey, W. W., Conkle, J. P., Miller, R. L.: Analysis of Trace Volatiles by Gas Chromatography/Mass Spectrometer Data System, NTIS order no. AD-A050 912, December 1977
317. Coleman, W. E., Munch, J. W., Slater, R. W., Melton, R. G., Kopfler, F. C.: Optimization of Purging Efficiency and Quantification of Organic Contaminants from Water Using a 1-L Closed-Loop-Stripping Apparatus and Computerized Capillary Column GC/MS, Environ. Sci. Technol. *17*, 571 (1983)
318. Ettre, L. S., Kolb, B., Hunt, S. G.: Techniques of Headspace Gas Chromatography, American Laboratory, October, 76 (1983)
319. McAullife, C.: GC Determination of Solutes by Multiple Phase Equilibrium, Chem. Tech. *1*, 46 (1971)
320. Piet, G. J., Slingerland, P., de Grunt, F. E., v. d. Heuveland, M. P. M., Zoeteman, B. C. J.: Determination of Very Volatile Halogenated Organic Compounds in Water by Means of Direct Head-Space Analysis, Anal. Lett. *5*, 437 (1978)
321. Veith, G. D., Kiwus, L. M.: An Exhaustive Steam-Distillation and Solvent-Extraction Unit for Pesticides and Industrial Chemicals, Bull. of Environ. Contam. Toxicol. *17*, 631 (1977)
322. Robbins, L. A., U.S. Patent No. 4,236,973, 2 December 1980

323. Nickerson, G. B., Likens, S. T.: Gas Chromatographic Evidence for the Occurrence of Hop Oil Components in Beer, J. Chromatogr. *21*, 1 (1966)
324. Godefroot, M., Sandra, P., Verzele, M.: New Method for Quantitative Essential Oil Analysis, J. Chromatogr. *203*, 325 (1981)
325. Godefroot, M., Stechele, M., Sandra, P., Verzele, M.: A New Method for Quantitative Analysis of Organochlorine Pesticides and Polychlorinated Biphenyls, HRC & CC *5*, 75 (1982)
326. Chian, E. S. K., Kuo, P. P. K., Cooper, W. J., Cowen, W. F., Fuentes, R. C.: Distillation/Headspace/Gas Chromatographic Analysis for Volatile Polar Organics at ppb Level, Environ. Sci. Technol. *11*, 282 (1980)
327. Peters, T. L.: Steatm Distillation Apparatus for Concentration of Trace Water Soluble Organics, Anal. Chem. *52*, 211 (1980)
328. Kuo, P. P. K., Chian, E. S. K., DeWalle, F. B.: Determination of Trace Low-Molecular-Weight Volatile Polar-Organics in Water by Gas Chromatography Using Distillation Method, Water Research *11*, 1005 (1977)
329. Hiatt, M. H.: Analysis of Fish and Sediment for Volatile Priority Pollutants, Anal. Chem. *53*, 1541 (1981)
330. Phillips, J. H., Zabik, M.: Analytical Techniques in Analysis of Municipal Sludges for Volatiles, American Laboratory, December, 46 (1981)
331. Stalling, D. L., Tindle, R. C., Johnson, J. L.: Cleanup of Pesticide and Polychlorinated Biphenyl Residues in Fish Extracts by Gel Permeation Chromatography, J. of the AOAC *55*, 32 (1972)
332. Nestrick, T. J., Lamparski, L. L.: Isomer-Specific Determination of Chlorinated Dioxins for Assessment of Formation and Potential Environmental Emission from Wood Combustion, Anal. Chem. *54*, 2292 (1982)
333. Nestrick, T. J., Lamparski, L. L.: Purification of Cylinder Gases Used in Solvent Evaporation for Trace Analysis, Anal. Chem. *53*, 122 (1981)
334. Curran, C. M., Tomson, M. B.: Leaching of Trace Organics into Water from Five Common Plastics, Ground Water Monit. Rev. *3*, 68 (1983)
335. Walker, D. G.: A Question of Sampling, Effluent and Water Treat. J. *22*, 184 (1982)
336. Liebetrau, A. M.: Water Quality Sampling: Some Statistical Considerations, Water Resour. Res. *15*, 1717 (1979)
337. Dandy, G. C., Moore, S. F.: Water Quality Sampling Programs in Rivers, J. Environ. Eng. Div. *105*, 695 (1979)
338. Shelly, P. E.: Sampling of Water and Wastewater, U.S. Environmental Protection Agency Report No. EPA-600/4-77-039, August 1977
339. Whitfield, P. H.: Evaluation of Water Quality Sampling Locations on the Yukon River, Water Resour. Bull. *19*, 115 (1983)
340. Dennis, D. S.: Surface Water Sampling Procedures for Environmental Contaminants, Environ. Chem.: Hum. Anim. Health *5*, 175 (1977)
341. Plumb, Jr., R. H.: Procedures for Handling and Chemical Analysis of Sediment and Water Samples, U.S. Environmental Protection Agency Report No. EPA/CE-81-1, May 1981
342. Carter, M. J., Huston, M. T.: Preservation of Phenolic Compounds in Wastewaters, Environ. Sci. Technol. *12*, 309 (1978)
343. Ogawa, I., Junk, G. A., Svec, H. J.: Degradation of Aromatic Compounds in Groundwater and Methods of Sample Preservation, Talanta *28*, 725 (1981)
344. Fujii, T.: The Determination of Traces of Organohalogen Compounds in Aqueous Solution by Direct Injection Gas Chromatography-Mass Spectrometry and Single Ion Detection, Analytica Chimica Acta *92*, 117 (1977)
345. Nicholson, A. A., Meresz, O., Lemyk, B.: Determination of Free and Total Potential Haloforms in Drinking Water, Anal. Chem. , 814 (1977)
346. Henderson, J. E., Peyton, G. R., Glaze, W. H.: A Convenient Liquid-Liquid Extraction Method for the Determination of Halomethanes in Water at the Parts-Per-Billion Level, in: Identification and Analysis of Organic Pollutants in Water, (ed.) Keith, L. H., p. 105, Ann Arbor MI, Ann Arbor Science Publishers Inc. 1976
347. Levine, S. P., Puskar, M. A., Dymerski, P. P., Warner, B. J., Friedman, C. S.: Cross-Contamination of Water Samples Taken for Analysis of Purgeable Organic Compounds, Environ. Sci. Technol. *17*, 125 (1983)

348. Whitlock, C. J., Paulson, V. A.: Priority Pollutant Sampling — Different from Conventional Sampling Requirements, in: Ind. Waste, Proc. Mid-Atl. Conf., 14th (ed.) Alleman, J. E., Kavanagh, J. T., p. 501, Ann Arbor MI, Ann Arbor Sci. Publishers 1982
349. Berg, E. L.: Handbook for Sampling and Sample Preservation of Water and Wastewater, U.S. Environmental Protection Agency Report No. EPA-600/4-82-029, Sept. 1982
350. Bachmat, T., Ben-Zvi, M.: Optimization of a Groundwater Quality Sampling Program, Studies in Environmental Science *17*, 607 (1981)
351. Schuller, R. M., Biggs, J. P., Griffin, R. A.: Recommended Sampling Procedures for Monitoring Wells, Ground Water Monit. Rev. *1*, 42 (1981)
352. Fetter, Jr., C. W.: Potential Sources of Contamination in Ground Water Monitoring, Ground Water Monit. Rev. *3*, 60 (1983)
353. Wilson, L. C., Rouse, J. V.: Variations in Water Quality During Initial Pumping of Monitoring Wells, Ground Water Monit. Rev. *3*, 103 (1983)
354. Seanor, A. M., Brannaka, L. K.: Influence of Sampling Techniques on Organic Water Quality Analyses, in: Manage. Uncontrolled Hazard. Waste Nat'l. Conf. 1981, p. 143, Hazard. Mater. Control Res. Inst., Silver Springs, MD
355. Pettyjohn, W. A., Dunlap, W. J., Cosby, R., Keeley, J. W.: Sampling Ground Water for Organic Contaminants, Ground Water *19*, 180 (1981)
356. Sahni, B. M., Bhuiyan, S. I.: Monitoring and Protecting Groundwater Quality in Stratified Aquifer Systems, in: Studies in Environmental Science 17, p. 761, Elsevier Scientific Publishing Company, 1981
357. Lee, G. F., Jones, R. A.: Guidelines for Sampling Ground Water, J. Water Pollut. Control Fed. *55*, 92 (1983)
358. Scalf, M. R., McNabb, J. F., Dunlap, W. J., Cosby, R. L., Fryberger, J. S.: Manual of Ground Water Quality Sampling Procedures, U.S. Environmental Protection Agency Report No. EPA-600/2-81-160, 1981
359. Guzman, C., Bloxom, S. R., MacWilliam, G. L.: Extraction and Injection of Soil Water with Hollow-Fiber Semi-Permeable Membranes, U.S. Energy Research and Development Administration Report No. ORNL/MIT-217, 1975
360. Levin, M. J., Jackson, D. R.: A Comparison of In-Situ Extractors for Sampling Soil Water, Soil Sci. Soc. Am. J. *41*, 535 (1979)
361. Wood, A. L., Wilson, J. T., Cosby, R. L., Hornsby, A. G., Baskin, L. B.: Apparatus and Procedure for In-Situ Sampling of Volatile Organic Compounds in Soil Profiles, Soil Sci. Soc. Am. J. *45*, 442 (1981)
362. Dunlap, W. J., McNabb, J. F., Scalf, R., Cosby, R. L.: Sampling for Organic Chemicals and Microorganism in the Sub-Surface, U.S. Environmental Protection Agency Report No. EPA-600/2-77-176, August 1977
363. Hodgson, J. M.: Soil Sampling and Soil Description, Oxford University Press, Fair Lawn, NJ 1978
364. Mason, B. J.: Preparation of Soil Sampling Protocol: Techniques and Strategies, U.S. Environmental Protection Agency Report No. EPA-600/4-83-020, May 1983
365. Apperson, C. S., Leidy, R. B., Eplee, R., Carter, E.: An Efficient Device for Collecting Soil Samples for Pesticide Residue Analysis, Bull. Environm. Contam. Toxicol *25*, 55 (1980)
366. Powers, C. F., Sanville, W. D., Stay, F. S., Schuytema, G. S.: Aquatic Sediments, Journal WPCF, June 1307 (1977)

Chemical Reactions in Alkali Metals

Hans Ulrich Borgstedt

Kernforschungszentrum Karlsruhe, Institut für Material- und Festkörperforschung II, P.O. Box 3640, D-7500 Karlsruhe, FRG

Table of Contents

Liquid alkali metals are of interest for several technical applications due to their physical and nuclear properties. Problems of safe handling and protection against atmospheric gases and water are caused by their chemical reactivity. Several chemical reactions occur even in purified liquid alkali metals.

Alkali oxides are thermodynamically stable up to very high temperatures, and even hydrides have saline character and considerable stability. Lithium nitride is a compound which can be isolated from the solution in the metal in crystalline form. Dissolved oxides have the ability to react with transition metal oxides to form complex oxides, or with hydrogen to form hydroxides of the beavier alkali metals. Lithium cyanamide is formed by means of the reaction between nitrogen and carbon dissolved in the molten metal. The reaction product in liquid sodium is sodium cyanide.

Carbon dispersed in liquid alkali metals is hydrided by the reaction with dissolved hydrogen or hydrides to evolve methane. Some reactions of non-metals dissolved in the molten metals are important for the compatibility of materials with the alkali metals. Transition metals are almost insoluble in molten alkali metals. Their solubilities can be considerably raised by dissolved non-metals. Several metals of the fourth and fifth group form one or more intermetallic compounds with alkali metals.

1 The Role of Alkali Metals in Technology

The alkali metals belong to the elements which are widely distributed in the earth crust. Some of them are in the group of the most abundant elements. Their chemical properties, however, cause severe problems in the technical processes of their isolation from the ores. They were discovered by means of electrochemical methods in the early nineteenth century.

Potassium was the first alkali metal isolated in its elemental state. Sir Humphrey Davy electrolyzed caustic potash in 1807 applying a powerful battery. He gained metallic globules of a reactive metal collected at the cathode. It was the first time that a metallic element was isolated by means of electrolysis. Davy discovered sodium in the same year. He used caustic soda for the electrolysis. Before Davy's discoveries, these alkalis were not thought to be elements.

Lithium was discovered by Arfvedson (1817) in Berzelius'laboratory in Stockholm. He discovered an unknown constituent element in the mineral petalite and called it lithium. The first isolation of this new element was again the work of Davy (and Brandes) in 1820. They succeeded to get small amounts of the metal by means of their electrolytic method. Bunsen and Matthiessen were able to obtain larger quantities of the metal. They electrolyzed lithium chloride in 1855.

Cesium was discovered in 1860 by Bunsen and Kirchhoff by means of their spectroscope at Heidelberg. They observed characteristic blue lines, when analysing the mineral waters of Bad Dürkheim in Germany. They could isolate 50 grams of the compound cesium chloroplatinate from 40 tons of the mineral water. The first electrolytical isolation of the metal was performed in 1882 by Setterberg. He used the cyanide as electrolyte. Bunsen and Kirchhoff also discovered rubidium. They observed the characteristic dark red lines in their spectroscope when analysing the mineral lepidolite. The electrolytic technique, which was so successful in the isolation of the alkali metals in the laboratories, was the basis for the technical production of the metals.

Due to their physical and chemical properties, alkali metals were not regarded as being attractive metals in the classical sense of application of metals. Therefore, these metals were mainly used as intermediates for chemical processes. Sodium, for instance, was largely produced for the synthesis of tetra ethyl lead on the basis of the reaction of ethyl chloride with the sodium lead intermetallic compound NaPb.

Modern technology, however, has an increasing demand for liquid alkali metals which make use of such attractive properties. Alkali metals have low melting points and large ranges of the liquid state. They conduct electricity and heat very well. This fact, as well as the stability of the liquid state at low pressures, makes them ideal heat transfer media in the temperature range from 400 to 700 °C. They also possess nuclear properties, which favour their application as coolants or blanket fluids in nuclear power generating plants. Their extreme position in the electrochemical series of metals favours them for the application in galvanic power sources.

The properties of alkali metals, which are of concern for their application as liquid metals are listed in Table I.

The nuclear properties of the light alkali metals are of importance as far as the metals are applied in nuclear fields. The most important facts are compared in Table II.

The application of lithium has been widened by the development of nuclear fusion as an energy generating process. The fusion reaction — the technical realization of

Table I. Properties of Alkali Metals

Element	Atomic number	Atomic weight	Melting point (°C)	Boiling point (°C)	Specific heat (kJ/K · kg) at 298 K	Density of liquid (g/cm^3) at 500 K	Thermal conductivity (W/K · m) at 298 K	Electrical resistivity (10^{-8} Ω) at 293 K
Lithium	3	6.941	180.5	1342	3.549	0.515	84.5	9.28
Sodium	11	22.9898	97.81	881	2.008[a]	0.920	132.3[a]	4.77
Potassium	19	39.0983	63.2	756	0.770[a]	0.791	102.5	7.20
Rubidium	37	85.468	39.3	686	0.356	1.397	58.2	12.84
Cesium	55	132.905	28.5	678	0.233	1.732	36.1[b]	20.46

[a] at 293 K; [b] provisional value

Table II. Selected Nuclear Properties of Alkali Metals

Target element	Energy of neutrons	Reaction and product	Half life of product	Cross section
Li-6	14.5 MeV	(n, p) He-6	802 ms	8.3 mb
Na-23	thermal	(n, γ) Na-24 m	20.1 ms	400 mb
		(n, γ) Na-24 g	15.02 h	530 mb
	fast	(n, p) Ne-23	37.6 s	1.5 mb
		(n, α) F-20	11.0 s	765 μb
		(n, 2n) Na-22	2.6 a	2.2 μb
K-39	thermal	(n, γ) K-40	$1.28 \cdot 10^9$ a	1.96 b
		(n, α) Cl-36	$3.01 \cdot 10^5$ a	4.3 mb
K-40		(n, γ) K-41	stable	30 b
		(n, p) Ar-40	stable	4.4 b
		(n, α) Cl-37	stable	390 mb
K-39	fast	(n, p) Ar-39	269 a	20 mb
		(n, α) Cl-36	$3 \cdot 10^5$ a	13 mb
K-40		(n, α) Cl-37	stable	31 mb
		(n, 2n) K-39	stable	1.6 mb

it is now under development — is based upon the deuterium — tritium nuclear fusion, and the only supply of fusion energy plants with tritium is the nuclear reaction of lithium isotopes with neutrons:

$$n + {}^{6}Li \rightarrow T + {}^{4}He + 4.8\ MeV \qquad (1)$$

$$n + {}^{7}Li \rightarrow T + {}^{4}He + n\ (-2.8\ MeV) \qquad (2)$$

Since the element lithium is essential for the fusion reaction, some concepts for reactor blankets are based on the application of liquid metals, lithium or the eutectic alloy $Li_{17}Pb_{83}$, as blanket fluids or also as reactor coolants.

The high ionization potential and the very low density of the metals are promising to make use of them in high-temperature batteries [2)]. Electrochemical cells using lithium as anode, a solid ceramic electrolyte and lithium polysulphide as cathode may reach a theoretical energy density of 3000 $Wh \cdot kg^{-1}$. Problems are caused by the bad compatibility of lithium with ceramic materials.

Liquid sodium has attractive properties for its application as a working fluid in a fast neutron reactor with the ability to breed plutonium fuel by the reaction of ^{238}uranium with the fast neutrons. Sodium does not act as a neutron moderator, its liquid state at atmospheric pressure reaches from 97.8 °C to 892 °C, its heat transfer properties are excellent and its nuclear reactions do not cause a long lasting activation. Sodium is the medium which is able to transfer the energy generated in the high density reactor core better than any other heat transfer fluid [3)].

The heat transfer capacity of sodium is also successfully demonstrated in a sun energy conversion plant, where it is applied to store the energy and to transfer it from the radiation receiver to the steam generator. The energy storage in the hot sodium tank helps to operate the plant even after sunset.

Another modern application of liquid sodium is its utilization in sodium sulphur batteries [4]. These batteries are based on a molten sodium anode, a β-alumina ceramic electrolyte and a molten alkali polysulphide cathode. The working temperature of such batteries is limited by the melting point of Na_2S_3 and the boiling point of sulphur at a temperature between 300 and 440 °C with an optimal working range of 300 to 350 °C. Sodium sulphur cells may be combined to form chains in order to receive high voltage and power. Batteries formed by such chains of cells are intended for storing electrical energy or to driving vehicles.

Other high-temperature applications of alkali metals are in the field of heat or energy transfer. Heat pipe make use of the latent heat of evaporation and condensation of the alkali metals. The advantage of these devices to transfer energy is the low temperature gradient between the heat source and the sink. The application of different alkali metals allows the use of heat pipe in the temperature range of 400 to nearly 1500 °C [5].

The thermal energy of the evaporated alkali metals may also be transferred into electrical energy by the utilization of the magneto hydrodynamic effect. The alkali metal vapor, containing droplets of the metals, transfers the electrical charges of the metal. The motion of the charged particles thus causes the generation of an electromagnetic field [6].

The application of alkali metals at high temperatures can utilize chemical properties, or may be influenced by chemical reactions. The solutions of non-metallic elements in the alkali metals change physical properties of the pure metals. Dissolved elements are able to cause or to influence the corrosion phenomena. Some compounds are only formed or made stable in the presence of excess liquid alkali metal. Due to such an influence of chemical reactions on the behavior or metals, the new applications have initiated many studies in alkali metal chemistry. Interest has been concentrated on the elements lithium and sodium. The heavier alkali metals have found further interest in more recent work.

This work has been mainly performed in the nuclear centres of several countries such as the USA, USSR, United Kingdom, France, Japan, the Federal Republic of Germany and in the Department of Chemistry of the University of Nottingham, UK. The results of alkali metal chemistry work of the past 25 years are the basis of this survey. It gives a state of knowledge report on the advance of chemical research work, closely related to the transformation of energy.

2 Alkali Metals-Oxygen Systems

The high affinity of alkali metals to form oxides, together with the influence of dissolved oxides on the compatibility of metals with metallic or ceramic materials, is the reason for an extensive study on the formation of oxides, their solubility and their chemical potential in solution, which governs their reactions with metals and solid oxides. Interest was concentrated on the sodium-oxygen system. More recently, data on the oxides of lithium and potassium have been established. The oxides of rubidium and cesium are less stable and soluble to a much higher degree in their molten metals. The existing data on Rb_2O and Cs_2O need critical examination.

2.1 Alkali Oxides and their Solubility in the Molten Metals

Alkali oxides, Me_2O, are stable when in contact with the alkali metals, and form crystals of the fluorite type. In the presence of air or oxygen, peroxides of the Me_2O_2 or MeO_2 type are formed. The peroxides of the heavier alkali metals are stable even at higher temperatures and they are formed by the combustion of the metals in air. The peroxides, however, are unstable when in contact with alkali metals. The physical properties of the stable alkali oxides are listed in Table III. The solid oxide in equilibrium with the solution of oxygen in the liquid metal is Me_2O. The suboxides of rubidium or cesium may also be transformed into Rb_2O resp. Cs_2O at higher temperatures.

Table III. Properties of alkali oxides

Oxide	Molec. Weight	Structure	Lattice Constant (nm)	Density ($g \cdot cm^{-3}$)	Melting Point (°C)
Li_2O	29.88	cub., CaF_2	0.462	2.013	> 1700
Na_2O	61.98	cub., CaF_2	0.555	2.27	1275 (subl.)
K_2O	94.20	cub., CaF_2	0.644	2.32	350
Rb_2O	186.94	cub., CaF_2	0.674	3.72	400
Cs_2O	281.81	rh., $CdCl_2$	0.675	4.25	490 (N_2 atmosph.)

The solubility of lithium oxide Li_2O in liquid lithium was recently determined by fast neutron activation analysis after sampling oxide-saturated lithium samples in the temperature range from 195 to 734 °C [7)]. The results can be expressed by the saturation Eq. (1).

$$\log c_s^{Li_2O}\,(\text{wppm}) = 6.992 - \frac{2896}{T\,(K)} \tag{1}$$

The enthalpy of solution of the oxide in liquid lithium calculated from the slope of the solubility curve is $\Delta H_{sol} = 55.6\ kJ \cdot mol^{-1}$. The results of this most recent study differ from earlier studies, which may is influenced by the fact that the solid oxide precipitates as a very fine and stable dispersion, making filtering techniques difficult.

Two publications summarize the numerous data on the solubility of sodium oxide in sodium [8,9)]. The latter, which refers to more recently generated data, gives a saturation Eq. (2).

$$\log c_s^{Na_2O}\,(\text{wppm}) = 6.2571 - \frac{2444.5}{T\,(K)} \tag{2}$$

The heat of solution corresponding to Eq. (2) is $\Delta H_{sol} = 46.8\ kJ \cdot mol^{-1}$. Equation (2) is the result of the data selection from twelve data sets, including data obtained by the improved distillation technique to determine oxygen in sodium. The agreement of Eq. (2) with the older one [8)] and even with the results of measurements with electrochemical oxygen meters [10)] and with the vanadium wire equilibration method [11)] is satisfying.

Only one saturation curve of oxygen in potassium has been published so far [12)].

However, these data have been generated at a time, when accurate methods to estimate oxygen in alkali metals have not been available. In a very recent study, oxygen saturation concentrations in the temperature range 70 to 200 °C have been measured in purified potassium applying the distillation method [13]. The results best fit Eq. (3).

$$\log c_s^{K_2O}\,(\text{wppm}) = 4.086 - \frac{767.3}{T\,(K)} \qquad (3)$$

The heat of solution $\Delta H_{sol} = 14.7\ \text{kJ} \cdot \text{mol}^{-1}$ deduced from this equation is much lower than for lithium and sodium oxide solutions.

Compared to the light alkali metals, rubidium and cesium can dissolve large amounts of their oxides, as can be seen from the phase diagrams in Fig. 1. These diagrams indicate that at low temperatures suboxides such as Rb_3O [14] or Cs_7O, Cs_4O, and Cs_3O [15] are also existent in dilute solutions in the metals. At temperatures above the 50 °C limit for rubidium and 160 °C for cesium the Me_2O type oxide should be the only stable one. In the region of stability of Me_2O, the saturation concentration of rubidium oxide in molten rubidium can be expressed by

$$\log c_s^{Rb_2O}\,(\text{at-\%}) = 1.5753 - \frac{93.15}{T\,(K)} \qquad (4)$$

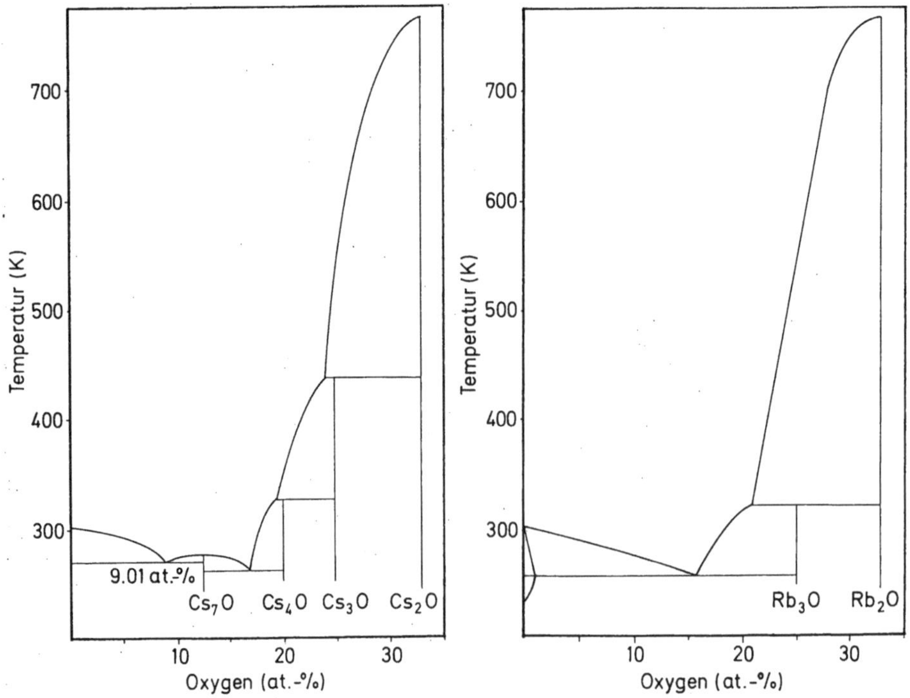

Fig. 1. Cesium-oxygen and rubidium-oxygen phase diagrammes, taken from Ref. [14, 15]

In the cesium-oxygen system, the saturation concentration-temperature relationship can be expressed by

$$\log c_s^{Cs_2O} \text{ (at-\%)} = 1.6188 - \frac{114.8}{T\,(K)} \tag{5}$$

The free enthalpy of formation ΔF_T depends on the temperature of the reaction according to Eq. (6). The constants of the solubility Eq. (1)–(5) and of the Eq. (6) for

$$\Delta F_T = -P + Q \cdot T \tag{6}$$

the alkali oxides and their solutions in the metals are listed in Table IV. It is obvious that the lithium oxide is the most stable one, which can be seen from the high value of P. The enthalpy of solution is high in the Li—O and Na—O systems and very low in the Rb—O and Cs—O systems, while the value of ΔH_{sol} of the K—O system is between the two groups.

Table IV. Thermochemistry and solution of alkali oxides in alkali metals

System	Saturation curve (wppm)		Saturation curve (at-%)		ΔH_{sol} (kJ · mol^{-1}	ΔF_T	
	A	B	A	B		P	Q
Li_2O/Li	6.992	2896	—	—	55.6	−606115	139.8
Na_2O/Na	6.2571	2444.5	—	—	46.8	−405763	128.9
K_2O/K	4.086	767.3	—	—	14.7	−360391	137.4
Rb_2O/Rb	—	—	1.5753	93.15	0.9	−334631	148.8
Cs_2O/Cs	—	—	1.6188	114.8	2.2	−321865	167.1

Analytical methods applied to estimate oxygen in alkali metals are the fast neutron activation [7] for lithium oxide in lithium, vacuum distillation of excess alkali metal and analysis of the residue by atomic absorption spectrometry [16] to estimate oxygen in sodium, as well as in the heavier alkali metals. Equilibration of oxygen between getters such as vanadium, liquid alkali metals [11] and solid electrolyte oxygen meters, can be applied in several alkali metals. They measure oxygen activities directly in alkali metal circuits or closed containers.

2.2 Reactions of Alkali Oxides Dissolved in the Liquid Metals

Alkali oxides dissolved in molten alkali metals are able to react with solid metals in several ways. The simple exchange of oxygen between the liquid and solid metals sometimes oxidizes the solid metal under formation of a stable surface oxide, which has a protective character and reduces the reaction rate. The kinetics of this type of reaction follow a parabolic rate law. Diffusion of oxygen or metal ions through the slowly growing oxide layer is the rate determining step. An example of this type of reaction is the oxidation of zirconium in liquid sodium at temperatures above 500 °C [17]. The oxygen exchange between alkali metals and solid alloys can also cause the phenomena and kinetics of internal oxidation. Such corrosion effects have been observed when vanadium alloys containing titanium have been exposed to liquid sodium [18]. The internal oxidation layers contain precipitated oxide (Ti, V)O. Some oxygen, however, is also dissolved in the matrix on interstitial positions, and such layers preceed the internal oxidation zones [18].

The oxygen exchange is also able to result in a deoxidation of the solid metal. Vanadium containing 1400 wppm oxygen loses a large portion of the interstitial element, as is shown in Fig. 2, due to the reaction with liquid lithium [19]. The leaching of oxygen causes the formation of cavities at grain boundaries. The cavities are formed at the positions of the oxide precipitated in the alloy before exposure to the alkali metal. The effect is suppressed by alloying the vanadium with small amounts of titanium, which forms more stable oxides at the grain boundaries.

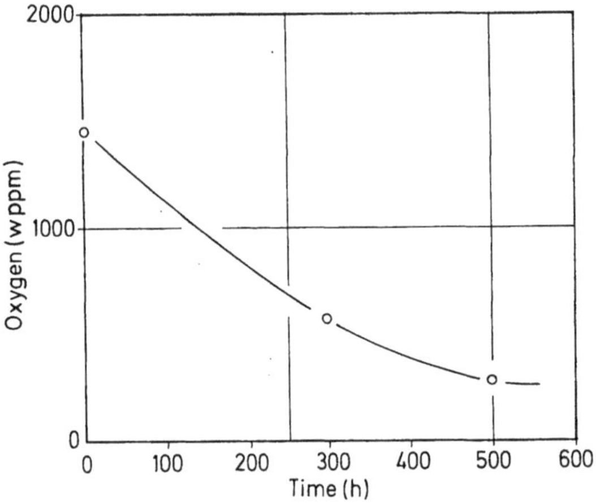

Fig. 2. Leaching of oxygen out of vanadium by lithium at 700 °C as a function of the exposure time [19]

The typical behaviour of metals in oxygen containing alkali metals is influenced by the alkali oxides, which are able to form very stable complex oxides with the reacting metals. The best known reaction of this type is the formation of sodium chromite $Na_2Cr_2O_4$ by the oxidation of chromium metal in liquid sodium containing oxygen. The hexagonal compound was identified by X-ray diffraction [20]. The standard free enthalpy of formation of the $Na_2Cr_2O_4$ from its constituent oxides has been measured directly by applying electrochemical oxygen meters:

$$\Delta H^0_{298} = -101.4 \pm 1.0 \text{ kJ} \cdot \text{mol}^{-1}$$ [21]

The oxygen meter measurements allow for the definition of a threshold value of the oxygen activity. The complex oxide is (only) stable and can be formed at activities above this threshold value. The threshold for the formation of sodium chromite is at relatively low oxygen concentrations in sodium, for instance about 5 wppm at 550 °C [22]. The results of such measurements [23] have been used to establish a diagram of the stability of the compound in sodium as a function of temperature and oxygen concentration or chemical activity, as is shown in Fig. 3.

The sodium-oxygen-iron system influences the compatibility of iron based materials with liquid sodium. There is some evidence that oxygen contents in sodium raise the solubility of iron, although the formation of complex oxides could not be observed under the conditions of the solubility tests [24]. However, the formation of a dark brown oxide Na_4FeO_3 was observed [25] after reactions of iron in sodium containing more than 0.1 wt-% oxygen at 600 °C.

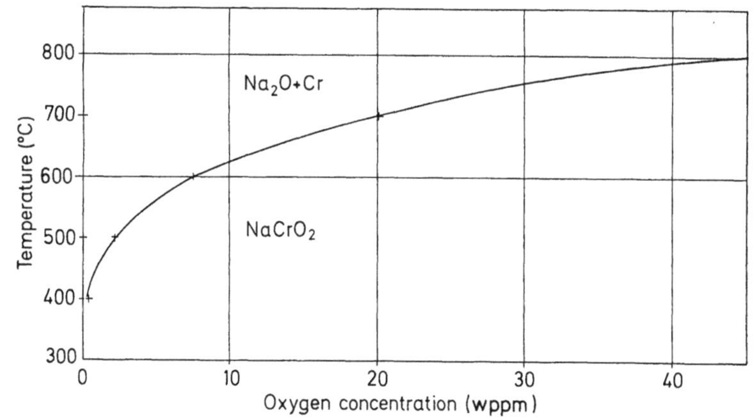

Fig. 3. Range of stability of sodium chromite in respect to temperature and oxygen concentration in sodium [23]

The free enthalpy of formation of this sodium iron double oxide was estimated to be $\Delta H = -9.2\ kJ \cdot mol^{-1}$ at 600 °V. This low value indicates that the compound can only be formed in an oxygen solution in sodium, the chemical activity of which is close to unity. The standard free enthalpy of combination of the constituent oxides was measured by solution calorimetry:

$$\Delta H^0_{298} = -104.9 \pm 2.3\ kJ \cdot mol^{-1}$$ [26]

Similar products can be formed by reactions of liquid sodium with solid oxides, and some of these reactions are of technical importance. The failure of fuel element canning tubes causes the contact of uranium dioxide fuel with liquid sodium at high temperatures. The stoichiometric UO_2 does not react with sodium at temperatures of 400 and 600 °C due to its very high thermodynamic stability. Non-stoichiometric compounds, however, which may contain some UO_3 or U_3O_8, are able to react. In this case, the sodium uranate-V, Na_3UO_4, is formed, a face-centered cubic cell with $a = 0.474$ nm [27]. The same product is formed at temperatures above 550 °C by the reaction

$$2\,Na_2O + UO_2 \rightleftarrows Na_3UO_4 + Na \quad (7)$$

It seems that the species MO^{n-} is relatively stable when in contact with liquid alkali metals. The latter reaction is of importance for the fast breeder reactor chemistry, since sodium normally contains enough oxide to promote this reaction. The reaction (7) occurs even at low oxygen concentrations in the region from 0.1 to 10 wppm depending on the reaction temperature [28]. This can be observed by means of the electrochemical oxygen meters.

The same type of reactions occur inside the fuel elements of nuclear reactors, where the two alkali metals rubidium and cesium are present as fission products. For instance, in the cesium-uranium-oxygen system two compounds, namely Cs_2UO_4 or $Cs_2U_4O_{12}$, are existent. In contact with liquid cesium, only Cs_2UO_4 is stable. In case of absence of cesium metal in the reaction mixture, the other uranate can also be formed [29].

The relatively high oxygen potentials in the heavy alkali metals, rubidium and cesium, cause the formation of several complex oxides, in which the relationships of alkali to heavy metal oxides are larger than in sodium chromite. In solutions with relatively high amounts of dissolved oxide even ortho-oxometallate can be formed. Different chromates or ferrates are formed in liquid rubidium containing different high oxygen levels, as is shown in Fig. 4 [30]. These compounds dissolved in the liquid alkali metal cause the same oxygen potentials as have been observed during the forming reactions measured by means of electrochemical oxygen meters.

Oxygen dissolved in liquid alkali metals also reacts with other non-metals, which may be present in the solutions. Hydroxides are formed with dissolved hydrogen. Carbonate is one of the reaction products formed in solutions containing oxygen and carbon.

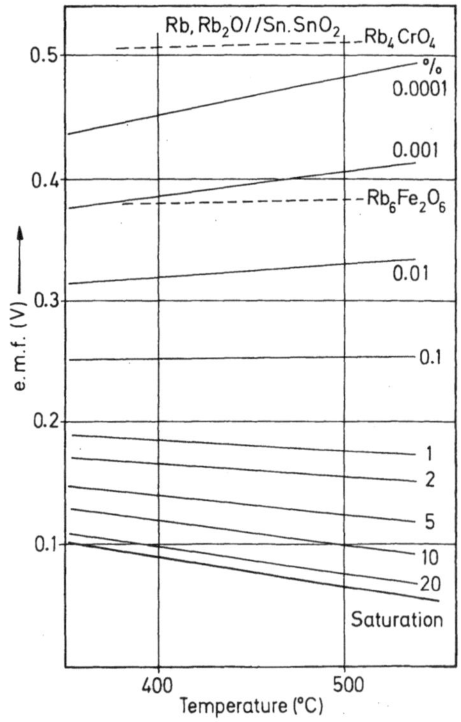

Fig. 4. Formation of different rubidium-oxochromates and ferrates at different oxygen activities and temperatures [3]

Lithium hydroxide cannot coexist with lithium metal as is shown in a thermochemical study [31]. Only oxide and hydride are stable in presence of the metal at any temperature and partial pressure of oxygen and hydrogen. In the sodium-oxygen-hydrogen system, hydroxide is stable at temperatures above 500 °C at high partial pressure of oxygen, as well as of hydrogen, as is shown in Fig. 5 [32]. Experimental studies have confirmed the thermochemical predictions. The reaction of sodium with sodium hydroxide leads to a fourphase equilibrium above 412 °C [33]. while only oxide and hydride are existent at lower temperatures.

$$Na(l) + NaOH(l) \underset{\text{heating}}{\overset{\text{cooling}}{\rightleftarrows}} Na_2O(s) + NaH(s) \qquad (8)$$

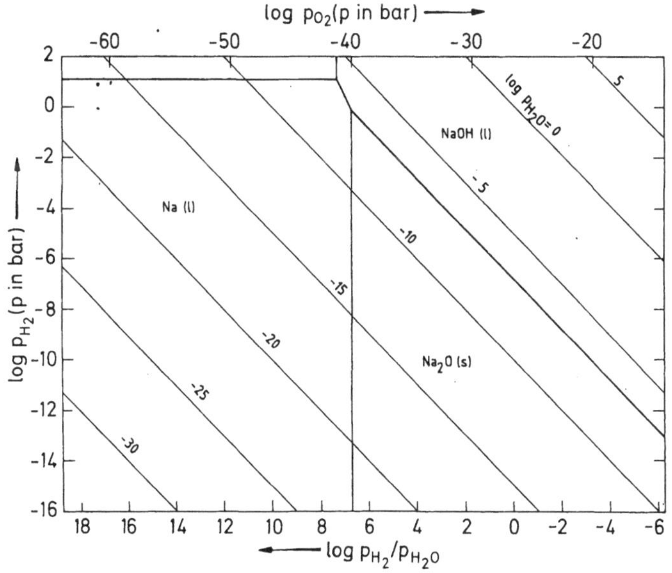

Fig. 5. Thermochemical data for the phases existent in the Na—O—H system at 800 K (527 °C) [32]

The dissociation of sodium hydroxide in liquid sodium can be observed when the oxygen und hydrogen chemical activities are measured by means of electrochemical probes. The hydroxide seems to be metastable at a low temperature, since a saturation concentration of this compound has been measured in liquid sodium.

The results of thermochemical studies of the potassium-oxygen-hydrogen system indicate that alkali hydroxides become more stable with increasing atomic weight of the alkali atom. Most recent calculations of the stability ranges of condensed phases in this system have shown that the potassium hydroxide can exist in contact with the liquid metal from its melting point to its boiling temperature, if the partial pressures of oxygen and hydrogen are high enough [34]. The range of its stability grows with increasing temperature as shown in Fig. 6, which demonstrates the differences between the systems Na—O—H and K—O—H. If this tendency were to continue, the rubidium and cesium hydroxides should also be stable in contact with the liquid metals. The relatively high chemical stability of potassium hydroxide may have influenced the early studies of the solubility of oxygen in metal. The early measurements have resulted in values of the saturation concentrations one order of magnitude higher than the values gained most recently.

It is also reported that oxygen contents in sodium influence the solubility of carbon in the molten metal. Measurements in the sodium-sodium carbonate system have resulted in an equation valid in the temperature range from 150 to 400 °C [35]:

$$\log c_s^{Na_2CO_3}\,(\text{wppm}) = 2.2496 - \frac{364.9}{T\,(K)} \tag{9}$$

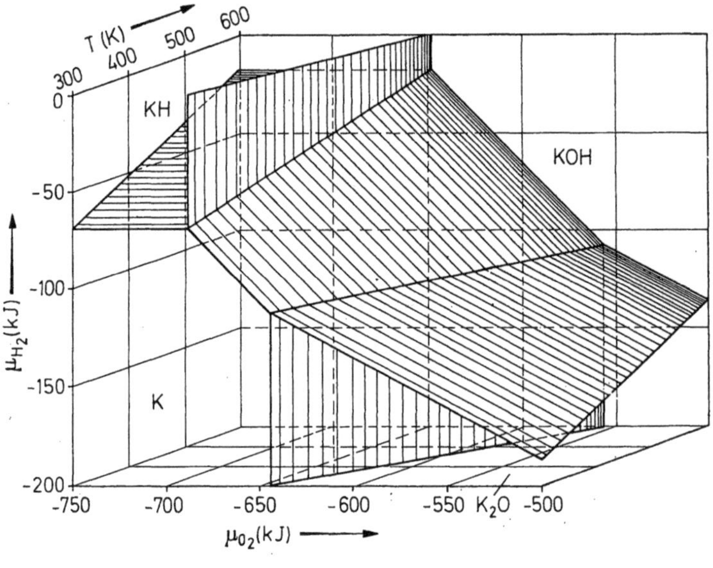

Fig. 6. The system potassium-oxygen-hydrogen as a function of the chemical potentials of oxygen and hydrogen and of the temperature [34]

The slope of this solubility relationship over the reciprocal temperature indicates a very low value of the free enthalpy of dissolution ($\Delta H_{sol} = 7.0$ kJ · mol^{-1}), which is not comparable to the solution of other non-metallic compounds in alkali metals. Indeed, thermochemical analyses of the Na—O—C system show an analogical behaviour to the Na—O—H system [36]. Sodium carbonate is chemically stable when in contact with liquid metal at high temperatures and high potentials of oxygen, as well as of carbon, (in the system) as can be seen from Fig. 7. The metastable carbonate decomposes at lower temperatures to form sodium oxides and carbon dissolved in liquid sodium. Information on the reactions of carbonates of other alkali metals with the molten metals is not available.

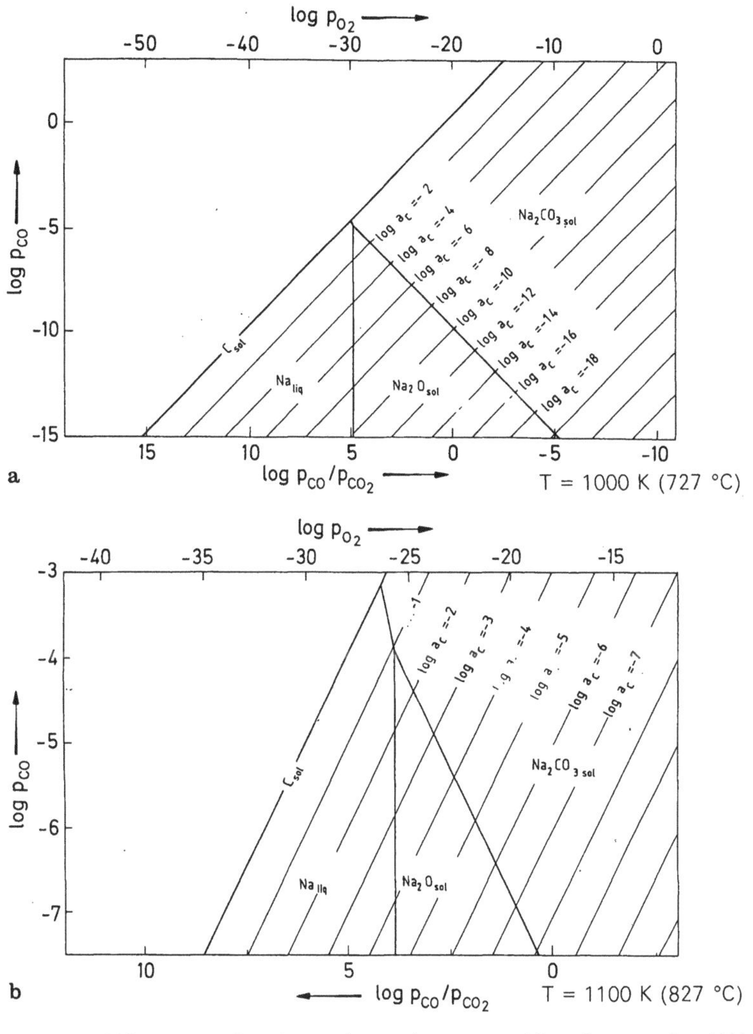

Fig. 7. Stability ranges of sodium carbonate in contact with sodium metal at 1000 and 1100 K [36]

3 Alkali Metals-Carbon Systems

The carbon potentials in liquid alkali metals are important in material compatibility problems. Carbon as a minor component of several materials of technical importance strongly influences the strength and ductility of the materials. The alkali metals have the ability to wet the surfaces of metals or alloys. In this state they tend to exchange carbon until they reach the chemical equilibrium. The carbon exchange between sodium and austenitic chromium nickel steels is extensively studied. As is shown in Fig. 8, in which the chemical activities of carbon in sodium and in the Cr18-Ni9 steel are compared as functions of temperature [37], sodium containing 0.1 wppm carbon decarburizes an austenitic steel with a carbon content of 0.05 w-% carbon at a temperature of 650 °C and carburizes the same steel at 550 °C.

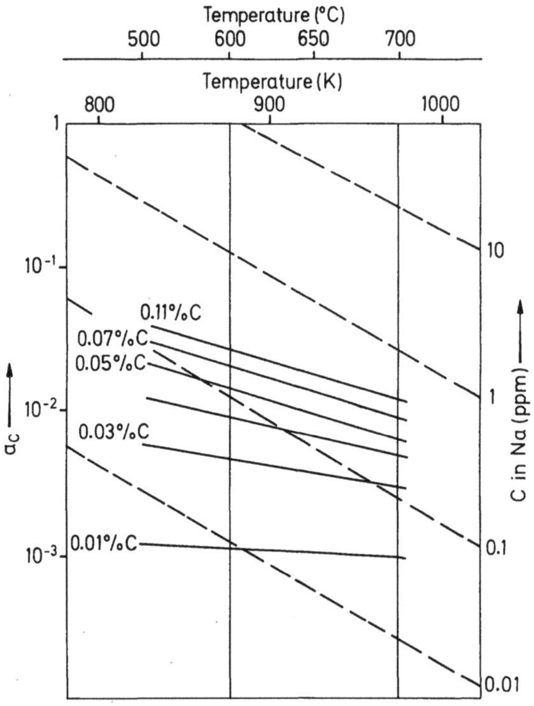

Fig. 8. Activity of carbon in Cr18-Ni9 steel and in sodium (dotted lines) as a function of temperature and concentration [37]

Such carbon exchange can be observed between alkali metals and ferritic or austenitic steels as well as alloys based on vanadium, niobium, or other refractory alloys. Carbon dissolved in alkali metals also has the ability to react with other dissolved nonmetallic elements. In some cases, rather surprising reaction products have been observed.

3.1 Alkali-Carbon Compounds

The light alkali metals form compounds of the acetylide type Me_2C_2. The product of the reaction of carbon with lithium metal is lithium acetylide Li_2C_2, which evolves acetylene gas by hydrolysis [38]. Lithium acetylide crystallizes at room temperature in the primitive monoclinic structure with a = 0.78 nm, b = 0.88 nm, c = 1.09 nm and $\beta = 76.8 \pm 0.1°$, 19 molecules of Li_2C_2 belonging to one unit cell [39]. The acetylide is stable up to 800 °C in contact with the liquid metal and with graphite. The free energy of formation of Li_2C_2 as measured by means of electrochemical methods at 600 °C has a value of $\Delta G_{873} = -89$ kJ · mol^{-1}, thus indicating the stability of this compound.

The structure of the white crystalline compounds Na_2C_2 and K_2C_2, which can be obtained by thermal decomposition of the $MeHC_2$ compounds in vacuo, has been determined by X-ray powder diffraction. The acetylides have a similar tetragonal structure as the peroxide K_2O_2 [40]. Sodium acetylide is less stable than the lithium compound, the free enthalpy of formation has been reported as $\Delta G_{298} = -21.0$ kJ

$\cdot$ mol^{-1}. However, the solvation energy of the sodium acetylide in the molten metal is high enough to stabilize it even at an elevated temperature in dilute solutions. Potassium acetylide should still be less stable. A value of the free enthalpy of formation has not yet been published. The heavy alkali metals, rubidium and cesium, do not seem to form stable acetylides.

Acetylides of lithium and sodium evolve acetylene gas when the solutions are treated with cold water. The absorption of acetylene by liquid lithium results in the formation of acetylide and hydride:

$$4\,Li + C_2H_2 \rightleftarrows Li_2C_2 + 2\,LiH \qquad (10)$$

Graphite reacts with alkali metals forming lamellar graphite compounds C_xMe, in which alkali metals are taken up into the graphite lattice. The structure of these compounds has been studied by Rüdorff and Schulze [41]. The reactions of the heavier alkali metals with powdered graphite at temperatures above 400 °C cause a penetration by alkali metals between the graphite layers, thus expanding the graphite lattice. Considerable amounts of alkali metals can be taken up into the structure of these compounds. The existence of stoichiometric compounds with carbon/alkali atomic ratios of 8, 16, 24, 36, 48, and 60 has been shown for the metals potassium, rubidium, and cesium.

Sodium is also able to form such compounds with the approximate formula $C_{64}Na$ [42]. The compounds with the highest alkali content (i.e. C_8Me) decompose under vacuum at elevated temperatures to yield alkali metal vapour and compounds with a higher carbon/alkali metal ratio according to Eq. (11).

$$3\,C_8K \rightarrow C_{24}K + 2\,K \qquad (11)$$

Graphite compounds of rubidium and cesium seem to be more stable and to be formed easily. This is of technical importance since the absorption of the fission elements rubidium and cesium by graphite immersed in liquid sodium will be applied to remove them from the sodium coolant of a fast neutron reactor [43]. The formation of a lithium compound of this type has never been observed.

3.2 Solutions of Alkali-Carbon Compounds in the Molten Metals

Solubilities of carbon in alkali metals can be expressed by the same type of equations as formulated for the Me–O systems, in spite of the fact that the compounds are less stable. The solubility of lithium acetylide in lithium determined first by Fedorov and Su [38] by means of a X-ray diffraction method has been recently revised [44]. In this study, the acetylene evolution method has been applied. The saturation Eq. (12) is based on this most recent study.

$$\log c^{C}_{s(Li)}\,(\text{wppm}) = 5.9894 - \frac{2645.5}{T\,(K)} \qquad (12)$$

The level of saturation concentrations represented by Eq. (12) is much lower than expected from older work. A comparison of the two saturation lines is shown in Fig. 9.

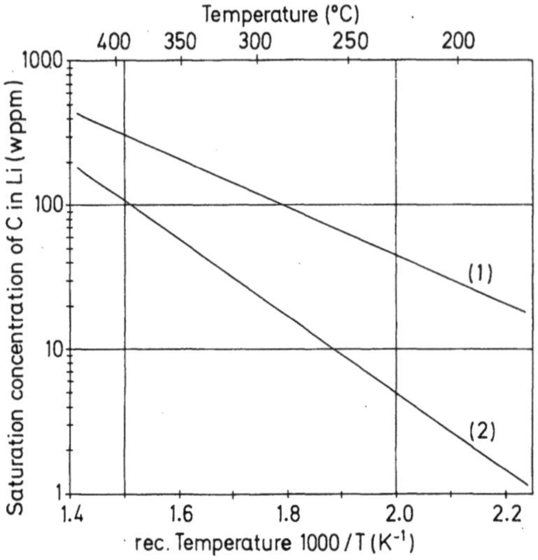

Fig. 9. Saturation concentrations of Li_2C_2 in liquid lithium, (1) after Fedorov and Su [38], (2) after Yonco et al. [45]

The discrepancies might be caused by analytical problems as well as by problems of proper handling of the alkali metal.

The results of the most recent measurements of the solubility of carbon in sodium show a better agreement. Some earlier studies have also contributed widely scattered results. The values of saturation concentrations determined by Ainsley et al. [46] and by Longson and Thorley [47] can be expressed by Eq. (13).

$$\log c^{C}_{s(Na)}\,(\text{wppm}) = 7.646 - \frac{5970}{T\,(K)} \tag{13}$$

These data consist with measurements of carbon concentrations and chemical activities with different types of diffusion or electrochemical carbon meters and with the data on the carbon exchange between sodium and stainless steel.

Saturation concentration values of carbon in heavy alkali metals are not yet available. The solubility of carbon in liquid cesium was estimated at two temperatures. The reported data do not seem to be sufficient for the establishment of a saturation curve. Carbon compounds like carbonates or cyanides in contact with liquid alkali metals tend to decompose.

Analytical methods to determine carbon in the light alkali metals have to be highly sensitive, as there are only very low concentrations present in the molten metals. Therefore, monitoring of the chemical activities of carbon seems to be more favourable than the classical analysis of combustion and determination of the carbon dioxid evolved. This method is based on an analytical vacuum distillation of the dissolving alkali metal samples collected in alumina crucibles. The sensitivity of the method is not sufficient to estimate the carbon contents in unsaturated solutions of carbon in lithium or sodium. The hydrolysis and evolution of acetylene has also been applied for the estimation of the lithium acetylide contents. This method may be disturbed by side reactions, which occur in the presence of higher amounts of nitrogen.

Equilibration methods based on the exchange of carbon between alkali metals and several solid alloys are established to estimate carbon activities in alkali metals. The solid alloys are inserted into the molten metals as foils. These foils – stainless steel, iron-nickel, or iron-manganese alloys – are exposed to liquid alkali metals at temperatures above 650 °C for 200 to 500 hours and then analysed by means of the combustion analysis. Conclusions can be drawn in respect to the carbon activity in the alkali metal in chemical equilibrium with the foil material based on the known relationship of concentration and chemical activity of carbon in the solid alloys.

The carbon monitors applied for the determination of carbon activities in lithium or sodium apply diffusion cells. Carbon dissolved in alkali metals contacting the probes diffuses through the probe wall, a thin tube wall of pure iron. The diffusing carbon in consumed by chemical reactions in the probe:

$$C + FeO \rightleftarrows Fe + CO \qquad (14)$$

The carbon monoxide gas is carried by the carrier gas passing the probe to a gas analyzing unit, which continuously measures the carbon content of the gas. The carbon monoxide is converted by catalytical hydriding to form methane, which is then determined by means of a flame ionization detector. This principle is applied in the Harwell carbon meter [48]. At 550 °C the sensitivity of such a probe allows the detection of a chemical activity of carbon in sodium in the level of $a_c = 10^{-3}$. This activity corresponds to a concentration of about 10^{-2} wppm carbon in sodium.

Carbon activities in alkali metals are also estimated by electrochemical meters. These are based on the activity differences between two carbon bearing electrodes separated by a carbon ions conducting electrolyte. The electrolyte is a molten salt mixture, consisting of the eutectic of lithium and sodium carbonate, melting at approximately 500 °C. The molten salt mixture has to be kept free from any impurities or humidity. The mixture, acting as liquid electrolyte is kept in an iron cup. The iron wall is in contact with both the liquid electrolyte and the liquid metal. Thus, it exchanges carbon with both up to the equilibrium. Iron, with the same carbon potential as the liquid metal, acts as one electrode. The reference electrode of graphite or any other material with a well defined and stable carbon activity is immersed in the molten electrolyte. The Nernst equation defines the potential of the electrochemical chain:

$$E = \frac{R \cdot T}{n \cdot F} \cdot \ln \frac{a_C^{Me}}{a_C^{ref}} \qquad (15)$$

In this equation, R is the gas constant, T the temperature in (K), F the Faraday constant and n the number of electrons involved. The logarithmic term relates the chemical activities of the two electrodes. The electrochemical cells are not yet developed to a technical state, which allows their application as analytical instruments in reactors or plants. They are, however, already successfully applied in laboratories [49].

3.3 Reactions of Carbon in Alkali Metals with Non-Metals

Carbon dissolved in alkali metals reacts with other non-metals present in the solutions. The solution of lithium acetylide in the molten metal reacts with nitrogen to form dilithium cyanamide, Li_2NCN [50], at elevated temperatures. The cyanamide is a stable compound in contact with lithium metal, it can be isolated by vacuum distillation of the excess metal. The reaction is expressed by the equation

$$Li_2C_2 + 4\,Li_3N \rightarrow 2\,Li_2NCN + 10\,Li \quad (16)$$

The product of the reaction of carbon dissolved in liquid sodium with nitrogen is sodium cyanide. The difference between the reaction products in the two alkali metals might be due to the different solubility of nitrogen and the different chemical stability of the nitrides formed in solution [50].

Carbon and carbon compounds react with hydrogen to form methane when dissolved in liquid sodium [51]. The reaction occurs at temperatures between 300 and 500 °C. The dissolved sodium acetylide has the highest reactivity of the carbon compounds and is able to form methane at the lower limit of the temperature range. Carbonate and cyanide require higher temperatures to react with hydrogen introduced into the mixture as a gas. It is also shown that reactions of natural coal and hydrogen also form the compound with the highest hydrogen content possible, which is methane [52]. Thus, the hydriding of natural coal takes place at unusually low temperatures in liquid sodium, which acts as a solvent for the reacting elements as well as a catalyst. The reaction with hydrogen is applicable to decarburize the alkali metals.

3.4 Reactions of Carbon in Alkali Metals with Metallic Elements

Reactions of carbon in alkali metals with carbide forming metallic elements are the driving processes of the carburization of stainless steels. The direction of the carbon exchange between the molten metals and the solid metallic materials depends on the carbon potential in the liquid metals and on the free energy of formation of the metal carbides and the chemical activity of the metallic element in the solid phase.

Chromium carbide is among the compounds detected as precipitating the low temperature regions of liquid metal circuits, and the system Na—Cr—C is one of the most intensively studied systems [53]. There is some evidence that the most stable chromium carbide $Cr_{23}C_6$ is formed at temperatures between 550 and 700 °C even in stainless steels, where the chemical activity of chromium is well below unity. This reaction is the chemical process causing the carburization of austenitic CrNi steels. $Cr_{23}C_6$ precipitates in the surface zones of the material.

Vanadium also forms a very stable carbide VC, and carburization of this metal is part of the corrosion reactions of vanadium based alloys contacted with liquid lithium as well as sodium. Vanadium alloys with contents of titanium have an even higher affinity to form solid carbides by absorbing of carbon from liquid metals. In systems in which vanadium titanium alloys and stainless steels are in contact with the same lithium or sodium, carbon migrates from the steel to the refractory metal alloy, thus passing the alkali metal serving as a transport medium [54,55]. The free energies of formation of the alkali acetylides are compared with the values of several metal carbides in Table V.

Austenitic steels containing titanium or niobium as stabilizing elements tend to absorb carbon from sodium [56], and they withstand decarburization by liquid lithium, thus suppressing a carbon transfer, which might be caused by the presence of vanadium based alloys.

Table V. Free energies of formation of some carbides [57]

Compound	Free energy of formation ($cal \cdot mol^{-1}$)
1/2 Li_2C_2	$-7800 + 7.1 \cdot T$ (K)
1/2 Na_2C_2	$-5290 + 6.28 \cdot T$ (K)
1/6 $Cr_{23}C_6$	$-16450 + 1.38 \cdot T$ (K)
V_2C	$-35200 + 1.1 \cdot T$ (K)
TiC	$-43700 + 2.25 \cdot T$ (K)
Nb_2C	$-46000 + 1.0 \cdot T$ (K)

4 Alkali Metals-Nitrogen Systems

Nitrogen is, similar to carbon, a minor alloying element in several technical materials. In austenitic stainless steels additions of nitrogen serve to strengthen the material or to improve the stability of the austenitic phase. Nitrogen contents are also applied to improve the mechanical strength of refractory alloys. On the other hand, the ductility of the materials is also influenced by nitrogen contents. Very high nitrogen concentrations cause brittleness of the materials, thus nitriding reactions by the exchange of the element between liquid alkali metals and solid alloys cause the formation of a more or less brittle surface zone. The embrittling is part of the material corrosion by alkali metals.

Nitrogen contents in molten lithium give rise to enhanced corrosion of iron based alloys due to the formation of complex nitrides stabilized by high chemical activities of nitrogen. Such souble nitrides are more or less soluble in the alkali metal and do not form protecting layers.

4.1 Alkali Metals-Nitrogen Compounds

The only compound formed by alkali metals and nitrogen being stable in contact with the liquid metal is lithium nitride, Li_3N. This compound is formed by an exothermal reaction of elemental nitrogen with lithium metal [58]. The nitride can be considered to have a typical iónic structure, N^{3-} being coordinated by 8 Li^+ ions in a regular way. Li_3N has a hexagonal structure with a = 0.365 nm, c = 0.387 nm, Z = 1 and the space group P6/mmm [59].

The very stable lithium nitride melts in a nitrogen atmosphere at 813 ± 1 °C and has a considerably high solubility in the liquid metal as indicated by the $Li-Li_3N$ phase diagram in Fig. 10 [60].

The solubility equation according to Ref. [58] is established by chemical analyses based on a micro Kjeldahl method. Its agreement with results of electrical resistivity measurements of saturated solutions in lithium [61] is excellent.

$$\log c_{s(Li)}^{N}\,(\mathrm{wppm}) = 7.597 - \frac{2098.5}{T\,(K)} \tag{17}$$

The standard free enthalpy of formation to the compound as estimated from dissolution and thermal decomposition studies [58] is

$$\Delta G^0\,(\mathrm{cal}) = -39100 + 32.2 \cdot T\,(K) \tag{18}$$

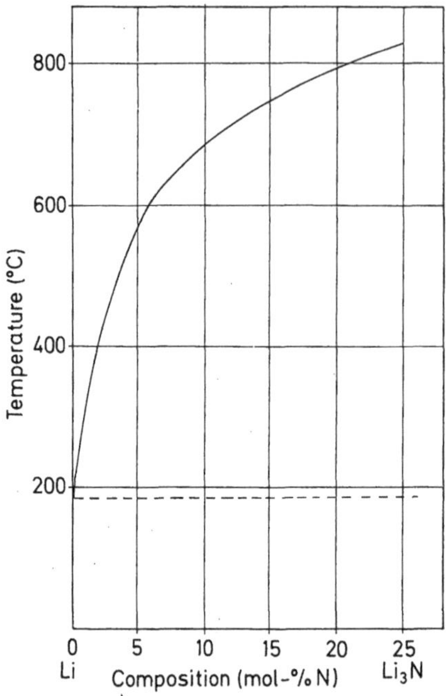

Fig. 10. The lithium-lithium nitride phase diagram [60]

The formation of Li_3N has also been observed as the product of the reaction of ammonia with the metal [61]:

$$6\,Li + NH_3 \rightarrow Li_3N + 3\,LiH \qquad (19)$$

Dissolution of lithium containing dissolved Li_3N in water, on the other hand, evolves ammonia as the product of the hydrolysis.

The nitride does not occur in the sodium nitrogen system, and the miscibility of the two elements is very poor. In the very dilute solutions of nitrogen in liquid sodium, the non-metal seems to be present in the elemental form. The solution behavior of N_2-molecules is similar to that of argon atoms.

The nitride Na_3N as a metastable compound is formed only under the influence of an electrical discharge. The formation of nitrides of the other alkali metals potassium, rubidium, or cesium has never been reported.

4.2 Reactions of Nitrogen in Alkali Metals

As already pointed out in Section 3.3 the N^{3+} ion, which is dissolved in liquid lithium, has a considerable reactivity to form compounds with non-metallic elements. Such reactions occur with dissolved carbon as well as in lithium as in sodium.

The nitrogen exchange between lithium and several transition metals gives rise to the formation of binary or ternary nitrides, which show analogies with the ternary oxides formed in Na—O—Me systems [62]. In the lithium-nitrogen-stainless steel system, nitrogen is picked-up by the stainless steel due to the getter reaction of the chromium present in the steel. The free enthalpies of formation of chromium nitrides are comparable with the potentials of lithium nitride in dilute solution in the metal as can be seen in Fig. 11. X-ray patterns of the reaction product formed on the steel surfaces indicate that a ternary nitride, probably of the formula Li_9CrN_5 should be the compound formed in this reaction. Table VI gives a survey on corrosion products, which are observed on several metals or alloys exposed to liquid lithium containing lithium nitride.

Even in cases in which we do not observe ternary nitrides among the corrosion products, such somponents are existent in solutions with high nitrogen potentials. Ternary nitrides, which can be formed under those conditions are Li_5TiN_3 [63] and Li_7NbN_4 [64].

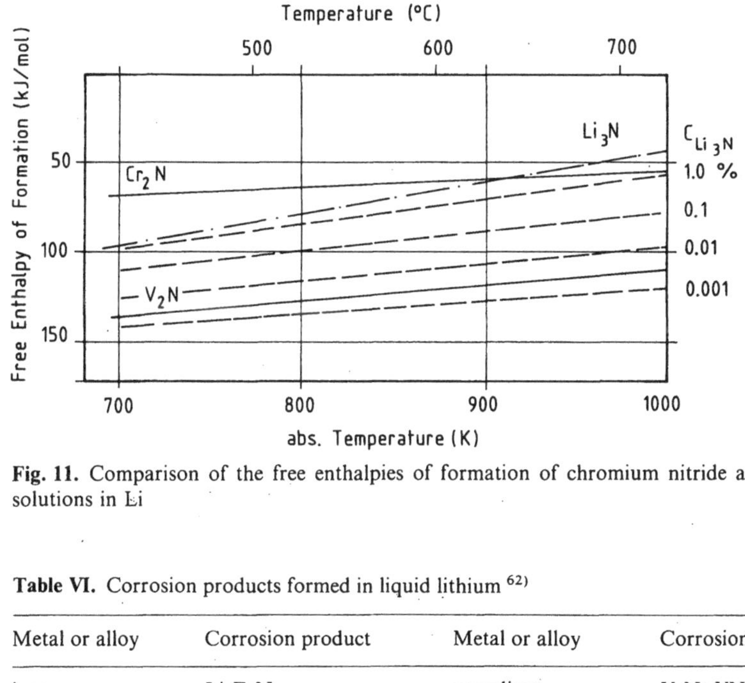

Fig. 11. Comparison of the free enthalpies of formation of chromium nitride and Li_3N in dilute solutions in Li

Table VI. Corrosion products formed in liquid lithium [62]

Metal or alloy	Corrosion product	Metal or alloy	Corrosion product
iron	Li_3FeN_2	vanadium	V_3N; VN; Li_7VN_4
chromium	Li_9CrN_5	titanium	Ti_2N
nickel	dissolution	niobium	Nb_2N
stainless steel	Li_9CrN_5	zirconium	Li_7ZrN_2; ZrN

A chromium nitride, CrN, was found on stainless steel surfaces as the reaction product, when stainless steel was contacted with sodium containing high amounts of nitrogen at 700 °C. Chemical analysis revealed the composition of the precipitated phase as Cr_2N. X-ray diffraction showed, however, that two phases, chromium nitride CrN and chromium metal were present. Probably, Cr_2N may have been formed as the first product of the nitriding. It seems to be metastable and to decompose during the cooling of the sodium containing tubes [66].

5 Alkali Metals-Hydrogen Systems

Solutions of hydrogen and its isotopes deuterium and tritium are important for technical application of alkali metals. The lithium-tritium system is of concern in fusion technology, since tritium serves as the nuclear fuel. Hydrogen chemistry is related to safety problems in fast breeder reactors applying sodium as a coolant. Increasing hydrogen concentration in the sodium of the secondary circuit indicates leakages in the steam generators. The early detection of water leakages by means of highly sensitive hydrogen analyses helps to improve the safety and reliability of reactors of this type.

Hydrogen present in alkali metals is reactive. It may cause harmful corrosion reactions with several structural materials. Brittleness is caused by penetration with hydrogen, and decarburization caused by the formation of methane weakens the materials. Several other non-metals react with hydrogen dissolved in alkali metals. Such solutions may even be applied as process fluids for hydriding reactions.

5.1 Alkali Hydrides

Direct reactions of liquid alkali metals with gaseous hydrogen at temperatures above 300 °C cause the formation of hydrides according to Eq. (18). Alkali hydrides are solid compounds crystallizing in the NaCl-type lattice, in which the hydride ions, H^-, take the places of the chloride ions. The apparent ion radius of H^- is about 0.15 nm. The standard heat of formation decreases with growing atomic weight of the alkali ion in the considered hydrides. The most stable compounds of the light alkali metals have considerably high melting points of 688 °C (LiH) and 800 °C (NaH). At high temperatures the hydrides tend to decompose.

$$\mathrm{Me} + 1/2\,\mathrm{H_2} \rightarrow \mathrm{MeH} \qquad (18)$$

The alkali hydrides are also formed by reactions of alkali metals with small amounts of water or by decomposition of hydroxides in the presence of excess alkali metals. Solutions of hydrides in molten metals develop a partial pressure of hydrogen, which can be applied to estimate the hydride concentrations [66].

5.2 Solubility of Alkali Hydrides in Molten Alkali Metals

The solid hydrides as well as gaseous hydrogen dissolve in liquid alkali metals. Their solubilities can be expressed by the Eq.

$$\log c_s^H = A - \frac{B}{T} \qquad (19)$$

The constants A and B of the Eq. (19) (for c_s^H in wppm) are listed in Table VII. The solubility of the hydrides of the heavier alkali metals has not yet been studied sufficiently to elaborate solubility equations.

Table VII. Solubility of hydrides in alkali metals

Solute	Solvent	A	B	Temp. range (K)	Ref.
H	Li	4.7054	−2322.9	523–775	[67]
D	Li	5.8057	−2888.9	549–724	[67]
D	Li	5.6605	−2841.4		[68]
H	Na	6.93	−3600		[69]
H	Na	6.52	−3180		[70]
H	Na−K	6.69	−2900	603–977	[71]
H	K	5.807	−2930		[71]

Tritium shows a similar solution behaviour as deuterium. The constants of solubility in the sodium-hydrogen system seem to need further improvement.

The decomposition of alkali hydrides at higher temperatures evolves a hydrogen partial pressure even on dilute solutions in alkali metals, which obey Sieverts' law:

$$n_H = K_s \cdot (p_{H_2})^{1/2} \tag{20}$$

In Sieverts' law, n_H is the hydrogen mole fraction in the solution, p_{H_2} the partial pressure of hydrogen on this solution and K_s the Sieverts' constant. The value of this constant is dependent on the temperature as expressed in Eq. (21).

$$\ln K_s = \ln (n_H/p_{H_2}^{1/2}) = C - \frac{D}{T} \tag{21}$$

By means of this equation one can estimate hydrogen concentrations in the liquid metals, if Sieverts' constants are known and the partial pressure are measured.

6 Miscibility of Alkali Metals with Metallic Elements in the Liquid State

According to Mott's rule [72] the miscibility of metals in the liquid state depends on the ratios of atomic sizes, on the vapour pressures and on the electronegativity of the solutes and solvents. The properties last mentioned are close together in the alkali metal group. Differences in the atomic radii, however, cause incomplete miscibility of light and heavy alkali metals.

Particularly lithium shows a tendency to incomplete miscibility with its homologues elements in the liquid state. For instance, the Li−Na system has a miscibility gap below 303 °C. The miscibility is even more limited in the solid state. Lithium does not form solid or liquid alloys with the heavier alkali metals potassium, rubidium, and cesium. The compound Na_2K exists as a solid phase below 6.6 °C in the Na−K system. This intermetallic compound crystallizes in the $MgZn_2$ type of structure with a = 0.75 nm and c = 1.23 nm. The eutectic alloy contains 66 at-% resp. 76.7 wt-% K. The melting point of the eutectic is at −12.5 °C (260.7 K). This low melting point is technically important. The alloy is liquid at room temperature and has a very large range of liquid state. Figure 12 shows the Na−K phase diagram.

Sodium is miscible with rubidium and cesium in the liquid state. Eutectics containing 75.5 at-% Rb resp. 75 at-% Cs occur. A Na_2Cs compound is indicated by magnetic measurements in the solid state. Potassium is miscible with rubidium as well as with cesium in both the liquid and the solid state.

Ternary mixtures of sodium, potassium and cesium form a eutectic with a very low melting temperature. The ternary eutectic contains 13.3 wt-% Na, 46.5 wt-% K, and 40 wt-% Cs. Its melting point is at −79 °C (194 K).

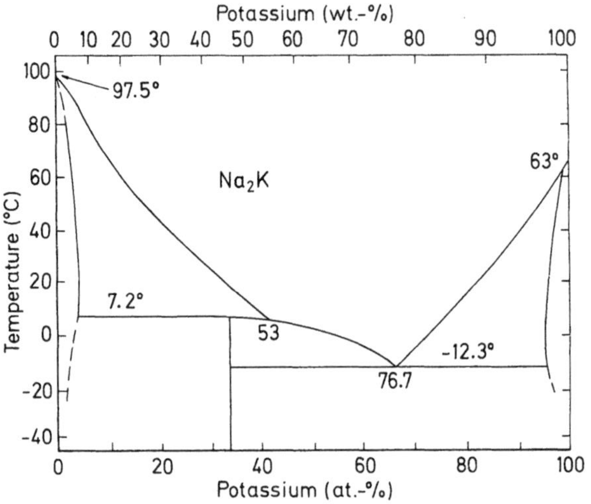

Fig. 12. The simplified Na—K phase diagram [74]

The metals of the group 1B are more or less miscible with the alkali metals. Silver and gold are miscible in wide ranges of concentrations and intermetallic compounds occur. The elements cesium and gold, for instance, are miscible in the liquid state. The mixtures show the typical behaviour of liquid metal solutions. Equi-atomic mixtures, however, behave more like molten salts. The electrical conductivity of the melt of the composition CsAu measured at 600 °C has a pronounced minimum [72], and an analogue minimum of the absolute thermoelectric power occurs at the same composition. The changes of properties in mixtures containing the metals in stoichiometric relationships indicate a gradual metal-non-metal transition induced by concentration changes in the Cs—Au system. The electric transport properties are determined by ionic conduction due to the formation of an ionic bond in the cesium melt.

The solubility of alkaline earth metals in molten alkali metals is limited. The elements of the third group of the periodic table of elements are still less soluble in alkali metals, only the aluminium-lithium system is an exception. This system contains two intermetallic phases, LiAl and the peritectic phase Li_9Al_4, and solid alloys of both metals are of technical importance. The metals of the fourth group have a better solubility in alkali metals. They tend to form intermetallics. Some of the liquid alloys have found technical interest.

The importance of the lithium-lead system is based on its usefulness as a blanket fluid of fusion reactors, which need lithium as breeding material for tritium. The eutectic with 0.68 wt-% (17 at-%) lithium has a melting point of F_p = 235 °C (508 K),

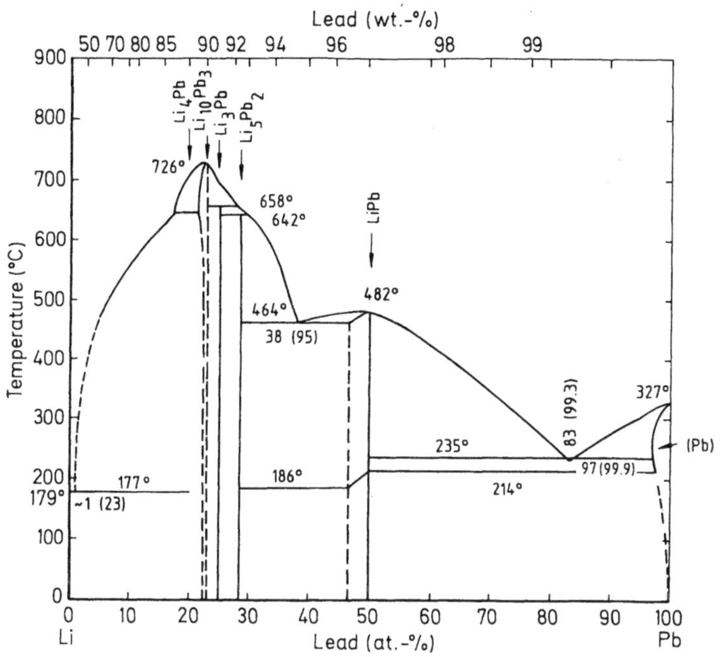

Fig. 13. The simplified Li—Pb phase diagram [74]

which is low enough to apply this alloy in the liquid state. Several higher melting intermetallics as Li_4Pb, Li_7Pb_2, Li_3Pb, Li_5Pb_2, and LiPb exist. Solid intermetallics may be applied as solid blanket alloys. Figure 13 shows the Li—Pb phase diagram.

The sodium lead system is important, since NaPb compounds are applied to chemical processes. The intermetallic compound NaPb is fabricated in large amounts as an intermediate for the production of tetra ethyl lead. The Na—Pb phase diagram indicates the formation of several compounds, as shown in Fig. 14. The solubility of lead in liquid sodium is considerably high, the saturated solution contains ~3 at-% Pb at 250 °C. The sodium-tin system shows a similar solution and compound formation behaviour.

The elements of the fifth group of the periodic table of elements are able to form compounds with alkali metals, which have properties of alloys as well as of salts. Bismuth and antimony form compounds with alkali metals of the cubic Li_3Bi and the KBi_2-type, which is also cubic. The compounds have high melting points, among these Li_3Bi has the highest, $F_p = 1145$ °C [75,76]. All the compounds within these systems are very reactive and tend to ignite in contact with air. This tendency is strongest among those compounds which have the highest alkali contents.

Transition metals are nearly insoluble in alkali metals compared to the metals of the groups just described. The concentrations of saturated solutions at 500 °C are on the level of a few wppm. Among these metals, nickel has a relatively high solubility in liquid metals, whereas molybdenum has an extremely low miscibility in the liquid state.

The solubility of some transition metals in alkali metals is influenced by the interfer-

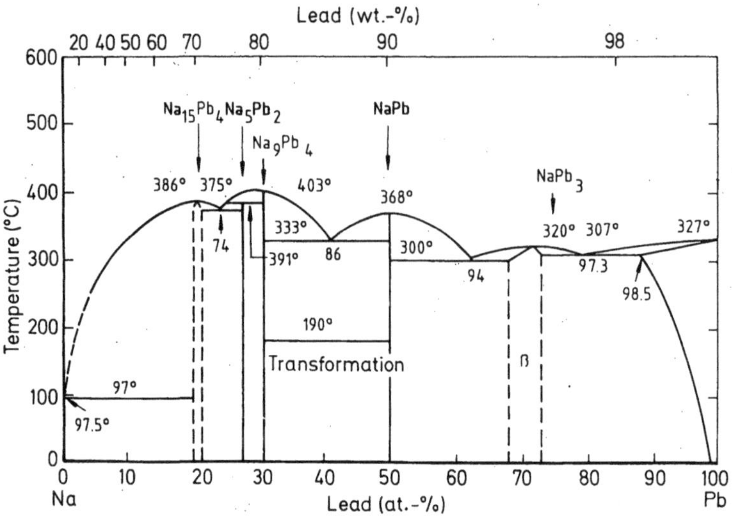

Fig. 14. The simplified Na–Pb phase diagram [74]

ing action of non-metals, which may be present as contaminants in either the solid or liquid metal. In the iron-sodium system, for instance, it is obvious that iron saturation is governed by a saturation equation valid for solutions in very pure sodium (Eq. 22) [24].

$$\log c_{sNa}^{Fe} \text{ (wppm)} = 4.720 - \frac{4116}{T \text{ (K)}} \tag{22}$$

The free enthalpy of solution, $\Delta H_{sol} = 78.7 \text{ kJ} \cdot \text{mol}^{-1}$, is relatively high. The saturation curve takes the form of Eq. (23) when oxygen is involved in the solutions. Equation (23) is valid for solutions of iron in sodium containing $\sim$5 wppm of oxygen. Raising oxygen content causes an increase of the constant term of Eq. (23) while the slope remains the same for different oxygen concentrations.

$$\log c_{sNa}^{Fe,O} \text{ (wppm)} = 1.804 - \frac{842}{T \text{ (K)}} \tag{23}$$

The free enthalpy of solution is much lower in this case ($\Delta H_{sol} = 16.1 \text{ kJ} \cdot \text{mol}^{-1}$). The range of oxygen concentrations, in which such behaviour has been observed, is 2 to 25 wppm. The formation of complex sodium iron oxides has not been detected in such solutions (see Fig. 15).

The solubility of some transition elements in liquid lithium is found to be influenced by the nitrogen content of the alkali metal. Solubilities of elements can only be measured in very pure lithium. Nitrogen contents of >50 wppm increase the saturation concentrations. The presence of nitrogen, however, does not evidently change the values of the free enthalpy of solution.

Solubilities of transition metals in heavy alkali metals are of the same order as in sodium. Very few data exist on the liquid metals potassium, rubidium, and cesium.

The solutions in these alkali metals are also influenced by non-metallic elements present as contaminants. Oxygen causes the formation of complex oxides as well as in sodium. These compounds are in chemical equilibrium with the dissolved species of the transition elements.

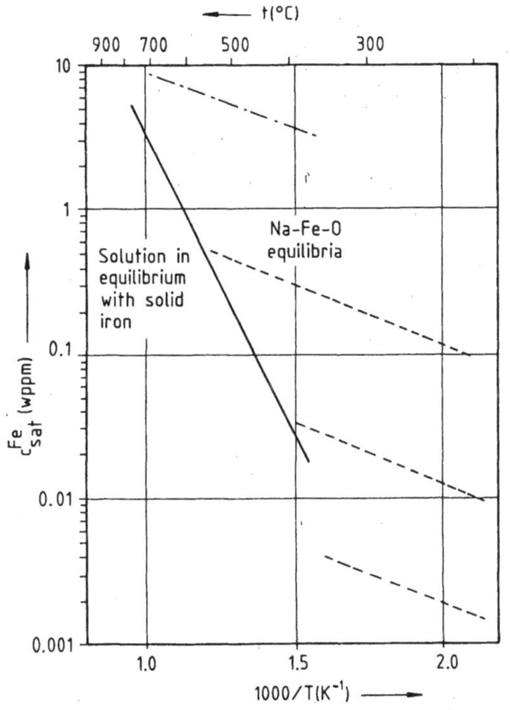

Fig. 15. The solubility of iron in liquid sodium [24]; regions of Fe equilibria with the solutions (left side) and region of dominating Fe—O—Na equilibria

7 Conclusions

The modern applications of liquid alkali metals in nuclear and energy conversion techniques have forced an intensive research work to gain information on chemical reactions in and with molten alkali metals, which may interact with the mode of their application. Their ability to dissolve metals as well as non-metals has to be considered when alkali metals are applied as heat transfer media. The heat transfer may, therefore, be accompanied by a material transfer. Thus, all chemical properties have to be taken into consideration for the designing or large energy conversion facilities.

The role of dissolved non-metals in the compatibility between liquid alkali metals and solid materials based on transition metals can be understood as a complicated system of local heterogeneous chemical equilibria. The chemical potentials of the non-metals such as oxygen, nitrogen, carbon, or hydrogen, are influenced by the formation of compounds. These compounds can be dissolved or precipitated. Several ternary compounds are of higher chemical stability than well known oxides, nitrides, carbides, or hydrides in systems, in which alkali metals, non-metals and transition elements can react. Thus, the complex compounds act as sinks for the non-metals due to the reduction of their chemical potentials. The fact that the solid materials have the ability to form compounds with the same non-metallic elements causes complications of the system of heterogeneous chemical equilibria.

Some reaction products formed by non-metals in alkali metals are less common or difficult to be prepared. The reactions in alkali metals might be considered as a new way to form such compounds, which are not easily produced in conventional chemical processes. Reactions of elemental nitrogen with carbon, for instance, and the formation of dilithium cyanamide, are examples of such chemical processes. The formation of methane by a reaction of hydrogen with coal in sodium or potassium is of concern for compatibility problems as well as for opening a new way to prepare methane from the elements at a moderate temperature.

Alkali metals are principally similar in their ability to form compounds with non-metals and to dissolve these compounds. There are, however, some differences between light alkali metals, lithium and sodium, and their heavier homologues, potassium, rubidium, and cesium. The extreme position of lithium is due to its very high affinity to form salts and to its similarity to the alkaline earth metals. Lithium oxide and hydride are the alkali compounds of highest stability. Lithium nitride is the only stable compound of this class, and probably, lithium acetylide is also the only stable alkali carbon compound, which occurs in contact with excess alkali metal.

Potassium has a transition position. The solubility of oxide in this metal is higher than in lithium and sodium, much lower, however, than in rubidium and cesium. The free enthalpy of solution shows the same tendency, its value is between the light and the heavy alkali metals.

Reactions of considerable extent occur even in very dilute solutions of non-metals in alkali metals. Small concentrations of dissolved non-metals also influence physical properties of the molten metals. Very exact analyses are necessary to define the chemical potentials of non-metals in alkali metals. Oxygen can be removed from sodium, for instance, to such a degree, that only 0.1 to 0.01 wppm remain in solution. Electrochemical cells have the ability to estimate such extremely low concentrations. Carbon in liquid alkali metals, which are in contact with austenitic stainless steels, is in the same range of concentrations. Thus, only activity meters, based on gasanalytical devices or electrochemical cells, are able to measure such low carbon concentrations. There is still need for the development of analytical procedures to estimate nitrogen in alkali metals with the same sensitivity and accuracy.

Sodium is the alkali metal, the chemical properties of which are best established in the molten state. Lithium chemistry has been improved during the last decade due to the interest of the fusion reactor technology. Nevertheless, several chemical properties are still unknown. Potassium and the heavy alkali metals still require research work concerning the solutions of their compounds with non-metals, as well as on the solubility of metallic elements. The solubility of transition elements may range at the same level as in sodium. The degree of solubility of the elements of the fourth and fifth groups and the formation of intermetallic compounds with them are not well known. Further research may detect some new aspects, which may help to improve the application of liquid alkali metals in modern technology and chemistry.

8 References

1. Klemm, A.: Angew. Chem. *70*, 21 (1958)
2. Cairns, E. J., Shimotake, H.: Science *164*, 1347 (1969)
3. Dreyer, S., Haubold, W., Goetzmann, C.: Ullmanns Enzyklopädie der technischen Chemie, Vol. 14, 102 (1977)
4. Weber, N., Kummer, J. T.: Proc. 21st. Annual Power Sources Conf. 21, 42 (1967); Adv. Energy Convers. 1967, 913
5. Brost, O., Groll, M., Schubert, K. P.: Reprints of the 1st. Intern. Heat Pipe Conf., Stuttgart 1973; Verein Deutscher Ingenieure, Düsseldorf 1973
6. Freund, J. H.: Atomkernenergie *11*, 221 (1966)
7. Yonco, R. M., Maroni, V. A., Strain, J. E., DeVan, J. H.: J. Nucl. Mat. *79*, 354 (1979)
8. Eichelberger, R. L.: Report AEC-AI 12685 (1968)
9. Noden, J. D.: J. Brit. Nucl. Energy Soc. 12, 57 and 329, (1973)
10. Minushkin, D., Kissel, G., in: Corrosion by Liquid Metals, Plenum Press, New York 1970, 515
11. Smith, D. L., Kassner, T. F., in: Corrosion by Liquid Metals, Plenum Press, New York 1970, 137
12. Williams, D. D., Grand, J. A., Miller, R. R.: J. Phys. Chem. *63*, 68 (1959)
13. Ganesan, V., Borgstedt, H. U., Adelhelm, Ch.: J. Less-Common Metals 113, (1985)
14. Touzain, Ph.: Canad. J. of Chem. *47*, 2639 (1969)
15. Knights, C. F., Phillips, B. A.: J. Nucl. Mat. *84*, 196 (1979)
16. Rohde, J. F. M., Hissink, M., Bos, L.: ibid. *24*, 503 (1970)
17. Borgstedt, H. U., Frees, G., Drechsler, G.: Werkst. & Korros. *21*, 568 (1970)
18. Borgstedt, H. U., Schneider, W.: J. Nucl. Mat. *37*, 114 (1970)
19. Borgstedt, H. U.: Werkst. & Korros. *28*, 529 (1977)
20. Chiotti, P., Wu, P. C. S., Fisher, R. W.: J. Nucl. Mat. *38*, 260 (1971)
21. Gross, P., Wilson, G. L., Gutteridge, W. A.: J. Chem. Soc. (A) 1970, 1908
22. Bhat, N. P., Borgstedt, H. U.: Nucl. Technol. *52*, 153 (1981)
23. Cavell, I. W., Nicholas, M. G.: J. Nucl. Mat. *95*, 129 (1980)
24. Awasthi, S. P., Borgstedt, H. U.: ibid. *116*, 103 (1983)
25. Barker, M. G., Wood, D. J.: J. Less-Common Metals *35*, 315 (1974)
26. Gross, P., Wilson, G. L.: J. Chem. Soc. (A) 1970, 1913
27. Addison, C. C., Barker, M. G., Lintonbon, R. M., Pulham, R. J.: ibid. 1969, 2457
28. Adamson, M. G., Mignanelli, M. A., Potter, P. E., Rand, M. H.: J. Nucl. Mat. *97*, 203 (1981)
29. Cordfunke, E. H. P., Westrum jr., E. F., in: Thermodynamics of Nuclear Materials 1979, Vol. 2, IAEA-SM-236 (1980) 125
30. Gadd, P. G., Borgstedt, H. U., in: Liquid Metal Engineering and Technology, Vol. 2, Brit. Nucl. Energy Soc., London 1984, 107
31. Migge, H., in: Proc. 2nd. Intern. Conf. on Liquid Metal Technology in Energy Production (CONF-800401-P2), Richland, Wash., USA, April 20–24, 1980, vol. 2, 18-9
32. Jansson, S. A., in: Corrosion by Liquid Metals, Plenum Press, New York 1970, 523
33. Myles, K. M., Cafasso, F. A.: J. Nucl. Mat. *67*, 249 (1977)
34. Ganesan, V., Borgstedt, H. U.: to be published
35. Carmichael, H. T., Meacham, S. A.: The Solubility of Sodium Carbonate in Sodium, Report USAEC-APDA-184 (1968)
36. Migge, H., in: Material Behavior and Physical Chemistry in Liquid Metal Systems, Plenum Press, New York 1982, 351
37. Borgstedt, H. U.: Metall *34*, 143 (1980)
38. Fedorov, P. I., Su, M. T.: Acta Chim. Sinica (Hua Hsuah Hsueh Pa O) *23*, 30 (1957)
39. Secrist, D. R., Wisnyi, L. G.: Acta Cryst. *15*, 1042 (1962)
40. Föppl, H.: Angew. Chem. *70*, 401 (1958)
41. Pulham, R. J., Hubberstey, P., Thunder, A. E., Harper, A., Dadd, A. T., in: Proc. 2nd. Intern. Conf. on Liquid Metal Technology in Energy Production (CONF-800401-P2) Richland, Wash., USA, April 20–24, 1980, Vol. 2, 18-1
42. Rüdorff, W., Schulze, E.: Z. Anorg. Allgem. Chem. *277*, 156 (1954)
43. Asher, R. C., Wilson, S. A.: Nature (London) *181*, 409 (1958)
44. Olson, W. H., Ruther, W. E.: Nucl. Techn. *46*, 318 (1979)
45. Yonco, R. M., Homa, M. I.: Trans. Amer. Nucl. Soc. *32*, 270 (1979)

46. Ainsley, R., Hartlib, A. P., Holroyd, P. M., Long, G.: J. Nucl. Mat. *52*, 255 (1974)
47. Longson, B., Thorley, A. W.: J. appl. Chem. *20*, 372 (1970)
48. Asher, R. C., Kirstein, T. B. A., in: Liquid Metals 1976, Conf. Series no. 30, The Inst. of Physics, Bristol and London 1977, 561
49. Salzano, F. J., Newman, L., Hobdell, M. R.: Nucl. Techn. *10*, 335 (1971)
50. Pulham, R. J., in: Material Behavior and Physical Chemistry in Liquid Metal Systems, Plenum Press, New York 1982, 429
51. Jung, J., Buckmann, U., Pütz, R., in: Material Behavior and Physical Chemistry in Liquid Metal System, Plenum Press, New York 1982, 265
52. Borgstedt, H. U., Konys, J.: Chem. Ind. *36*, 404 (1984)
53. Natesan, K., Kassner, T. F.: J. Nucl. Mat. *37*, 223 (1970)
54. Borgstedt, H. U.: ibid *51*, 221 (1954)
55. Konys, J., in: Liquid Metal Engineering and Technology, British Nuclear Energy Soc., London 1984, Vol. 2, 71
56. Borgstedt, H. U., Frees, G., Schneider, H.: Nucl. Techn. *34*, 290 (1977)
57. Smith, D. L., Natesan, K.: ibid. *22*, 392 (1974)
58. Yonco, R. M., Veleckis, E., Maroni, V. A.: J. Nucl. Mat. *57*, 317 (1975)
59. Rabenau, A., Schulz, H.: J. Less-Common Met. *50*, 155 (1976)
60. Adams, P. F., Hubberstey, P., Pulham, R. J.: ibid. *42*, 1 (1975)
61. Adams, P. F., Down, M. G., Hubberstey, P., Pulham, R. J.: J. Chem. Soc. (Faradey Trans. I) *1*, 230 (1977)
62. Barker, M. G., Frankham, S. A., Gadd, P. G., Moore, D. R., in: Material Behavior and Physical Chemistry in Liquid Metal Systems, Plenum Press, New York 1982, 113
63. Juza, R., Weber, H. H., Meyer-Simon, E.: Z. Anorg. Allgem. Chem. *273*, 48 (1953)
64. Juza, R., Gieren, W., Haug, J.: ibid. *300*, 61 (1959)
65. Marin, A., de la Torre, M., Borgstedt, H. U., in: Proc. 2nd. Intern. Conf. on Liquid Metal Technology in Energy Production, (CONF-800401-P2), Richland, Wash., April 20–24, 1980, Vol. 2, 13-20
66. Meacham, S. A., Hill, E. F., Gordus, A. A.: The Solubility of Hydrogen in Sodium, USAEC Report APDA-241 (1970)
67. Adams, P. F., Down, M. G., Hubberstey, P., Pulham, R. J.: J. Less-Common Met. *42*, 325 (1975)
68. Smith, F. J., Talbot, J. B., Land, J. F., Bell, J. T., in: Radiation Effects and Tritium Technology for Fusion Reactors, (CONF-750989), Vol. II, 1975, 539
69. Addison, C. C., Hubberstey, P., Oliver, J., Pulham, R. J., Simm, A.: J. Less-Common Met. *61*, 123 (1978)
70. Compère, E. L., Savolainen, J. E.: Nucl. Sci. Engng. *28*, 325 (1967)
71. Ivanovskij, N. N., Arnol'dov, M. N., Morovzov, V. A., Moireeva, T. J., Pletenet, S. S.: Izv. Akad. Nauk. USSR, Metal., 214 (1980)
72. Mott, B. W., in: The Alkali Metals, The Chem. Soc., Special Publ. no. 22, London 1967, 92
73. Schmutzler, R. W., Hoshino, H., Fischer, R., Hensel, F.: Berichte der Bunsen-Gesellschaft *80*, 107 (1976)
74. Hansen, M., Anderko, K.: The Constitution of Binary Alloys, McGraw-Hill Book Comp., Inc., New York 1958
75. Gnutzmann, G., Klemm, W.: Z. Anorg. Allgem. Chem. *309*, 181 (1961)
76. Dorn, F. W., Klemm, W.: ibid. *309*, 189 (1961)

Author Index Volumes 101–134

Contents of Vols. 50–100 see Vol. 100
Author and Subject Index Vols. 26–50 see Vol. 50

The volume numbers are printed in italics

Bei Fragen zur Produktsicherheit wenden Sie sich bitte an:
If you have any questions regarding product safety,
please contact:

Walter de Gruyter GmbH
Genthiner Straße 13
10785 Berlin
productsafety@degruyterbrill.com